AWAKENING THROUGH

THE NINE BODIES

AWAKENING THROUGH

THE NINE BODIES

Exploring Levels of Consciousness in Meditation

PHILLIP MOFFITT

North Atlantic Books
Berkeley, California

Published by
North Atlantic Books
Berkeley, California

Cover and book design by Gail Segerstrom
Printed in the United States of America

Cover illustration: *The Cosmos in Movement* by Sri Swami Balyogi Premvarni

This book is for the general reader of writing on yoga in English, and uses phonetic Sanskrit without diacritical marks.

Awakening through the Nine Bodies: Exploring Levels of Consciousness in Meditation is sponsored and published by the Society for the Study of Native Arts and Sciences (dba North Atlantic Books), an educational nonprofit based in Berkeley, California, that collaborates with partners to develop cross-cultural perspectives, nurture holistic views of art, science, the humanities, and healing, and seed personal and global transformation by publishing work on the relationship of body, spirit, and nature.

North Atlantic Books' publications are available through most bookstores. For further information, visit our website at www.northatlanticbooks.com or call 800-733-3000.

Library of Congress Cataloging-in-Publication data is available from the publisher upon request.

2 3 4 5 6 7 8 9 KPC 22 21 20

DEDICATION

THIS BOOK is dedicated to Pawan Bareja, without whom it would never have come into existence.

After my first few trips to study with Balyogi Premvarni in Rishikesh, India, Pawan, a native of that country, accompanied me on subsequent trips as a valued colleague. She sat in on most of my study sessions, taking notes, as was permitted by Balyogi. I missed her presence on those occasions when she was not there as it was impossible for me to both take comprehensive notes and to engage in the teachings, which were more like a transmission than a didactic presentation.

On many occasions Pawan acted as a translator, helping me and Balyogi to understand each other. Her handwritten session notes of Balyogi's teachings, which she later transcribed, were often what I used as the final research reference for the book, particularly in regard to Balyogi's interpretations of his illustrations. In the evening Pawan and I would review the day's teachings so that I could prepare for the next day's study. I deeply enjoyed these sessions, and they were essential because the material I was being taught was complex and often the circumstances surrounding the teachings made understanding and integrating the material more difficult.

Pawan often played a vital role in helping Balyogi and me communicate with each other. Pawan also served as a cultural translator in relation to the many challenges of spending time in India—from the basics of travel to the complexity of the rituals and expected behavior at Balyogi's ashram. She was always willing to do whatever was necessary to keep the project moving.

When I describe life at Balyogi's ashram, picture both Pawan and me trudging up the hilly path carrying books, recorders, cameras, yellow notepads, and food offerings. When Balyogi was having me do various cleansing and health rituals, you can imagine Pawan being given her own to do. Pawan would keep an eye out for my well-being and for the book project while I was completely immersed in various meditations.

Thank you, Pawan, for all this and more.

CONTENTS

Foreword by Anam Thubten Rinpoche ix

How to Use This Book xii

Introduction xiv

Chapter 1 Balyogi's Ashram Life Is Integral to His Teachings 1

Chapter 2 Insights into Consciousness 17

Chapter 3 The Nine Bodies Teaching 37

Chapter 4 Connecting to the Nine Bodies in Meditation 63

Chapter 5 How to Work with Balyogi's Illustrations 85

Chapter 6 Balyogi's Cosmic View of Reality and Consciousness 93
The Eternal Journey of the Transmigration
of Spirit and Consciousness 94
The Cosmos in Movement 102
The Cosmos in Repose 106

Chapter 7 Three Levels and Nine Bodies 109
Three Levels Teachings of Liberation 110
Auras of the Three Levels 114
The Three Centers Awakened 118
Nine Bodies 122

Chapter 8 The Flame of Consciousness 125
Flame of Consciousness with Nine Bodies 126
Flame of Individual Consciousness 132
Details of the Flame of Individual Consciousness 138

Chapter 9	Awakening in the Subtle Level	143
	Explosive Awakening	144
	Side View of the Nine Chakras	150
	Back View of the Nine Chakras	156
	The Tortoise Channel	160
	Thousand Petals of Consciousness	166
Chapter 10	The Awakened Heart	171
	Luminous Consciousness in the Spiritual Heart	172
	Three Hearts	178
	The Radiating Heart	184
	The Eye of Awareness	186
Chapter 11	Mandalas of Awakening	191
	Mandala of Antah-Karana	192
	The Mandalas of the Subtle Body	194
	Shri Yantra and Om Mandala	200
	Epilogue: The Nine Bodies and Liberation	206
	Appendix A: The Traditional Teachings on Levels of Being	212
	Acknowledgments	216
	Glossary	218
	Resources	222
	Index	223
	About the Author	229

For guided audio meditations, go to www.ninebodies.com.

FOREWORD

by Anam Thubten Rinpoche

VAJRAYANA, the Tantric tradition in which I was trained, might be the only one in Buddhism that teaches extensive knowledge on energetic elements of the human body, along with complex techniques to work with them for the purpose of inner purification that leads to spiritual awakening. Its practice was part of my daily life while growing up in Tibet, so wisdom teachings about human subtle body and alchemistic transformation of consciousness have never been too esoteric to me, rather some kind of intuitive science that derives from direct experience instead of mentally fabricated doctrine. That is not to say that following this path is a simple matter. Like any other scientific understanding, it requires a whole endeavor of practice and experimentation to gain direct experience.

Many do not have the interest or the right kind of opportunities to go through such a process. This sometimes becomes a cause for people to think that Tantric and yogic teachings are a nonpragmatic system developed by the old civilization. The truth is not only are they authentic, but we need them to heal ourselves from suffering that runs deep.

Many ancient traditions are going through difficulties in an increasingly secular modern culture that is in great need of spiritual healing to overcome various forms of neurosis, partly developed by the way we live. In part this has to do with the fact that those traditions are still using archaic language and methodologies that don't resonate with people anymore or are hard to relate to. The forms need to be updated from time to time as they meet a new era. The mind-blowing popularity of hatha yoga is not an indication of those ancient traditions being alive or well understood by the masses. Yoga is becoming more and more like a fitness exercise imported from India, spreading all over the world after much of its profundity has been stripped off to fit consumerism. This is neither a good nor bad thing. It's just what is happening. No doubt that such a trend has many beneficial aspects. There is also a longing among many of us for something deep and profound.

Many of you know who Phillip Moffitt is. He is a wonderful meditation teacher in the Buddhist tradition in the lineage of Insight Meditation. This lineage has been passed down by prominent Western Buddhist pioneers— authentic spiritual teachers, who have been inspiring us with their wisdom, compassion, and humility. Phillip is an author who has the ability to articulate things in an engaging and clear fashion, as demonstrated in his previous book *Dancing with Life*.

I have never met Balyogi Premvarni in person. I've never had the chance to interact with yogic masters from the Hindu world except for a few scholars. But I always love to meet people from different traditions and enter into dialogue to learn their wisdom as well as where we share commonality. Phillip Moffitt has studied with Balyogi and practiced his teachings in depth with keen diligence. He delved into this system and came out with very complete knowledge and practices to share with others for their spiritual healing. Phillip is a man who is committed to walking the path of awakened ones and has the altruism to help others.

Balyogi Premvarni's teachings are based on the system of Nine Bodies encompassing the wholeness or multidimensionality of a human being—mind, consciousness, body, spirit, vital energy, and more. His system has roots in the ancient Tantric and yogic traditions combined with his own understanding. This fusion can be seen right away in his illustrations, which marry the ancient and contemporary. In Buddhist Tantra there are three bodies, known as the coarse body, subtle body, and very subtle body. These categories point out the multidimensional nature of a human being that can elude our ordinary awareness. How many people have direct understanding of things like prana? Yet, prana is not an abstract concept that was created by a philosopher. It's a vital energy that sustains our life with many amazing functions.

To have more complete healing or spiritual awakening, it's important to work with subtle dimensions of our own being and to purify psychophysical karmic habitual patterns that hold us back in invisible chains of pain and suffering. Tantra was developed to fulfill such a purpose. Countless individuals have had life changing epiphanies that might be hard for others to understand. Many of them have profound experiences through Tantric and yogic practices—such as "unblocking the knot of the channels"—in which the body becomes healthier, the mind becomes more wholesome, and a sense of openness develops through which new streams of joy, love, and creativity flow.

It would be a great loss to humanity if these ancient Tantric teachings were forgotten or become obsolete. Personally, I see Phillip is doing a great job contributing to their longevity by writing this book to make them accessible to the mainstream through the magical work of clear presentation endowed with profound understanding. Performing such a job is not easy; it requires so much experience, dedication, and special gifts. Because of this, I offer my sincere reverence to him and his work.

This book illuminates the most important topic—consciousness. It's pretty much everything. Without consciousness, you or I wouldn't be having a life and witnessing the cosmic wonder of existence. Even our sense of "I am" is the work of consciousness. We feel, taste, see, hear, sense, and recognize because there is consciousness in each of us. Sadness, joy, anger, love, confusion, despair, falling in love, spiritual awakening—none of these would be there if there were no consciousness. It's a realm that has many realms within it. There are realms we can tap into that yogis and mystics have entered. Even though rational mind is an expression of the consciousness, it often fails to comprehend the myriad aspects of the Buddha-mind, original mind, inborn wisdom, or luminous consciousness. The more we understand the world of consciousness, the more we're able to understand who we are and find a means to alleviate suffering, as well as to evolve by widening the circle of love and compassion toward all living creatures.

This is why ancient civilizations of the East have been studying consciousness through a variety of meditation practices for thousands of years. The book is quite rare in that it shares such rich knowledge in contemporary language. This book shows a complete methodological system that explores a Nine Body–based practice to heal and expand our consciousness to its higher potential. Let me welcome this book as a new light to illuminate the beautiful world of our own consciousness.

Dharmata Foundation
Richmond, California
January 2017

How to Use This Book

This book is intended to be a guide to meditation practice, not just a theoretical or philosophical text. As such, it will only be effective if you actually do the practices it contains, not just read about them. Each chapter is densely packed with information and concepts that must be read over and over again—and repeatedly investigated through your own experience—before they can be understood.

In that way, it is analogous to a travel guidebook to a vast country you have never visited before. You can orient yourself to the country by flipping through the guidebook and learning some useful facts. Perhaps you will get excited about the multiple possibilities of cities to visit, hikes to take, hotels to stay at, and cuisine to sample.

But at a certain point, you need to actually travel to the country to get the full experience. At that point, you will need to focus in on one section of the guidebook at a time—and details that might have been boring to read about (such as the location of train stations) will become vital for the success of your journey.

For ease of use, guidebooks often map out suggested itineraries for their readers. In the same way, I will suggest a few practice and study pathways you might take through this book.

1. For everyone: It is important to embark on your journey by reading the Introduction and Chapter 1. This will give you an essential orientation to the context in which the Nine Bodies teachings were developed. You should also at least look over the overview of the Nine Bodies teachings that is presented in Chapter 3 and pay particular attention to the chart on page 42.

2.   If you're someone who learns best through verbal explanations and presentations of systems, after reading the Introduction and Chapter 1, proceed through the book chapter by chapter. Pay particular attention to Chapter 2, which gives an overview of Balyogi's teachings on consciousness. Then, after reading Chapter 3, begin the meditations on the Nine Bodies in Chapter 4.

3.   If you learn best through imagery, after looking over Chapter 3, you may want to proceed to Chapter 5 and begin working directly with Balyogi's illustrations to access the Nine Bodies that way. After working with the illustrations in Chapter 6, try going back to the guided meditation in Chapter 4 (referencing the overview in Chapter 3 as needed).

4.   If your background is primarily as a student of mindfulness meditation (rather than yoga philosophy), you may wish to go straight to Chapter 4 after reading the introduction and Chapter 1 (and looking over Chapter 3). At that point, go back and read Chapter 2 (and read 3 more thoroughly).

5.   If you're especially interested in yogic energy systems and classical yoga philosophy, the material in Chapter 3 and Appendix A will help you locate these teachings in the frame of yoga philosophy. If your yoga background is more focused on asana practice, you might be especially interested in starting your practice with the illustrations in Chapter 7 of Bodies Three and Nine.

For guided audio meditations to support your practice, you can go to www.ninebodies.com.

Introduction

The contents of this book represent my understanding of a set of teachings about the nature of consciousness that were transmitted to me by the Himalayan yoga master Sri Swami Balyogi Premvarni, whom I refer to simply as Balyogi throughout this book.

Over fifty years ago, during a time when he was immersed in intensive *samadhi* (deep concentration and absorption) meditation practices, Balyogi had a series of revelations and visions about the structure of consciousness and how *nonspecific energetic potential* manifests in both the mind and the body. He saw that there are multiple, interactive "levels" or "bodies" of being within each of us. Gradually, it became clear to him that all our experience is composed of nine such bodies and that exploring these "Nine Bodies" yields insights into the nature of body and mind, which in turn bring "happiness, joy, bliss, and the peacefulness and stillness of realizing emptiness."

Balyogi says that these teachings are not instructions for realizing full spiritual awakening (*nibbana*), but rather they are a means for accessing, understanding, integrating, and balancing the Nine Bodies through meditation. They are instructions for clearing obstacles from your path to full awakening and for fully utilizing the meditative states and insights that occur during your journey to freedom.

Supporting his teachings of the Nine Bodies is a series of beautiful and mysterious illustrations capturing the nature of consciousness, which Balyogi says he created during his time of intense samadhi explorations. These drawings are reproduced in this book with Balyogi's blessings. He refers to these drawings as "scientific illustrations of consciousness." In these images, you can literally see one man's inner experience of the relationships between mind, spirit, and consciousness. When he uses the word "scientific," Balyogi does not mean that his drawings belong to the world of medical anatomy, but rather that they capture dimensions of inner experience that can't be identified by neurological science with tools such as magnetic resonance imaging.

When Balyogi first showed me his drawings, I was captivated by their insight and originality. As a long-time practitioner and teacher of meditation, I immediately saw that the illustrations reflected certain aspects of the inner experiences that occur during meditation and are almost impossible to express with language. These inner experiences are manifestations of various energetic dimensions of consciousness that are "felt" but not "thought" at times during meditation. I discovered subsequently that the illustrations have the power to elicit some of the energetic dimensions that arise

Sri Swami Balyogi Premvarni circa 1979

when meditating, even among people who do not have a meditation practice.

I have worked fruitfully with the Nine Bodies teachings since 1999. For half this time, I have shared the Nine Bodies teachings with experienced meditation students on a limited basis. Many students find them to be of great value and ask for more in-depth exposure. Due to this student response and at Balyogi's urging, I resolved to write a thorough explanation of my own understandings of consciousness that have arisen from working with these teachings. Doing so turned out to be a more formidable challenge than I had anticipated, but the book you are now reading constitutes my own insights regarding consciousness that have arisen from so many years of exploring these teachings. You will discover that in its essence the book is a description of how it is possible to move beyond ordinary mind states into a new direct awareness of the nature of consciousness itself.

My primary goal in sharing what I have learned from Balyogi's Nine Bodies teachings is to make them available for meditation students from all spiritual traditions to use as gateways for exploring the nature of mind. While the Nine Bodies teachings are intellectually stimulating (particularly in light of recent scientific studies about the brain and consciousness), I find that their greatest value comes from utilizing them to explore consciousness through meditation.

I have filtered Balyogi's teachings through my own experience and practice. For the sake of clarity and consistency, I have sometimes used terms that he does not use and organized the material in a way that he has not. This is because in traditional oral teachings, language is often used metaphorically and even inconsistently to describe different aspects of the indescribable and to evoke an inner experience in the listener—an approach that does not always translate well to the written page. The reflections and meditations in Chapter 4 and those in the later illustrated chapters (Chapters 6–11) come from my own practice experience and are not derived from the way Balyogi himself teaches this material.

The Value of the Nine Bodies to Students of Mindfulness Meditation

If you practice mindfulness meditation, the Nine Bodies teachings offer you an additional means for tracking and classifying meditative experiences, which can help you stay present with whatever arises. These explorations may also increase the clarity and specificity of your mindfulness, which can help you gain insight into how you may be causing suffering. They may also help you see the truth of *anicca* (the constancy of change) and *anatta* (not-self). However, in no way are these teachings a substitute for your lineage practice. Rather, they may help you be more effective in your lineage practice.

Each Buddhist lineage or *yana* (Theravada Hinayana, Mahayana, and Vajrayana) has its own means for identifying the progress of insight and measuring the degree of realization in a student. In general, Buddhist teachings don't focus on the phenomena of energetic levels or bodies in the manner that Balyogi's Nine Bodies system does, although they are a strong focus of some Tibetan Tantric teachings. However, extraordinary and altered mind states do occur in all forms of intense meditation practice, and Balyogi's teachings can add perspective and orientation when such experiences arise.

For instance, sometimes you may have experiences during meditation that are confusing, alarming, intoxicating, or captivating. When such experiences occur, you may become stuck or fixated on the experience as you try understand it, or make it happen again, or make it go away, or prevent it from happening again. Many of these seemingly mysterious and exceptional experiences can be examined and understood utilizing the Nine Bodies map. Additionally, the perspective of the Nine Bodies creates a container for your intense meditation experiences that normalizes them and breaks your fascination or your fear of them. Once you have some means for normalizing an exceptional experience, you can move forward in your insight practice. Likewise, in doing *jhana* (concentration) practice or even concentrated *metta* (loving-kindness) practice in the Theravada tradition, very powerful experiences can occur, which these teachings can help put in perspective.

Value of the Teachings for Students of Yoga

For yoga students, the Nine Bodies teachings provide a means for contextualizing and connecting with what you may have learned about the *chakras* (energy centers), *koshas* (sheaths), *gunas* (qualities of nature), and what are traditionally called the Three Bodies (physical, subtle, and causal levels of being). Balyogi's teachings are strongly correlated to Patanjali's Yoga Sutras. They also relate to Samkhya thought and share commonalities with Kashmir Shaivism. Moreover, his explanation of the Nine Bodies may help provide a framework for you to begin to contemplate the extraordinary claims that yogis throughout the ages have reported, but which are difficult to verify or study. Depending on the type of yoga you practice, you may be learning a variety of intense energetic practices that in turn manifest in your meditation practice where they create confusion or disturbances in the mind. If so, the Nine Bodies teachings may help you move beyond your confusion and into deeper meditative states of mind that actually bring you peace and understanding.

The Nine Bodies as a Tool for Teachers

In my experience, the framework of the Nine Bodies provides an additional tool for teachers to help guide students through the meditative process. Whenever I teach the Nine Bodies, the most common response from students is that they feel they have a new means of understanding a particular meditation experience or a way to identify how they got stuck during meditation. Students have not shown a tendency to get attached or fixated on Balyogi's teachings or to regard it as a competing system to the one they already practice. Instead, the teachings seem to provide these students with a language and perspective for examining and responding to mind states that either are causing them concern or are overly exciting.

Inevitably, if students practice meditation with intensity, altered mind states will arise for most of them. These mind states can be extremely pleasant and involve altered sense perceptions, or a dazzling sense of well-being, or clarity of mind that are so enticing that students obsess about wanting to have more of such an experience. It is easy for these states to distract them from the true purpose of meditation, which is to liberate the mind from greed, hatred, and delusion. Likewise, certain unusual mind states can arise that are so confusing and disorienting that students fear they may arise again and so hesitate to meditate. It can be very liberating to have a means of normalizing these unusual states of mind. By locating them on the spectrum of the Nine Bodies, students can receive the insights they offer without getting lost in them. Moreover, even in daily life, such unusual mind states can sometimes seemingly come out of nowhere. In these instances, having a means of identifying and containing such experiences can be essential.

If you are a yoga teacher, dedicated yogi, psychotherapist, or a mindfulness meditation practitioner, you may well discover information about how the mind relates to itself that will help you understand and deepen your practice or help you in guiding your students or patients.

Keeping the Ancient Teachings Alive in the Twenty-First Century

Besides wanting to share what I believe are unique teachings about the nature of consciousness, I have a secondary motivation for writing this book—to preserve the teachings of the Himalayan forest yogis. Balyogi is one of a disappearing group of elder master yoga teachers in India who were initiated by their teachers in the knowledge of the forest tradition. They lived the old ways and learned in that style through incredibly intense practice. As a fourteen-year-old boy, having run away from home to seek the spiritual life,

Balyogi lived with and served his master, who initiated him into a realm of knowing that is not widely available in today's India. Then he lived in a small, isolated cave for twelve years, ate wild plants and berries, and learned secret oral traditions from his fellow cave-dwelling yogis. In that sense, Balyogi is not only a yogi, he is a shaman as well. What Balyogi and these other yogis mastered is not easily separated from the conditions under which they learned. Those conditions—simple, isolated, harsh living conditions—are vanishing in India as its economy continues to prosper and as modern life extends into remote locations such as Rishikesh, a mountain village on the Ganges River in the foothills of the Himalayas whose caves and riverbanks have long been a sanctuary for spiritual seekers. Therefore, it seems vitally important to preserve the ancient teachings. (Of course, new teachers of knowledge will emerge from the new environment, but what they offer will not be quite the same.)

Furthermore, Balyogi's illustrations were already in an advanced state of deterioration when I first saw them. Without this book, both the illustrations and the teachings associated with them could easily have been lost to posterity. It is not possible to know how you or some future yogi may be inspired by these teachings nor how you will build upon them or "correct" them. But they will be available as a resource to you and future spiritual seekers.

The Personal History I Bring to These Teachings

In the early 1970s at the age of twenty-three, I began to study *hatha yoga*, meaning the asanas or poses, which are now widely practiced and many people think of as yoga. Upon the recommendation of my teacher, I visited an ashram created by Swami Vishnudevananda, who was one of a small group of Indian yogis who popularized the study of yoga in the West. There I encountered the full breadth of the teachings that are referred to as Raja yoga, or the royal path of yoga. I became devoted to a daily practice that included yoga postures, various breathing techniques called pranayama, and meditation. I went on to study in the Iyengar tradition of yoga for a number of years as well.

After ten years of intense yoga practice, I had my first experience with the Buddhist practice of Vipassana or Insight Meditation, which is built upon the practice of mindfulness and is a key part of Theravada Buddhism, the predominant Buddhism of Southeast Asia and Sri Lanka. This practice seemed extraordinarily complementary to my yoga practice—the Buddha's teachings provided me with the depth of understanding and practical guidance that I longed for. I eventually chose Vipassana as my primary practice, and it remains so today although I have continued my yoga studies with Balyogi. I have not found myself conflicted over differences in the teachings. Instead, these disparities led me to explore my personal experience further.

A few years after starting Buddhist meditation practices, I left my leadership position at *Esquire* magazine, where I was editor in chief and CEO, to devote myself fully to these practices and to explore the inner life more fully. The year was 1987 and I was forty years old. During the next ten years, in addition to practicing Vipassana and yoga, I studied the writings of C. G. Jung and underwent analysis with the Jungian analyst Dr. Joseph Henderson. Dr. Henderson was an expert in the symbols and interpretations contained in a thirteenth-century alchemical text about the human inner journey titled *Splendor Solis*, which had been introduced to him by C. G. Jung.[1]

In the 1990s I was invited by Spirit Rock Meditation Center to undergo training to become a Vipassana meditation teacher, and I became a full-time teacher of the dharma. In recent years, I have written a book about the Buddha's Four Noble Truths, *Dancing with Life,* based on the teachings that I received from my Buddhist monastic teacher, the Venerable Ajahn Sumedho. This was followed by a second book on wise living based on Buddhist psychology, *Emotional Chaos to Clarity*. I teach silent meditation retreats and lead multiyear training programs for other teachers and for dedicated practitioners. Among the trainings is one for yoga teachers in how to incorporate mindfulness practice into the asana classes they teach.

When I encountered Balyogi and his illustrations, my three main areas of interest—the interpretation of symbols, the psychological, and most importantly, the nature of consciousness—came together. When Balyogi stated that the Buddha was foremost in fully mastering the realization of the Nine Bodies, my interest in the teachings was further heightened. Here was a teacher integrating the two lineages of spiritual understanding that were the focus of my adult life. I recognized that his teachings and illustra-

1   You can read about *Splendor Solis* in Joseph Henderson's book *Transformation of the Psyche* (Hove, UK: Brunner-Routledge, 2003). You can also read about the role of symbols in *C. G. Jung, Man and His Symbols* (New York: Doubleday Windfall, 1964) to which Henderson contributed a section titled "Ancient Myths and Modern Man."

tions captured something rare and genuine. They do not represent academic or conceptual thinking about the mind. (Balyogi had no formal education or even artistic training.) Instead, these teachings and illustrations are an inspired, nonintellectualized reflection of the mind in meditation experiencing consciousness as its object. Of course his insights and illustrations reflect the Indian yoga forest tradition that he is a part of, but they don't merely echo a belief system or repeat ancient teachings. They are what I call "the thing itself," meaning the intuitive or direct knowing of experience.

My Aspiration for This Book

The teachings presented in this book are my best effort to discern and point to what is true and useful for you to explore regarding the Nine Bodies in your meditation practice. The Nine Bodies teachings can be difficult to comprehend without guidance, yet they can be stimulating and inspirational once understood. They can help provide direct insight regarding the misperceptions that cause disquiet and delusion in your heart and mind.

My deepest aspiration is for this book to be helpful to Buddhist and Patanjali yoga practitioners in their meditation practice by pointing to and explaining some of the varieties of experiences of consciousness in meditation. I make frequent reference to the teachings of Patanjali, the Buddha, and my Buddhist teacher, the Venerable Ajahn Sumedho. I make such references in order to capture the integral, nondenominational, nonsectarian vision of Balyogi's teachings.

Although I teach meditation in the Theravada Buddhist tradition, I am not a Buddhist scholar, and, while I used to teach hatha yoga, I am certainly not a scholar of Patanjali's sutras or of the other great Indian yoga treatises. Nor do I claim perfect understanding of Balyogi's teachings of the Nine Bodies. All I can offer are my understandings and experiences coming from my own explorations. I hope they are sufficient to provide insight and practical guidance to you in your practice.

When it is particularly helpful or relevant, I have included the Pali or Sanskrit words for various philosophical terms. These words can be transliterated into the Roman alphabet in a variety of ways. I followed the recommendation of a contemporary yoga scholar in this regard, and in some cases the spelling is different from that used by Balyogi. Balyogi also made many cross-references between yogic and Vedic traditions that I have generally not included because they are beyond the scope of this book.

Beware of Trying to Reconcile Different Teachings

Each spiritual map that has stood the test of time offers the possibility of some insight that may help you relate more effectively to your own body, energy systems, and mind. The most effective way to gain understanding is to study each map within its own system and take whatever insight you gain with gratitude. Rather than trying futilely to reconcile them, you should practice using those descriptions that coincide with your own experience.

Balyogi's teachings have some overlap with those of Kashmir Shaivism and other lineages, but it isn't productive to compare and contrast these maps in your meditation practice and development. It only creates conceptual chaos and confusion. Leave such intellectual study to the scholars. The same is true with comparing Vipassana, Zen, or Tibetan Buddhism with these teachings. There are differences in all lineages and traditions, but they will not prevent you from gaining new understandings, more flexibility in your meditation, and possibly a new energetic facility in your mind. For this reason, despite being a Vipassana teacher versed in key Buddhist teachings, I don't attempt to correlate or explain the differences between Vipassana and Balyogi's teachings when they conflict.

In the present-day Indian state of Bihar, there was once the legendary Nalanda International University, which flourished from the fifth century BCE to 1197 CE. It is described as being one of the first great universities in recorded history, a place where students of many different Hindu and Buddhist persuasions studied and practiced together to the benefit of all. Hindu and Buddhist rulers alike supported the university financially and politically. I share the same ecumenical perspective that we can all learn from each other. Therefore, as you explore the teachings of the Nine Bodies, do as Ajahn Chah, the renowned Thai forest meditation master of the last century, advised his students: "Take what is useful with you and leave the rest here."

Phillip Moffitt
Northern California, 2017

1

BALYOGI'S ASHRAM LIFE
IS INTEGRAL TO HIS TEACHINGS

Balyogi's Ashram Life Is Integral to His Teachings

Since most Western students of meditation and yoga have never been exposed to teachings quite like Balyogi's, and in order to fully absorb their meaning it is helpful to know a few things about Balyogi and to review the classical yoga foundation from which his teachings have emerged. It is almost impossible to understand Balyogi's teachings outside of the context in which he lives and offers his wisdom. Quite literally, his knowledge and his life are not separate. He uses his life as an analogy for his teachings directly and implicitly. His teaching style is the most unusual combination of form and nonform I have encountered.

Balyogi offers his teachings at his ashram in Rishikesh, which is about four hours by train north of New Delhi. Rishikesh is located just a few miles from Haridwar, one of the four sites of the Kumbh Mela, a holy festival held every four years. The Kumbh Mela is the largest spiritual gathering in India, which millions of people attend. Rishikesh sits at the bottom of a large valley where the great Ganges River flows out of the Himalaya mountains. Rishikesh itself is a small, thriving town. But in the foothills above the town on both banks of the Ganges there are an extraordinary number of ashrams and other spiritual centers, which attract thousands of Indian, Asian, and Western spiritual seekers who come for as little as a weekend or for many months and years to study with the many teachers who live there.

Balyogi's ashram is located across the main road and up the hill between two bridges, Ram Jhula and Lakshman Jhula. Neither of these bridges is open to auto traffic; therefore, the area surrounding the ashram feels remote. The ashram sits on four-and-a-half acres about a third of a mile from the river. To get there you have to make your way past a few stores and vendor carts until you come to an area that feels cut off from the bustle on the other side of the bridge. The riverbank is empty of development; there are only a few dwellings—the huts and caves of the *sadhus* (spiritual seekers) who live there. From the river you pass through an opening in a walled-off pasture and walk along a dirt path until you see the gate of the Yogant Foundation, which is Balyogi's ashram. There is a sign stating the hours during which visitors are welcome.

Sometimes the gate is open during those hours, and sometimes it remains locked. The message is clear from the start—that spiritual "tourists" should not bother coming here. There is also a sign with a phone number urging you to call for an appointment; again sometimes

Balyogi, circa 1957.

you will get an appointment, sometimes not. It definitely helps to know someone who has walked the path up that hill before.

If the gate is open and you are able to venture up the steep winding pathway, after a five-minute walk, you will find yourself on the flat part of a hill. On your left will be one of the most unusual trees you are ever likely to see. Close examination reveals that it is actually four trees entwined as one. Around the tree is a stone and sand meditation terrace with a small Shiva *lingam* (an abstract representation of the god Shiva, usually as an ovoid stone) and a pot for burning incense. When you sit facing the tree with your back to the path that brought you to this inspiring spot, you are looking straight up the beautiful, pristine valley from which the Ganges flows. If you look in the direction of the path that led you to the ashram, the opposite riverbank and the many ashrams along the river are visible, and the sound of children playing floats up from the small school down below. The feeling standing there is that you have entered another world, one that moves more slowly and has a different focus than that of the Western world or modern India.

Unless there is an event or class being held, there is little activity at the ashram. Only a few people live there and not many classes are offered, although there are some rooms available for long-term students. You may not even see anyone at first, but eventually someone will come out to greet you and ask you to have a seat until Balyogi can see you. If you happen to come on a day when he is sitting nearby, you will be asked to wait or to come back another day. If you happen to come when a student is sitting under the tree meditating, chances are that student will continue to sit there without offering to help you. This is as it should be; the student's mind is not to be focused on worldly questions or responsibilities at that time.

Finally, Balyogi will greet you. You will discover that he is a man in his eighties with thinning, flowing black hair, the soft unblemished skin of a baby, and deep dark eyes that are like bottomless wells. If you become a regular visitor, you may hear about the time robbers attacked him and bashed his head in. Although his attackers left him for dead, he survived by going into deep samadhi. (A large piece of bone is missing from the top of his skull; he often has episodes of intense pain and reports that his brain is not working well enough to teach. He uses sunlight and meditation as his medicine to alleviate these problems. He refuses to take any medicine that clouds his mind.) He will speak to you in halting but understandable English. You might catch a glimpse of his daughter Divya (who teaches hatha yoga classes at the ashram) or his grandchild—both of them live at the ashram part-time.

If you are there to just ask a question, he will listen and give you what advice he has. For instance, one day while I was studying at the ashram, a young Japanese man who was a pearl diver came seeking advice because he had suddenly become afraid of swimming into the depths of the ocean, and his fear was blocking him from his only means of economic survival. (Balyogi taught him how to stay in his body while looking at the nature of his mind, and he returned to Japan hopeful that he would be able to dive again even if fear continued to arise.) Oftentimes, a visitor will have had a big spiritual experience and want Balyogi to interpret it or tell them how to recreate it; or else they are looking for someone to teach them asana, or pranayama, or a shortcut to altered mind states. Balyogi is not interested in teaching asana himself, but he will have Divya teach it to visitors. And he is not interested in providing shortcuts for getting into altered mind states; he's interested in offering teachings that bring about an understanding of consciousness and that lead to freedom.

If you are an "honored guest," you may see Balyogi's scrapbook of the time he taught in the U.S., Japan, and elsewhere while you are being served delicious chai. But you are not likely to hear about the day in the 1960s when the Beatles wandered by and asked for instruction, particularly "Georgie" (George Harrison), nor about the many senior Indian teachers who come for visits. If you seek meditation, you may be taken to the altar room or directed to sit under the mysterious tree.

Balyogi, circa 1980.

Among the many striking things that set the Yogant Foundation apart from other ashrams is that neither the ashram nor Balyogi have much to sell you in the way of movement classes, health services, lodging, or tourist "holy moments." For some visitors, this lack of an agenda can be a letdown or a point of confusion. Common reactions I've heard include, "Why am I here?" "What do I say to this man?" and "What happens next?" But the lack of a set program at the Yogant Foundation can expand your mind in a new manner. You may learn to simply be open and available to experience the moment without needing to judge it against some view you may have of what your time is worth. You may discover that even the boring or mundane can bring ease and insight. Of course, no spiritual tourist is willing to put up with such uncertainty, and certainly not with being bored, so they disappear almost as soon as they arrive.

On the other hand, if you have come on a quest that Balyogi feels he can help you with—an illness, or you and your spouse are hoping to heal your marriage, or you are looking to serve in an ashram—he welcomes you and makes you part of the ashram for an afternoon, a few days, weeks, or months, or for periodic visits with phone calls in-between.

Balyogi does not conceal his personality from you. He is not worldly, but he possesses an innate sense of how to manage in the world. He is a swami, a guru, and his occasionally imperious manner of interaction reflects the style that such teachers traditionally employed in India, which is quite different from Western style student-teacher relationships. "Gu" means "darkness" and "ru" means "remove," so a guru is "a remover of the darkness" or "one who shines light on the darkness"; the guru's role, therefore, is to help

Balyogi and Phillip Moffitt sitting under the meditation tree at the Yogant Foundation, circa 2001.

you free yourself from the *kleshas*, or hindrances of mind, and to help you see where your innate knowledge has been obscured by *avidya*, or ignorance. Balyogi demonstrates genuine care for the well-being of those who come seeking his attention, but because he is a swami with hundreds of years of patriarchal tradition conditioning his behavior, you have to take care of yourself and your own personal boundaries in your interactions with him. In the past there have been controversies and accusations of misconduct regarding Balyogi's attitudes and behavior toward Western female students. While I do not know what is true and not true, I do not condone or approve of any such behavior. In my view, as is the case with all people, including spiritual teachers, he is an imperfect human being who is not always skillful in his actions. It is the teachings and practices that Balyogi shares that makes the journey to spend time in his presence valuable and that is the focus of this book.

Upon meeting Balyogi, you quickly realize that you are in the presence of a teacher with true knowledge. True knowledge is the kind of knowing that can only belong to someone who has had the realizations and insights that constitute that knowledge. In Balyogi, you can feel the accumulation of knowledge that he has been acquiring since he ran away from home at the age of fourteen to look for a Buddhist teacher, but instead found the holy men of the Patanjali yoga tradition. You can feel his knowledge of the plants, healing herbs, and ease with nature that comes from living for many years in a cave deep in the jungle. You can feel the knowledge of his sixty years of practice and teaching of asana, pranayama, chanting, meditation, and so much more. You can feel his decades of *bhakti* (devotional) practice that he still engages in at least twice every single day. The result of all this knowledge combined with his "humanness" is that there isn't the usual gloss that so often obscures a teacher. You realize that Balyogi is upholding a tradition and that he is one of the few remaining great Himalayan teachers whose presence in the last century introduced so many Westerners to Eastern thought.

Maybe, just maybe, you are someone Balyogi feels for reasons of his own he really wants to teach. Without asking anything of you, he becomes more assertive—telling you how to spend your time, how much of your time he wants, and when it is to be. He expects you to honor this and to accommodate his vision; it is this classic respect for the teaching that is his primary payment. For this reason, you bring fruit, flowers, or little gifts each day you visit as a way of honoring the teacher, and you leave money at the end of each day on the altar as an indication of your respect and appreciation.

My Encounters with Sri Swami Balyogi Premvarni

My first encounter with Balyogi occurred in 1999. Having learned about him from a friend, I planned to visit the Yogant Foundation briefly to ask Balyogi a question about how to release an energy blockage in my throat chakra that had caused me discomfort and restricted my speech. I brought fruit as an offering, looked at his scrapbook, sat in meditation under the tree as he directed, received an answer to my question in the form of a mantra, took a tour of the ashram, and then left a donation on the altar. Just as I was preparing to leave, Balyogi reappeared and told me I needed to spend the next couple of days there. I had plans to be in another part of India, but I let those go, for how often will a teacher take this kind of initiative? (In my forty years of practice with wonderful Buddhist and yoga teachers, this has only happened twice; both times were life-changing.)

The teachings that Balyogi transmitted to me over the next two days inspired me to return numerous times over the ensuing years to study with him. (Ironically, the energy blockage in my throat that first brought me to him persisted and continues to persist to this day—perhaps because I was not consistent in working with the mantra that he gave me. However, I did learn to work with it much more precisely so that my throat is less of a problem.) During one of my visits, Balyogi locked the ashram gate some days, thereby making me the sole recipient of his teachings on those occasions. This immersion was instrumental in helping me develop insights regarding the teachings. Other days I had to sit and wait several hours for him to be ready to teach. I assume the delays were the result of the pain he experienced because of his brain injury. If he was interrupted or distracted during one of our sessions by some other commitment, then hours of my precious few days at the Yogant Foundation would appear to be lost.

It was in this context that I came to receive the teachings of the Nine Bodies. The context is important because Balyogi does not teach in a linear style; his style is elliptical, scattered, turns back on itself, has many interruptions and cross-references, and is laced with stories that don't seem to be related to anything but later prove to be relevant to what is being taught at the moment. He is often interrupted by daily ashram activities and will stop in the midst of making a crucial teaching point to do a task; he may not come back to that point until days later and then do so in a manner such that you have to figure out for yourself that he has returned to the earlier subject!

The natural environment itself is part of Balyogi's teaching—the animals, the jungle sounds, the hot sun or cold wind, the activity of the ashram, and the exotic vegetation that is now being studied by the India Department of Agriculture for its healing powers. Once when a tiger appeared at the ashram and had to be chased off, that became the illustration for a teaching about the dangers of desire. (Amazingly, it was Balyogi's then nine-year-old daughter who hit the tiger to chase it away from threatening her beloved dog—but that's a story to hear from her.) Another time, when I encountered a small herd of wild elephants on my way to the ashram, that too became a teaching on not giving in to strong emotions. I was often given plants or berries to eat or to apply to my skin. I participated in his "eco-therapy" activities (ecological healing practices involving trees, herbs, plants, water, and sun) during which I was given various *kriyas* (cleansing practices) for my eyesight, sinuses, and overall rejuvenation. Balyogi would sometimes prepare meals for me and the food would become a teaching analogy.

All of this teaching was presented as a pastiche; therefore, I was sometimes unsure whether I understood the point Balyogi was making or the specific meaning of the words he was using, which in the ancient texts often

Balyogi meditating in Mulabandhasana pose, circa 1970.

have multiple meanings. Balyogi says that the purpose of these activities is to induce "neutralization" of the physical being in order to prepare for the transmission of the teaching.

In this style of teaching and learning, transmission is key; the understanding evolves within you in response to the energetic field of the teacher. The mind has to let go of trying to interpret or bring order to what you're hearing, and you have to surrender control of the learning process. It is a style of teaching and learning that involves transmission of knowledge via osmosis, and spontaneous realization comes from certain conditions having been created. This style of learning is not reinforced by a sense of cognitive completion or by relating to a cognitive whole. Nor are there step-by-step rewards and reassurances along the way. You simply keep going until an understanding of the whole arises. Then you can go back and fill in the conceptual parts yourself.

This meandering and nonstructured teaching method is certainly not my favorite way to learn. That I have continued to study with Balyogi for all these years reflects the great respect I have for him and his knowledge. Learning in this way forced me to stretch how I learn and to conquer my frustration. Fortunately, my intuition often served me when I felt cognitively limited, but this required me to keep my mind alert and focused.

Since in many ways I was not an ideal student to receive Balyogi's teachings, I repeatedly had to let go of my unease by reminding myself that I did not choose him, he chose me. He has often said happily, "Now you get it," or "I knew you could understand." My inner response to such reinforcement was that I was glad he thought so, because I did not share such confidence! I simply had to trust his evaluation since I lacked an overview. At no other time in my forty-five years of studying yoga and Buddhism have I ever felt so lost for so long.

After each visit to Balyogi, I would discover that I had gained a new piece of knowledge. Upon recognizing this, Balyogi began to urge me to teach what I had learned from him. As the years went by, he began to voice impatience with me because I failed to do as he asked. But I always replied that there was too much that I did not understand and it would not do his teachings justice for me to merely parrot what I had heard him say.

Finally, after much study, I have arrived at my own relationship to Balyogi's material and feel ready to share his teachings. This is not to say that I fully understand his teachings, but rather that I have reached my own understanding of them, can apply them in my meditation practice, and am able to utilize them in working with meditation students. In some instances, I have had different insights than those Balyogi was pointing toward in his teaching.

Balyogi, twenty years old, sitting with his teacher Yogeswarananda.

The teachings in this book reflect my experience, my insights, and how I have integrated what I learned from Balyogi's teachings. I have done my best to accurately present what he taught me, but inevitably there will be misunderstandings. For this reason, while writing this book, whenever I have had uncertainty about a point that I could not clarify in discussions with Balyogi, I have stayed true to my own experience with the teachings. Therefore, you at least have the assurance that what is being taught accurately reflects someone's experience rather than a mere concept. Any misrepresentation occurring in this text is my responsibility alone.

A Day Studying with Balyogi

One day during a two-week period I spent studying with him, Balyogi announced that the following day the two of us would go to a deserted cave several miles away for an extended period of meditation without interruptions. I was thrilled at this news, as I always found meditating with him to be very powerful for collecting and unifying my mind. So the next day we hired a taxi and traveled along a treacherous road for more than an hour, arriving finally at a location that had no outward sign of being anything. Balyogi explained that the cave was on the site of an abandoned monastery. He told me that the cave extended over a mile, but most of it had been blocked off because there were venomous snakes in the deepest parts of it.

We proceeded on foot down a hill and around a bend and then came upon the monastery, which unbeknownst to Balyogi was being rebuilt. There were workmen everywhere pounding nails and pouring concrete. There were also numerous Indian tourists milling about because the monastery had recently been written up in a magazine. As we walked toward the cave entrance through the throng of people, I became increasingly disappointed because I thought we would not have a chance of finding any solitude. We entered the cave, which became very dark quickly. After a few moments we rounded a corner where a teacher sat on a rock ledge leading a group of about ten people in a chant.

We proceeded further into the cave until we were in complete darkness. Balyogi reached out and took my hand to guide me. Seconds later, I brushed up against something and realized it was someone seated. A few more steps, and I could see nine or ten people sitting in a chamber of the cave. The room

was dimly lit by a candle, which sat on a three-foot wide stone altar that had been carved out of one wall. Along with the candle were some icons. The chamber was still and silent. No sounds filtered through from outside, not even the sound of the students chanting in the previous chamber.

When we walked into the chamber, the people seated there began to bow to Balyogi. He proceeded to the altar with me in tow and then indicated with a hand

Balyogi with Swami Satchidananda, circa 1965.

gesture that I was to sit on a stone directly in front of the altar. He then boosted himself up onto the altar, which was about four feet off the ground.

I closed my eyes and we sat silently for about twenty minutes until the people in the group who had been sitting there when we arrived started to whisper among themselves. "Quiet," Balyogi boomed, "no talking!" Shortly after, I heard the others leave the chamber and the two of us continued sitting for a while. Then I heard Balyogi rustling around on the altar, but I kept my eyes closed. The next thing I knew, he had hopped off the altar. I opened my eyes and started to stand as well, but he indicated that I was to continue sitting. He handed me a small tin, the type that sardines come packed in, and said, "Put this in your backpack. Whatever you do, do not open the lid of the tin." I dutifully put the tin in my backpack and resumed sitting. Balyogi then left without further instructions.

He had not told me how long to sit nor given me any direction for continuing my meditation. Not long after he left, Indian tourists began trickling into the chamber. They ignored me sitting in silence and spoke to one another, sometimes going up to the altar and touching their foreheads in a sign of respect, talking all the while and even stepping on my feet! But since my assignment was to just sit, I continued to do so.

I've sat in stillness for many hours in even more uncomfortable situations, so I was not flustered. On the other hand, it was not how I thought the day was going to turn out, and there were only three days remaining before I had to leave India, so it did not seem like a good use of my time. Still, I sat there without many reactive thoughts—when you practice meditation you learn to let the circumstances be in the background and pay attention to the present moment. I trusted that Balyogi would either return for me or rejoin me in sitting, or that at some point I would know it was enough.

Finally, a feeling arose inside of me that it was time to move. I left the cave and found Balyogi standing outside surrounded by a group of people listening to his explanation of some spiritual topic. He left them, came over to me, and asked, "Do you still have the tin?" I told him that I did. He nodded his approval and then directed me to go sit by the Ganges, which was about a five-minute walk from the monastery. Again, he offered no explanation as to why I should do this or how long it would be before he rejoined me. I dutifully went and sat by the river.

Soon a group of French "spiritual tourists" arrived and their guide began teaching them Patanjali's Yoga Sutras as they stood or sat by the river. The guide's interpretation of the sutras contained some major misunderstandings, in my view. Despite their presence, I continued to sit there. Was this what Balyogi wanted me to reflect on—the danger in clinging to anyone's version of a teaching? Again, after a certain point, I knew I'd sat there long enough and went back to the monastery where Balyogi stood waiting for me. "What took you so long?"

Balyogi with B. K. S. Iyengar.

he asked. I said nothing. What could I say? In this kind of learning situation, you simply assume that there is a teaching in the moment, whether or not the teacher intends it.

Balyogi then announced that we were going somewhere else, and the hired car mysteriously reappeared. We drove for fifteen minutes and stopped again at an unmarked location. We walked down a hill and over a small rise to where an oarsman sat in a small rowboat. Balyogi announced that we were first going to meditate sitting in the middle of the great Ganges and then we would go to the other side. The oarsman rowed us out to the middle of the river, where we sat in silence for a short while, and then Balyogi directed him to take us to the far shore.

Once we reached the shore, we walked half a mile down the rocky beach and sat down. "Give me the tin," Balyogi directed, and I took it out of my backpack. "It is a good thing you did not open it," he says. Then he very carefully opened it and out fell one very mad scorpion! "Look how upset he is," Balyogi said. "This scorpion was where he was not supposed to be, and getting to his right place has been very unsettling for him." I asked where it had come from and Balyogi explained that when he was sitting in the cave he had seen the scorpion moving around on the altar. "I had to remove the scorpion," he explained. "With people placing their foreheads on the stone, someone could easily have been stung."

Keep in mind that Balyogi at that point was in his seventies and had almost died from having his skull bashed in. Yet in the darkness of the cave, he observed the scorpion and found a way of safely dealing with it. I said that I didn't feel that we had done our job leaving the scorpion out in the open. So we scooped it back into the tin and released it in a pile of rocks further from shore. "Look how he is completely settled now," Balyogi said. "He is no longer a danger to himself or anyone else."

Balyogi and I sat in silence for a short while on the beach. He then talked about an aspect of the Nine Bodies teaching. Afterward, we walked back to the rowboat and retraced our journey back to the ashram. We said very little on the way back and the scorpion was not mentioned at all. Nor was it mentioned the next day. But on the third day, Balyogi asked if I remembered the scorpion, and I replied that of course I did. "Well," he said, "just so with the students you teach. The ego identity is their scorpion; it needs to get to the far shore where it can find a natural home. If the ego does not make the journey, then it can cause harm to the person or to others. But it is not a comfortable journey to the other shore, and like with the scorpion you have to be careful while carrying it there. The teachings and practices are the tin, the container that constrains the ego while it makes the journey."

The way Balyogi is using the word "ego" in this instance is different from the way it is commonly used in Western psychotherapy. In his teachings, Balyogi generally uses the word "ego" to mean an identification with the personality—and its desires and aversions—that causes suffering.

When I tell students this story, they often ask, "But what if you had opened the tin and been stung? Why didn't he warn you?" I am never sure how to reply to such questions. First of all, Balyogi told me not to open it, and it never occurred to me to not honor his wish. I realize this may challenge your modern sense of accountability, but I was not likely to be in danger unless I violated a fundamental precept of Buddhism, taking only what is freely given. In this instance, knowledge of what was in the tin had not been freely given, so I was in danger only if I violated

Sri Swami Balyogi Premvarni, circa 2001.

the precept. I did not consider opening the tin, even when I sat down by the Ganges and it would have been easy to do. It was not my tin; I was carrying it for him. Respecting his boundary and not trying to second-guess what he was doing *was* my protection. In your life, you are sometimes given something to carry that is not yours. If you handle it with this respect, then you are much less likely to cause suffering to yourself and others.

Secondly, yes, the tin could have fallen open accidentally, and that would have put me at some risk when I removed stuff from my backpack. But studying with this kind of teacher is not risk-free. There were many ways I could have been stung by Balyogi during my years of study with him. But even more dangerous is the scorpion-like nature of the ego itself. When you are engaged in spiritual practice, you are constantly in danger of being stung by your ego, but do you acknowledge that risk with the same urgency as being stung by a scorpion?

I have witnessed others being stung by teachers throughout my four-and-a-half decades of practice. There are many risks in spiritual practice. For instance, you may put a lot of time and effort into doing a certain practice or studying with a particular teacher and then discover that it won't carry you forward. This is where surrender applies to spiritual practice. You surrender any attachment to choosing the right teacher, the right practice, or achieving a particular outcome. You just do the practice—carry the tin mindfully until the conditions are such that you can release the scorpion of your own ego. What makes surrender so poignant is that although you let go of the outcome, you continue to take responsibility for yourself.

At no point in all my time studying with Balyogi have I ever felt less than fully responsible for myself. Any injury to my feelings, my body, or my energy was my business. I trusted his good intentions, but I also knew I was going on a journey that involved risk and that I needed to be awake and cautious. I never assumed that he necessarily knew what was best for me.

It is empowering to acknowledge to yourself that the scorpion of your ego can be contained through self-awareness and reflection. Developing these capacities will enable you to carry the container to the far shore even though it will be challenging and even dangerous at times. In my experience, curiosity, modesty, humor, compassion, loving-kindness, and commitment to know the truth are your best companions on the journey. What I have found thus far in my own journey is that love (not romantic, self-referenced love, but rather the mysterious, interdependent oneness that is beyond the ego) is both the motivator for the journey and its final destination. It can never be said too many times that staying committed to the journey is your responsibility, not arriving at some distant destination. May these teachings serve you skillfully during your journey to the far shore.

2

INSIGHTS INTO CONSCIOUSNESS

Insights into Consciousness

The Nine Bodies teachings are an exploration of how to utilize the many dimensions and manifestations of consciousness in meditation. The teachings map out a journey that starts with the kind of consciousness that arises in the physical body and is directly observable, and then takes us through ever more subtle levels of consciousness to that which is not manifest and is only potential; therefore, it has to be inferred.

Through this journey, we discover how layered and tangled the mind's experience is. We also come to have faith that through meditation we can know these levels of consciousness and interact with them directly and skillfully. Initially, we learn about the characteristics of consciousness through study and reflection, and then we start to explore them through meditation and contemplation practices. As we make this exploration, bear in mind that our intent is to broaden and deepen our awareness of consciousness in order to be more effective in the particular path of practice we are following.

To begin with, let's define a few terms. When I refer to the "Nine Bodies," I am not referring to structures that can be located and verified using the tools of Western science. Rather, the Nine Bodies are universal realms of subjective human experience that we can experience, explore, and get to know more intimately through the use of our attention—especially when that attention is focused and directed through the tools of meditation. (In that sense, the Nine Bodies are analogous to other realms of exploration that mindfulness students may be familiar with, such as the Four Foundations of Mindfulness.) You could look at them as "layers," "levels," "aspects," or "dimensions" of your multilayered, multidimensional human life (and I'll use all of these different words in referring to them).

Some of the Nine Bodies are easily experienced in day-to-day life, such

as the Physical Body or the Emotional Body. (I'll tell you more details about these different bodies in Chapter 3.) Others (such as the Astral Body and the Intuitive Body) are more subtle and may only be experienced when consciousness is refined and focused through meditative practice, or in altered states such as dreams or trance.

Through focusing on each of these Bodies in meditation practice, we can illuminate more fully that particular dimension of our human experience. This can help us to clear areas of blockage, nonclarity, or stagnation that may be impeding our movement toward clear seeing and liberation from greed, hatred, and ignorance. We can also use our investigations in each of the Nine Bodies as an opportunity to turn our attention back toward the nature of consciousness itself.

The meditative work with the Nine Bodies develops and depends upon our ability to direct our attention into particular realms of experience—and is inextricably entwined with the exploration of the nature of consciousness itself. So before going forward, we first need to develop clarity around what is meant by the word "consciousness." This is not an easy task since the nature of consciousness has been a continual source of speculation, debate, and contention among Asian spiritual teachers for more than three thousand years. Moreover, spiritual teachers often use the word consciousness loosely, signaling different meanings based on context.

Consciousness has also been a source of debate and speculation among Western philosophers and psychologists and is now being intensely researched by neuroscientists, among whom there is no agreement as to what the mind is versus the brain. In this chapter I am not trying to resolve this debate but rather providing you with an understanding of how consciousness is used in the Nine Bodies teachings so that you can gain access to the felt sense of each of the Bodies. Nor are the Nine Bodies teachings about consciousness trying to compete with neurological explanations. Instead, their purpose is to help you come into direct contact with your experience of consciousness.

In traditional Buddhist teachings, what we call "consciousness" has two different functions or dimensions:

1. The process of being conscious of something, i.e., the *mental activity of cognizing*. In this dimension or function of consciousness, consciousness is linked with and known through the experiences of the senses

and the mind. It arises and passes away as these experiences—and the knowing of them—come and go. When I'm referring to this aspect of consciousness, I'll often call it "sense-consciousness" to distinguish it from the second dimension of consciousness.

2. *The phenomenon or capacity of consciousness that allows cognizing to happen.* Regardless of what you are being conscious of, there is a certain capacity of the mind called "consciousness." It has its own unique nature and characteristics, which are often described with words such as "luminous" or "timeless." This capacity of the mind—which I will refer to as "luminous consciousness"—can be directly experienced through meditation and investigation.

Sense-Consciousness

In order to fully comprehend the teachings associated with the Nine Bodies, it is helpful to have a depth of understanding about each of these qualities of consciousness.

In the first usage, the word "consciousness"—what I'm calling "sense-consciousness"—refers to the process of a stimulus coming into contact with one of the sense gates, such as the eyes, the ears, or the mind in the form of a thought or emotion. Once sense contact has been made, the stimulus is perceived by the sense organ and is then interpreted by the brain. In other words, this kind of consciousness is always consciousness *of* something—or, more precisely, consciousness that co-arises with a stimulus. This use of the word consciousness refers to the activity of something being known or cognized in a given moment. For example, when your hands get cold, it consciously registers in your brain that your hands are cold. If your hands are cold, but you're engrossed in watching a soccer match, consciousness of your cold hands may not arise until that moment in which the game ends, your team triumphs, and you suddenly notice your numb fingers.

It helps to understand this if you keep reminding yourself that sense-consciousness is a process, not a static or separate thing. This is very clear in the Pali language, which is based upon verbs rather than nouns—so *vinnana*, the Pali word for "sense-consciousness," could perhaps be more accurately translated as "sense-consciousnessing." Or, said another way, as "sense-consciousness is occurring." It is a *process* whereby sight, sound, smell, taste, physical sensation, and mental thoughts and emotions are being known.

In order to directly experience what is meant by sense-consciousness, you may try the following meditation exercise.

▶ MEDITATION EXERCISE ONE: Sense-Consciousness

Rest your hands on your thighs and focus on your right hand. As soon as you focus on the hand, you will start to feel sensations or a lack of sensations. You may feel the weight or hardness of the bones in the hand, the softness of the tissue, tingling or pulsations in the fingers, warmth or coolness in the palms. Such sensations in the hands are arising and passing away all the time, regardless of whether or not you notice them. But now you are awake to them as they happen; they are registering in consciousness. This is what I mean by consciousness being a process, an activity. Some form of contact arises through one of the senses, the mind focuses on that sensation (no matter how briefly), and you are conscious of it occurring.

This kind of fluency with experiencing and directing your sense-consciousness is important to the Nine Bodies work because we access the Nine Bodies through sense-consciousness.

Mindfulness and Sense-Consciousness

As Buddhist meditation students discover, it's possible to bring a quality called "mindfulness" (*sati*) to sense-consciousness as it arises. When sense-consciousness is accompanied with mindfulness, we meet our experience as it is without judgment or resistance. This nonresistance allows us to know our experience just as it is rather than through the filter of our reactive interpretations. And when we utilize mindfulness for attaining freedom from clinging and craving, it is called right or wise mindfulness (*samyak smriti* in Sanskrit, *samma sati* in Pali).

Mindfulness occurs when you are being *present for and attending to* what you are experiencing in the moment. For example when your hands are cold, you not only know your hands are cold, you *know you know* your hands are cold. You feel the cold directly and you watch how your mind reacts to the cold. Do you have an aversion to it? Does your mind panic? With mindfulness you are able to say to yourself, "Cold hands are like this," so that you are not completely lost in your reactions to your cold hands. When you utilize consciousness to be mindful, you quickly discover you have many more choices for acting wisely and maintaining a balanced perspective.

When you "know you know" that some experience is being cognized, you are still utilizing the process of sense-consciousness, and the consciousness is still focused on the objects of experience. However, mindfulness has a feeling of being *awake* and *present* that adds an extra dimension or context to consciousness beyond just registering that your hands are cold. This additional depth of attention allows profound insight and wisdom to occur. In the Theravada tradition of Buddhism in which I teach, the cultivation of insight is the direct means for liberating the mind and heart.

Much of your mind's reactivity in the form of wanting or aversion happens because you are reluctant to feel fully in your body and heart what is occurring in your consciousness. In contrast, when you are being mindful of what you are experiencing and how you are reacting, you develop a *nonobjecting attitude* to what is true at the moment. This nonobjecting attitude of mindfulness allows you to sit through all kinds of difficulty in your meditation practice and daily life and to stay true to your deepest values during challenging times.

Wise mindfulness is one of the factors in the Buddha's teaching of the Eightfold Path, which leads to the end of suffering. Wise mindfulness has a *remembering* quality, meaning that you are remembering to be conscious of your *intention* to live from your wisest *understanding*. Learning to access the aspect of consciousness that "knows this moment is like this" is most readily cultivated through Buddhist mindfulness meditation.

In order to directly experience mindfulness accompanying sense-consciousness, you may try the following meditation.

▶ MEDITATION EXERCISE TWO: Mindfulness

Sit with your hands on your thighs and take some time to become aware once again of the right hand, as you did in the first exercise. Keep directing your attention to the sensations of the right hand until the mind is stable, you can maintain focus on the hand for some time, and you are able to return quickly to it after taking a moment for reflection. Feel these sensations *directly*—they are not concepts. Also, confirm that you are genuinely present for what is occurring in this moment in your mind.

Now, become mindful of the consciousness of the sensations of the hand. Observe that you can know or be conscious that hand sensations are being known. This is mindfulness—you are *conscious of being conscious* of a moment's experience. Please note that your mindfulness experience is not removed from the experience of your hand. The spotlight of attention is still on the hand, but you have expanded the dimension of your consciousness. You are now able to be consciously present with what your mind is experiencing while your focus remains *with* the sensations of your hand. It may take some reflection and practice to understand and be able to do this, but if you persevere, your understanding of mindfulness will deepen in a manner that enhances your sense of being *present or having presence* in your daily life. If you start to feel like a removed observer, pay more attention to the physical sensations of the hand. Then with each sensation that arises in the hand, note that you *know you are knowing* that specific sensation even as it arises in consciousness.

Stay in this mindfulness state for a few minutes and observe what happens. Most likely the mind will find your hand sensations to be pleasant, unpleasant, or neither. The mind will either stay with the experience or start to wander away. If it stays with the hand sensations, the mind will start to comment on the sensations or the exercise itself or start to manipulate the experience. Imagine being able to do this mindfulness practice with memories, fears, desires, dislikes, old stories, and unskillful states of mind until you cease to be controlled by all of the desires and disturbances arising in the mind.

Developing this capacity of mindfulness supports your work with the Nine Bodies in two ways. First of all, you'll get out of your own way by not impeding your progress with your own reactivity, grasping, and aversion. Secondly, with mindfulness, you'll be able to penetrate your experience on a more refined level, thereby accessing the subtler of the Nine Bodies, such as the Etheric Body.

Luminous Consciousness

Now let's look more deeply at the second way the word "consciousness" is used in this book, as well as in the broader Buddhist and yogic traditions. In this usage, the word refers to consciousness as a phenomenon in and of itself. In other words, regardless of what you are being conscious of, there is a certain capacity of the mind, which I'm calling "luminous consciousness," that has its own unique nature and characteristics. When Balyogi refers to this dimension of consciousness, he often uses the Sanskrit word *chiti*.

When describing this dimension of consciousness, the Buddhist and yogic traditions often use words like "unconditioned," "radiant," "without seed," "unborn," and other terms that at first might seem mysterious. But as you practice, you may start to have your own foretaste of this dimension and the terms will begin to resonate with you. More importantly, by learning to directly access luminous consciousness, you will develop insight, which will liberate the mind from grasping and clinging.

It would not be surprising if you have neglected exploring the nature of *luminous consciousness itself* (chiti) because of how stimulated you are by what you become *conscious of*. But upon reflection, it is clear that there is a distinct difference between the process of sense consciousness, in which you become momentarily conscious of an object of experience, and the actual phenomenon of luminous consciousness.

You can experience this difference for yourself through the following meditation.

▶ MEDITATION EXERCISE THREE: Locating Luminous Consciousness

Repeat the earlier steps of locating the sensation experience of your right hand, confirming you are conscious of it and being mindful of your mind's moment-to-moment response to the sensations of the hand. Once you are established in your attention in this manner, *turn the spotlight of consciousness back on itself*, just as though you were in a movie theater and stopped looking at the screen and looked back at the projector. To do this, let go of noticing objects and make the phenomenon of consciousness the object of attention.

Just notice what you notice; do not try to figure it out, or you will fall back into the knowing of objects. If you persist, you will start to feel directly the capacity of consciousness. You can continue meditating in this manner even when consciousness starts doing its act of knowing. Just let go of the objects, let go of any interest in them, and *turn around once again* to gaze at the capacity of knowing that is simply there, regardless of what, if anything, is being known. Act as though you can do this meditation exercise even though you will likely fail many times before succeeding. Be patient, curious, and amused at your mind's independence.

When this shift of attention occurs, you are resting in the empty mind that is very awake and aware. The empty mind is characterized by a spacious stillness. You are not *doing* in this meditation but rather *being* in meditative awareness. Your attention is not focused on the hand, but the knowing of the hand remains in the background as the object of consciousness and grounds the entire experience in the moment. Remember there are many layers of depth to this experience. Most us already have some sense of this capacity and how it is different in some way than being conscious of some specific object. So, if the previous guidance seems too complex, just relax your mind and turn toward luminous consciousness.

When you turn your attention in this way to luminous consciousness, beware of the danger of identifying with it. The knowing aspect of consciousness can create the illusion that there is an unchanging *knower* who is in control of itself. We usually identify the knower with our ego, personality, or body, or our mind, or some combination of the four. We tend to envision this knower as a single permanent, fixed, and unchanging entity.

However, when closely examined we see that "knowing" can be more accurately described as the flow of consciousness from one moment to the next.

Freedom through Consciousness

You can easily see why a key part of the spiritual journey is exploring the nature of consciousness. The goal is to free your mind from the illusions that keep it fluctuating in ebbs and flows with which we identify. To the extent we are able to attain insight as to the true nature of consciousness, that is the degree to which we cease being caught in the endless cycle of wanting the desirable and not wanting the undesirable.

Balyogi frequently cites Patanjali's Yoga Sutras to illustrate how understanding the role of consciousness is a major factor to moving through the spiritual journey. Moreover, he states that of all the great meditation masters, it was the Buddha who most fully developed this capacity for finding freedom from suffering through consciousness. He says that most religions focus on honoring and expressing gratitude for their creator and emphasize behavior that will appease their God or Gods through living by certain rules and carrying out necessary rituals. However, the Buddha did not attain freedom from suffering through belief or through rules and rituals. Instead, he focused on directly experiencing insight and realization through consciousness. Thus, it was the Buddha's own practices, actions, and perseverance that carried him to freedom from the suffering caused by craving and aversion. For that reason, Balyogi offers the Buddha as a role model of how dedication to a practice of transformation and transcendence can free our hearts and minds.

The Activity of Consciousness: The Light Bulb Analogy

Balyogi uses the analogy of a light bulb and how it functions in giving off light to illustrate the distinction between sense-consciousness, luminous consciousness, and the functioning and physiology of the brain.

Consider a light bulb that is lighting up the objects in a dark room. Each object in the room—the furniture, food, people, and so forth—is bathed in the light of the light bulb. The process of the light illuminating the objects so that we can see them is analogous to the arising of sense-consciousness.

We tend to mistakenly identify the light bulb as the *source* of the light; after all, the light bulb is what is giving off the light. In the same way, we tend to assume that the brain and all its attendant functions—memory, reason, thoughts, a sense of self, etc.—are the source of our consciousness.

However, if you pause to examine this situation more closely, the light bulb itself is also being illuminated. You can easily see this is occurring, but does that mean that the light bulb has self-illumination? No, of course not. But then what illuminates the light bulb? Electricity. Electricity empowers the components of the light bulb to function so that light occurs.

Therefore, the power that actually lights up a dark room is a current of electricity. The existence of that electricity is not *caused by* the light bulb, nor does the electricity create the bulb. They exist independently. However, for the electricity to *manifest* as light, the light bulb is a necessary condition.

In this analogy, the light bulb is like the brain, the nervous system, and its various functions. Luminous consciousness is the electricity that streams through them, interacting with them to create the light that bathes the room. This is very different from the modern Western neurological model in which consciousness is an emergent property that arises from the functioning of the brain. Just as the electrical current is a necessary condition for the light to occur, so it is with luminous consciousness and the objects being known. For experience to be cognized, you need the appropriate mental capacities of your brain and nervous system, i.e., memory, association, and reasoning. The *interdependence* of the various capacities allows mind functions to occur, just as the combined parts of the light bulb enable light to be emitted. There is no mental function that is separate from these various conditions and capacities. But all the mental faculties share the requirement that luminous consciousness be present in order for knowing to manifest in the mind. Yet, the electricity of consciousness could not create mental activity without the mental functions, just as the electricity cannot create light without a light bulb.

The Electronics of the Mind

Another metaphor Balyogi uses for looking at the brain and its attendant functions is the "electronics of the mind." Just as the electrical devices in your home or office display videos, prepare coffee, wash dishes, etc., the *electronics of the mind are the instruments that produce thoughts, cognition, perceptions, hearing,* and so forth.

In traditional yogic philosophy, one term for referring to these electronics is the *antah-karana*. In the illustrations section of this book, images of the antah-karana are used to distinguish between luminous consciousness and the regular functions of the brain and mind. The antah-karana is sometimes referred to as "the four instruments of inner knowing." It is comprised of *chitta* (contents of consciousness or "mind stuff"); *ahamkara* (ego); *manas* (ordinary processes of thinking); and *buddhi* (intuitive intelligence and higher wisdom).

The electronics of your mind perform such amazing functions of knowing in such splendid diversity that they seem to be everything. However, they are always dependent on the "electricity of consciousness." They are not the actual power of luminous consciousness; rather they are the beneficiaries of luminous consciousness manifesting. Therefore, *if you genuinely want to understand the nature of consciousness, you need to investigate the unseen electricity or electrical current of luminous consciousness.*

I am not saying that luminous consciousness created the mental faculties, only that its presence is necessary for any particular mental function.

Also, any particular mental function is not necessary for luminous consciousness to exist. Luminous consciousness is there alongside planning, remembering, multiplying, composing, and identifying as each arises and disappears in the mind. Luminous consciousness is the constant in perception—smelling needs consciousness, so does hearing and seeing, but consciousness is not dependent on any one of them. If you lose your sense of smell or sight, you retain the capacity of luminous consciousness.

As I said earlier, this is a different model of consciousness from that of the dominant scientific paradigm in which consciousness is seen as a phenomenon that arises from the interaction of these mental faculties—a byproduct of them rather than a separate energy that powers them. I am not asking you to take this on faith but to hold this as a possibility as you practice ways to directly experience the nature of luminous consciousness.

In Balyogi's map of the Nine Bodies, each Body has its own "organs of consciousness," its own electronics as it were, that are powered by luminous consciousness.

Luminous Consciousness as Energy

In your meditation practice, when you put aside the objects of consciousness temporarily and start to investigate luminous consciousness as a phenomenon, you discover that the core characteristic of consciousness is an unseen and mysterious energy that, like electricity, enables moments of sense-consciousness to happen. Balyogi refers to this mysterious energy as *rahasyatmic* energy. He describes rahasyatmic energy as one of the three "flames of consciousness," which he portrays in his *Flame of Consciousness* illustrations in Chapter 8.

Because luminous consciousness has this energetic power, it is uniquely characterized by *the capacity for self-illumination*. Consciousness can know it is knowing an object of experience because of its self-illumination capacity. In contrast, the memory function cannot know that it is memory, nor can the planning function know it is planning. The capacity of luminous consciousness to know is always there when you are awake, whether or not there is consciousness of objects occurring. For instance, in certain samadhi states, knowing is vibrantly present in the mind, but the knowing is not in relation to objects. It is a knowing that is at rest within itself, which is a satisfying experience for the mind.

You can deepen your understanding of this particular teaching by spending five minutes of your meditation constantly noting, "Illumination is occurring," meaning that knowing is occurring. Then take the next five minutes to note all the specific electronics of consciousness, for example: "Hearing is being known, seeing is being known, remembering is being known." Doing these two meditation exercises several times a week for a few weeks will help you cultivate a new ability for discernment that will enable you to be mindful of the nature of luminous consciousness. You will discover that consciousness as a phenomenon or capacity is clearly separate from all individual moments of knowing and all brain functions that are involved in knowing. You can see for yourself that moments of knowing or cognizing occur because this unseen capacity is lighting them up.

Luminous Consciousness Arising as a Field of Awareness

Whenever you bring the mind into stillness through deep meditative absorption or samadhi and then make luminous consciousness itself the object of your meditation inquiry, you may experience luminous consciousness as a subtle *field of awareness* radiating with mysterious energy. You see that objects of experience arise and pass in this field of awareness. And you see how intrinsically peaceful, spacious, and nonattached the mind actually is when it is *resting in awareness*. The mind's capacity of attention is simply *being*, not *doing* or *knowing* in this field of awareness. The field of awareness does not identify with what is arising within it because it is not viewing these objects of momentary experience from the point-of-view of a self; thus the ego is not at the center thinking it is doing the knowing. Moreover, the field of awareness does not change based on what arises. This field of awareness invites deep exploration because it does not fit into conventional views of the mind. A few words of caution: it is easy to start thinking you are the field of awareness, but whatever it is, it's impersonal and not "me" or "mine." When you experience luminous consciousness as this impersonal field of awareness, it helps you to explore luminous consciousness directly through the felt sense. By felt sense, I mean the direct comprehension of the experience as it's registering in the senses as opposed to our views and concepts about the experience. For instance, if my knee hurts, I say, "Knee throbbing is like this," meaning burning, twisting, stabbing, contracting—instead of saying

"Oh, my knee is strained, the ligament is pulled" or some other conceptualization of the experience.

Meaning of Attention

When the word *attention* is used in this book, it always refers to the mind's ability to focus on an experience stimulated by one of the six senses (thoughts being the sixth sense) or to focus on an object simply by choice. For instance, mindfulness practice involves choosing to keep the attention on what consciousness is *knowing* in a moment and, when appropriate, deliberately maintaining attention on the object in order to investigate what makes up the experience and the mind's reaction to it.

Attention functions as the spotlight of the mind. It fully "lights up" an experience that is registering in the mind, that is, it makes that experience the primary focus so that it can be seen and therefore known. It takes practice to be able to sustain attention by choice, but such ability will develop even in the most wandering mind. Being able to direct attention to the field of awareness is the first difficulty, but having it stay or rest there for even a few minutes is even more difficult; however, with practice it becomes possible. Ironically, when conditions are favorable, resting in awareness can seem totally effortless, but most likely that ease will not last. When consciousness explores itself, instead of being interested in what is being lit by the spotlight, you become interested in the nature of light itself.

Directly Experiencing the Energetic Awareness of Luminous Consciousness

Balyogi compares one's first *direct* experience of the energy of luminous consciousness to going outside into the light of the sun for the first time. Imagine that up until that moment you have always stayed indoors and only known sunlight coming in through closed windows and reflecting off objects. Therefore, you have only known sunlight by what it illuminated in the room. Ordinary knowing of consciousness is like being in that room and seeing consciousness only as the illuminated objects in the mind. But when you focus on the *awareness that knows that knowing is occurring*, you are not knowing consciousness through objects, you are knowing it directly. Either way, consciousness is the same *illumination*, but now you are feeling it directly as it emanates from within the field of awareness. It is as though you are able to *see* and *feel directly* the electricity that powers the light bulb even as the light bulb is lighting up the room. Imagine how amazing it would be to see the actual electricity, not just its effects.

Using the example of the cold hands again to contemplate the nature of consciousness, you know your hands are cold and can observe (or know you know) your mind's reactions to the cold. Now move your attention to *knowing* itself as a phenomenon. The cold hands and your mind's reaction to them are in the background; your focus is on knowing directly the *feeling* of consciousness. This is how you start your investigation of luminous consciousness. Gradually, as the mind becomes sufficiently concentrated in meditation, the electronics and what they produce in the mind fall away and all that remains is your focus on the presence of awareness itself in the mind. This is an experience of spaciousness, peace, and stillness that is beyond description. It can temporarily interrupt the way you habitually construct the world. Such an experience often results in a change of view regarding what you believe your identity to be and the nature of this reality.

I have deliberately not tried to define the mind in relation to the brain as it invites over-conceptualization, whereas the terms I have defined are all subject to direct experience. The instructions given in this book apply whether you treat mind and brain as completely or somewhat different or as the same thing. The instructions also apply whether you believe the mind is independent and exists individually or is part of an interdependent co-arising. Such questions are fascinating to think about and discuss, and I certainly have my own views. But as the Buddha stated repeatedly, they are not helpful to bringing an end to the suffering that comes from attachment, resentment, wanting, and fear of uncertainty and difficulty.

Unchanging Awareness in the Sea of Changing Objects

In addition to sense-consciousness and luminous consciousness, Balyogi refers to a third aspect of consciousness, which he describes as the "generator" for the electrical, energetic capacity of consciousness. When referring to this aspect of consciousness, Balyogi uses the Sanskrit word *chit*—usually translated as pure awareness.[2] (This is different from, though related to, *chiti*,

2   Patanjali calls the energy that radiates from the emptiness of pure awareness *chiti-shakti*. (4.34.)

or luminous consciousness, and *chitta*, the contents of the mind and memory.) The experience of pure awareness is empty of consciousness—so only when you come out of it do you know you've had a direct experience of it. Yet its radiating nature is the source that generates the electricity of luminous consciousness. Later in the book, you will see that Balyogi's illustrations often include symbols that represent the radiating energy of pure awareness.

Pure awareness is not a "thing." In the Indian tradition, this aspect of consciousness is associated with *purusha*. The word *purusha* is often translated as "Supreme Self," but to my understanding the "Self" of purusha does not refer to an actual self, nor is it personal. (There are many different interpretations of purusha; the way I am defining it here is for the sole purpose of teaching the Nine Bodies.)

Pure awareness is also present in various Buddhist traditions. In the Theravada suttas, the Buddha makes various references to it directly and indirectly. The most dramatic may be the Udana Sutta (8.3) when he describes nibbana as the realization of that which is "unborn, uncreated and un-conditioned." The Buddha's teaching points to a pure awareness that is luminous, radiating, empty and yet responsive.

Mysterious and not comprehensible to ordinary mind states, pure awareness is beyond the personal, beyond time and space. Thus, pure awareness does not relate to ordinary categories of identification of things that are aggregated, meaning composed of other things. Pure awareness exists *beyond* ego and is without ego, thus it has no identification with the vagaries of moment-to-moment experience. This empty awareness is not doing anything, not even cognizing, nor is it an *entity* of any sort or a *thing, space,* or *place* in the mind. It is empty of all such concepts, but it is not nothing either. No such words apply, which is why it can only be described as mysterious. Buddhist teachings on pure awareness have some of the characteristics of Patanjali's teaching of it, but they are not the same. (Remember, at the beginning of this book I stated that is not helpful to try and create exact correlations between, or even within, traditions when exploring consciousness as a phenomenon.)

What distinguishes luminous consciousness from pure awareness is that luminous consciousness is conscious of its own existence. It has consciousness itself as an object while pure awareness has no objects, no subject. There is no self, no entity to experience any subject or object; the awareness simply is.

Exploring Consciousness Is Observation, Not Opinion

I realize how confusing descriptions of consciousness can be. You do not have to immediately understand what is being pointed to in this particular teaching. Just acknowledge the mystery of consciousness, drop any fixed views you may have about it, and keep practicing.

Different traditions and even different lineages within a tradition describe the experiences of pure awareness and luminous consciousness in their own way and give varying instructions as to how to practice with the experiences. The result is that it can be confusing to you as you try to interpret particular meditative states and figure out what to do next. My advice is to stay focused on your experience, do not try to interpret it, and, above all, beware of feeling as though you are special for having the experience. At the same time, do not deny that you "know what you know."

As I stated at the beginning of this chapter, the nature of consciousness has been debated for centuries. One of the main arguments centers around this question: Is there some aspect of consciousness that is independent of objects that arise and are known in the mind or is all consciousness bound up in time and space and with the arising and passing of objects in the mind? In other words, do pure awareness and luminous consciousness really exist?

While there is no way to objectively prove their existence, the experience of luminous consciousness (and less often of pure awareness) regularly occurs in meditative practice and is a central part of the Nine Bodies teachings. For this reason, *learning to distinguish between sense-consciousness and luminous consciousness* is central to your getting the most out of the Nine Bodies teachings. It can take some time to comprehend this distinction in a fluid manner, but once you do, you may find that your meditation practice has an added dimension.

The Felt Sense of Knowing and of Energetic Experiences

At the risk of introducing some additional terms that may cause further confusion, I feel it would be remiss to not add a few additional words and explanations that you will eventually need as you start directly exploring the power of consciousness. Before I start, just remember that *sense consciousness*, *luminous consciousness*, and *pure awareness* are the key terms used in this book. All three have been defined and explained in the above paragraphs. However, in meditation practice, certain events of consciousness may arise that feel so profound that you naturally want to have a way of classifying or contextualizing them.

The first of these meditative events is when the mind's primary experience becomes strongly collected around the impersonal phenomena of knowing that is involved in sense-consciousness as described earlier in the chapter. When this particular stability of attention occurs, you may have a sense that the mind is simply "resting in knowing," meaning you can see all the objects of experience arising in the mind without feeling "caught." The mind may feel sheltered from any hindrance of mind while this is occurring. Additionally, you may discover it is quite easy to direct your attention to any object of experience, such as the breath or the flow of thinking, and the mind will stay focused on that object without a lot of effort. It can be exhilarating and empowering to have such experiences.

A second empowerment of your consciousness comes when you experience moments of what I term "pure consciousness," which I distinguish from pure awareness in the following way. In this situation, the mind is strongly concentrated on luminous consciousness to the exclusion of most other objects coming to your attention. If they do appear, they only arise briefly and do not hold interest for you. Often this experience is deeply satisfying and freeing to the mind. It brings with it inspiration and insight. Other times it is felt as stillness or emptiness and as profound presence. Although it is inspiring and brings great relief from the tension of ordinary mind states arising from grasping after sense objects, in times of accessing pure consciousness there is still a sense of a "knower" and of "something being known." In contrast, when accessing pure awareness as described earlier, there is no sense of knowing, no sense of anything being known, and no sense of a knower.

In summary, the mysterious power of consciousness manifests in endless mind states and energetic sensations. Some of those manifestations occur in daily life experiences, and some arise in deep concentration states to include rapture and other ecstatic mind states. Likewise, it is the energy of consciousness that accounts for the so-called powers of mind such as precognition and distant knowing. Through the mysterious power of consciousness, the mind-body truly does on occasion have spiritual visions, powerful energetic experiences, major altered mind states including extreme states of bliss, and much more. Such occurrences are a normal part of deep meditation. Everybody has some degree of these experiences, but they vary in frequency and intensity.

As you learn the map of the Nine Bodies and utilize the illustrations in this book for study, reflection, and meditation, the many aspects of consciousness are likely to become clearer and you may well have more access to them in your practice. Just remember, mindfulness and yoga, despite their distinct differences, share the goal of liberating the mind and are not for the purpose of maximizing momentary *special* mind states.

3

THE NINE BODIES TEACHING

The Nine Bodies Teaching

Balyogi says, "My own experience with the Nine Bodies or Nine Levels of consciousness began in the Himalayas near Gomukh where the Ganges River originates.[3] I was under the care of Swami Yogeswarananda Maharaj at his ashram. I prepared my body for deep meditation by ensuring that once I entered I would not be disturbed by any exterior conditions or bodily elimination needs. Then I began my meditation practice and cultivated samadhi.

"It was not until after I completed my meditation that I was told that it had been three days since I entered deep samadhi. During that time, I did not know time, place, or have a sense of a physical body. This deep *yog-samadhi* meditation awakens you automatically into another level of inner world consciousness and awareness. I was just in existence and continuing to use the eye of intuitional vision to reveal deeper and deeper parts of my being. I discovered at this time that the body has three parts: physical, energetic, and spiritual.

"As I continued my practice, the existence of the Nine Bodies became clear. I realized that each Body has a different nature, frequency, and vibration and that each level has a distinct function and activity. The practice is perfected with time as you continue to focus with the eye of intuitional knowing. Living a *sattvic* (pure) life free from all distractions is a prerequisite to attaining this knowing."

Balyogi attributes his ability to access intuitional knowing to having opened his "third eye" and to the visualization capability of the *vijnana chaksu*, the "eye of awakening" where intuitional knowing that is even more refined than that of the third eye can be found. Both the third eye and the

---

3   Editorial note: The Ganges River begins from a glacier near Gomukh. You can observe this glacier, which is at a height of 12,000 feet, in videos on YouTube.

vijnana chaksu are illustrated and explained later in the Eye of Awareness section in Chapter 10. For now, it's important to understand that direct access to such experience requires a heightened state of consciousness, usually arising from deep samadhi, although such consciousness can arise spontaneously in meditation or in a moment of intensity in daily life.

A scientist uses research and experiments as tools to achieve knowledge. In a similar way, the spiritual practitioner uses meditation and reflection as tools for the attainment of intuitional vision or insight. Thus, a yogi's intuitional knowing is a rational process—just like that of a scientist—but the process is internal and subtle. For that reason, the Dalai Lama describes Buddhism as "the science of the mind." When Balyogi refers to his own deep concentration work as "scientific research in spirit," he is expressing this same understanding.

What the Nine Bodies Map Offers

The Nine Bodies teachings offer a map for systematically and specifically directing your attention to your inner experience in your meditation practice in a manner that brings you knowledge and understanding regarding consciousness and the nature of existence. Except for the Ninth Body, which has to be inferred, all the Bodies can be felt directly, meaning they can be comprehended directly as opposed to conceptually. It is this felt experience of knowing that provides you with the deepest realizations about your internal experience of mind and heart. Importantly, just as the Physical Body is composed of bones, tissues, and organs, each of the other levels of being is also made up of a collection of phenomena that constitutes its Body. Each Body has distinct characteristics and is capable of being understood and accessed independently (the Ninth Body being an exception). The Nine Bodies can also be studied as an interdependent, interactive whole.

Through the study of the Nine Bodies, you begin to see the subtleties of your internal experience. In meditation practice, you can use the Nine Bodies as a map to orient yourself when you are confused about what is occurring, uncertain as to what to do next, afraid of what might be happening, or getting attached to or identified with some mind state or body phenomenon that might be arising. Utilizing the Nine Bodies as a skillful means of approaching spiritual practice can both ground you and allow you to take your inner exploration deeper.

These teachings are not meant to supplant or replace your vehicle of practice. It's as if you were planning to drive across the country and someone gave you a descriptive map of interesting geographical features you could see on your journey. You would still use a road map to reach your destination, but you would use this additional map to enrich the journey.

Moreover, at times this other map might help you find your way if you get lost because it provides certain details that are not contained in a conventional road map. In meditation, an experiential map like the Nine Bodies may be what you need to keep moving forward to your destination. It provides inspiration, stimulation, and orientation so that you continue on your journey rather than abandoning it.

Whatever your motivations and goals for meditation are, paying attention at the depth of subtlety represented by the Nine Bodies makes life a richer, more interesting experience. In working with these teachings, you may recall experiences you've had whose meaning you could not penetrate. Or you may read about a particular Body and be surprised at how important it feels to you to discover more about that particular Body. Also, if you have questions about various psychic phenomena you have experienced or heard about, these teachings may provide a new perspective.

Experiences and insights about consciousness can arise at any time, not just from meditation. However, having your mind fully collected and unified through meditation allows you to systematically make this exploration. According to Balyogi, the advantage in accessing the Nine Bodies through meditation is that each Body has what he calls its own "organs of perception" that can lead you onward to the next, more subtle Body.

Relationship of the Nine Bodies to Traditional Yogic Teachings

Balyogi's teachings on the Nine Bodies are an elaboration and refinement of ancient teachings about the "levels of being" that have long existed in the Indian forest or mountain traditions of yoga. In many cases, Balyogi uses the language of these classical teachings to describe his own "scientific research" through meditation.

In the classic yoga tradition, *rishis* (sages) living in the Himalayas taught that we each have three main Bodies or levels of being—a "Gross

Body," a "Subtle Body," and a "Causal Body." An analogy is often made between these three "bodies" and the three states of water—ice, liquid, and steam. Despite being composed of the same molecule, all three forms are used in distinct ways and must be handled differently for safety and comfort. In this book, I will refer to these three traditional Bodies as "Levels" to avoid confusion with the Nine Bodies.

Another traditional yogic model depicts five koshas, or "sheaths" of existence—energetic dimensions of being that emanate from the most refined level to the most material level. Yet another classic map is that of the chakras and *nadis* (energy pathways), which details the energy systems in the body and mind.

If you wish to learn more about these traditional teachings and their relationship to the Nine Bodies teachings, they are described in more detail in Appendix A. As I discuss the Nine Bodies teachings, I will sometimes make reference to these traditional systems—however, it is not necessary to know them in detail in order to do the Nine Bodies practices.

The Nine Bodies in Three Sets

In the remainder of this chapter, I describe the Nine Bodies in three sets of three. This division reflects the way each set of three relates to the traditional yoga teaching of the "Gross," "Subtle," and "Causal" Levels (see Appendix A for more information). Each set of three begins with a general introduction to all three Bodies within that set.

Traditional System	Nine-Body System
Gross Level	Physical Body Vital Body Emotional Body
Subtle Level	Etheric Body Astral Body Intuitional Body
Causal Level	Spiritual Body Divine Body Cosmic Body

Following the general introduction, I provide specific details about each of the Bodies in that set. Additionally, I include comments on the capacity of consciousness that is available in each Body and how love manifests in each Body. Finally, I state what is needed to nourish each Body and the color associated with each. Concentrating on the appropriate color can be helpful in gaining access to a particular Body, according to Balyogi.

These descriptions of each Body contain much detail that requires assimilation in order to be fully understood. Despite this linear presentation, the teachings of the Nine Bodies are not meant to be conceptual, nor are they meant to be memorized or intellectually mastered; rather they are to be utilized in meditation and in times of reflection and inquiry such that your own "knowing" and "being" arise. You accomplish this by doing the experiential meditations offered in Chapter 4 and by meditating on the drawings (as detailed in Chapters 5–11) to discover what is true regarding your own experience of the Nine Bodies. This experiential investigation takes substantial time and commitment. Not knowing, feeling lost, feeling critical of the teaching, and doubting yourself are all part of the process of discovering the wisdom in these teachings.

In Balyogi's system of the Nine Bodies, there is a clear cause and effect among the various levels of being, which can be experienced and worked with in meditation and in everyday activities. The effect is both "up" and "down"—the more subtle levels affect the coarser body levels, and if the coarser levels are blocked, you can't directly access the more refined levels.

Bodies One Through Three:
The Physical, Vital, and Emotional Bodies

The first three Bodies we will discuss are what Balyogi calls the Physical Body, the Vital Body, and the Emotional Body. We discuss the first three Bodies together because they are the ones that can be most easily and directly felt. Balyogi says that these three Bodies are all contained within what the traditional yoga teachings term the Gross Level. These first three Bodies are actually "results" arising from the more subtle energies that exist in Bodies Four through Six (the Subtle Level).

Balyogi compares these first three Bodies to the layers of a coconut: "Just as a coconut has three unique and separate parts—husk, meat and milk—so too does the human body have three separate and distinct bodies." Just as the word "coconut" represents all three parts of the coconut without actually capturing a specific one, the usual use of the word "body" does not capture the physical, emotional, and vital parts it is comprised of.

The Physical, Vital, and Emotional Bodies can each be observed separately and each can be affected by the cultivation of various skillful means, including not only pranayama, meditation, and hatha yoga but also Western psychological, athletic, health, and medical practices. Both the Physical and Emotional Bodies are dependent upon and are empowered by the Vital Body. The Vital Body is the energetic power that runs the Physical Body; this energy is called *prana*. Although prana manifests in the Vital Body, it originates in a more subtle form in the more refined levels of the Nine Bodies.

Now let's look at each of these Bodies in more detail:

1. Physical Body *(Sthool Sharir)*

The Physical Body contains the five elements of earth, water, wind, fire, and space (ether) in varying combinations. In meditation you can evoke the elements of the Physical Body and utilize them for spiritual development. For example, the fire element burns away obscurity, allowing knowing and clarity to arise; the water element flows through the mind, cleansing and bringing purity; the wind element creates movement by giving of itself so that life can happen and carries with it the value of serving others; the earth element is receptive and gives nourishment and stability, reflecting the capacity of generosity. Learning how to access space can help you deal with the difficult emotional situations in life and to find a new way to be with your mind. The physical heart, which Balyogi says is the first of your three hearts, is located here.

- Corresponding kosha: In the yogic five-kosha system, which some yoga students may be familiar with, this Body corresponds to the *annamaya kosha*. For those who are interested in the five-kosha system, I will list the corresponding kosha for each of the Nine Bodies; however, it is not necessary to understand the kosha system in order to do or benefit from the Nine Bodies practices. (For more information about the koshas and their relationship to each of the Nine Bodies, see Appendix A.)
- How it's nourished (what it needs): The Physical Body needs hatha yoga and a good diet incorporating the six kinds of tastes—sweet, saline, pun-

gent, bitter, astringent, and sour—every day. It also needs the *shatkar-mas* (yoga purification techniques).

  ▍ How it expresses love: Through sensuality, including sexuality, or any form of expression of affection through touch, such as in caring for a person who is ill, or in taking care of a child, a friend, or even a pet.

  ▍ Color: Beige, as in wheat brown.

2. Vital Body *(Pranamaya Sharir)*

The Vital Body contains the ten pranas that sustain the life force. For this reason, Balyogi sometimes refers to it as the Prana Body. There is a prana that is vital for breathing, one for digestion, one for circulation, and so forth. Balyogi teaches that the Vital Body is nourished by oxygen and élan, by which he means the sense of aliveness that comes when you are genuinely engaged with life. (Élan is a French word that means vigorous spirit or enthusiasm.) To describe the Vital Body, Balyogi uses the analogy of a papaya. It is still vital, fully alive, while it remains connected to its tree, but the papaya that sits in your fridge is no longer connected to life in the same way. By focusing on your own sense of vitality and noticing when that vitality is diminished by disease, emotional turmoil, or exhaustion, you can take steps to correct it. If you fail to do so, you start to age in an accelerated manner, like the papaya in the fridge.

The Vital Body is the channel through which you access the more refined Bodies Four through Six (the Subtle Level). The prana in the Vital Body protects the Physical Body and provides the movement that keeps the body alive.

Balyogi likens the Vital Body to a ladder that allows you to climb up on the roof; you focus on the Vital Body in order to reach more subtle states. Therefore, you need a balance between aliveness and awareness on the inner journey. This focus on the Vital Body is reflected in the Anapanasati Sutta, the awareness of breath meditation that the Buddha taught.

  ▍ Corresponding kosha: *Pranamaya kosha.*

  ▍ How it's nourished (what it needs): The Vital Body needs cleansing kriyas, asanas, oxygen, pranayama, *bandha* practice, *mudra* practice, and shatkarmas (physical cleaning practices). Because the Vital Body and the Physical Body are so closely connected, anything that nourishes prana also nourishes the Physical Body.

▌ **How it expresses love:** Giving life energy to who or what you care about. Compassion and healing are both manifestations of love in the Vital Body. The Buddha was the incarnation of *karuna* (compassion).
Color: Blue.

3. Emotional Body *(Bhavanatmak Sharir)*

The Emotional Body is where all emotions and sentiments manifest, including excitement, frustration, depression, exertion, humor, anxiety, worry, generosity, joy, jealousy, insecurity, fear, panic, and satisfaction and dissatisfaction. Ambition also resides in the Emotional Body.

The Emotional Body is also where attachment arises because the emotions can create expectations and demands; however, emotions are not the problem because they are only energetic states. Like waves in the ocean, emotions do not create themselves; they are created by the mind. "You should observe whether you are acting or simply reacting from the Emotional Body," Balyogi advises.

If you don't relate to your emotions in a wise manner, the emotions will distort what is real and cause suffering to arise. Everybody has dark and light emotions; the question is, which will you develop? In order to develop positive emotions, you must practice mindfulness of what is arising in the mind that is causing the emotional waves.

For instance, one of the strongest and most confusing emotions we experience is love. We hold it in an exalted state, yet we often experience it with the corrupting emotions of greed, jealousy, possessiveness, resentment, and exploitation. Thus, many people come to spiritual practice seeking to be healed from a lack of innate self-worth, childhood trauma, or a broken heart, and wanting to feel unconditional love. Speaking about how the Emotional Body is healed in regard to love states, Balyogi says, "As the mind attains liberation from identification with wanting, it becomes more and more passion-proof and possessiveness-proof."

The activities of objective and subjective thinking or what is traditionally called the "lower mind," meaning the intellect and the psyche, first appear in association with the Emotional Body and continue through the Etheric Body (Body Four) and Astral Body (Body Five).

▌ **Corresponding kosha:** Balyogi says the Emotional Body is located between the pranamaya kosha and the *manomaya kosha* and is connected to both; therefore, it is hard to work with.

- How it's nourished (what it needs): The Emotional Body needs purification, self-love, harmony, and purification of sentiments. It also requires education in what is appropriate and helpful when expressing feelings. It also needs to surrender its own self-centered importance through doing selfless activity, cultivating unselfish sentiments, and practicing bhakti yoga or devotional attention.
- How it expresses love: The Emotional Body is the center of love. Love grows in the Emotional Body. The Emotional Body allows the expression of love and provides the means to explore love. When the Physical, Vital, and Emotional Bodies are unified in purpose, love is expressed as compassion and kindness.
- Color: Pistachio green.

Bodies Four Through Six:
The Etheric, Astral, and Intuitional Bodies

Bodies Four through Six are the Etheric, Astral, and Intuitional Bodies. They are discussed together because they are all energetic in nature and more subtle than Bodies One through Three. Balyogi says that these three Bodies are all contained within what the traditional teachings call the Subtle Level. In Balyogi's Nine Bodies map, the Etheric Body connects to the Vital Body and through the Vital Body affects the Emotional and Physical bodies. The Etheric Body functions like an antenna for *receiving information* that is in the larger field of human consciousness but is not known by the individual who mysteriously comes into this knowledge. The Astral Body operates like a *carrier for the mind* that allows for astral or out-of-body experiences. The Intuitional Body is a source for *direct realization*, meaning direct knowing or understanding that is beyond that of the *visioning capability* of the intellect, even in its highest form.

Emotions are manifested and expressed in the Emotional Body but originate in the Etheric Body. Balyogi explains how this works with an analogy: just as a hot pepper's essence is manifested as heat in the body, energetic states are expressed in the Physical Body as comfort or discomfort, in the Emotional Body as emotions, and in the Vital Body as robust or weak vitality.

The energy associated with the Etheric, Astral, and Intuitional Bodies is *jnanatmic*, the energy of knowledge. By contrast, the Physical, Vital, and Emotional Bodies has energy that is *kriyatmic* or action-oriented. (Both of these energies are visible in *The Flame of Individual Consciousness* illustration in Chapter 8.) The Etheric, Astral, and Intuitional Bodies are where we can most affect our inner growth through meditation, combined with the spiritual disciplines of precepts and austerities and the development of concentration and intention.

As you become more mindful of your relationship to each of the Subtle Bodies, you start to see how to adjust your meditation practice to have more vitality. For instance, someone who repeatedly has altered reality experiences in which he leaves his body in meditation and loses any sense of mindfulness can identify himself as getting stuck in his Astral Body and, therefore, needs to bring more of the earth element into his practice to counter this tendency. Or someone suffering from chronic low energy can learn to access their Etheric Body and start to connect to their more subtle energy or "chi," which is felt directly in the nervous system.

Each of the three Bodies in the Subtle Level is accessed through *intention*. Intention is the capacity to incline the mind toward a certain level of being such that the mind just naturally moves to that level. The more sattvic the mind is, the more amenable or responsive it is to such to inclinations. Intention functions like a request, such as "May this Body arise," rather than a demand. It requires steadiness of mind and confidence or trust that this level of being is indeed reachable, as well as patience and humility.

4. Etheric or Energy Body *(Akasha Sharir or Tanmatra Sharir)*

The Etheric Body is the *container* for the Physical, Vital, and Emotional Bodies. The word etheric is a translation of the Sanskrit word *akasha*, which means space; therefore, it contains all things. This space is not energetically dead or empty of energy, just the opposite; it is composed of energy, and it is "alive-space." According to Balyogi, the Etheric Body is more subtle than the wind, but it has a "felt sense" for those who can still the mind sufficiently. It also has presence and aliveness. By presence, I mean it is substantial and real. By aliveness, I mean it has vitality and an energetic quality that is as palpable as the Physical Body. *If you are going to focus on exploring only one of the Nine Bodies, I suggest that it be this Body.*

In my experience, learning to access the Etheric Body is one of the most important steps you can take in your inner development for three reasons. First, it enables healing in the Physical, Vital, and Emotional Bodies and, therefore, can dramatically affect your health. Second, it allows you to gather key information regarding the mind and heart that is obscured from ordinary awareness. This information is extremely valuable for empowering meditative insight. Third, it facilitates the directing and balancing of energy in all three of the Physical Bodies. Therefore, it is the most relevant Body for affecting both your body and mind in daily life.

Exploring the Etheric Body is also vital in creating the conditions for realization because developing access to this level of being helps you attain access to the Intuitional Body. The Etheric and Intuitional Levels of Being are closely linked for the cultivation of insight, which liberates the mind from grasping and attachment.

The Five Subtle Elements, the Psychic Heart, and *Kundalini*

The Etheric Body is where the subtle elements (*tanmatra*) of earth, water, fire, air, and space originate and then manifest in the physical world as the five material elements. These five elements are readily identified in the body but require reflection to be seen in the emotions. Every emotion is composed of a combination of the five elements and, upon close examination, can be found to be either heavy or light, warm or cool, vibrating or still; it also has a form, is connected or disconnected to what you truly value, and occurs in a mind that is either contracted or spacious. Thus, the Emotional and Physical Bodies are more similar than you might think, and they can be investigated in meditation in similar ways.

Since the subtle elements that make up emotions arise here, it is not surprising that the second of your three hearts, which Balyogi calls the Psychic or Subtle Heart, is located in the Etheric Body. The Psychic Heart is the center of discernment. It is embodied energy as well as the source of sentiment or resonance with others that we experience. (See the *Three Hearts* illustration in Chapter 10.)

All of the chakras operate in the Etheric Body and it vibrates with the same frequency as kundalini energy. Thus, it is in the Etheric Body that the experience of kundalini rising occurs. You may be familiar with the classic yogic teaching that the sound of *Om* is responsible for creating all space.

According to Balyogi, the Etheric Body is where this subtle vibration of sounds originates and creates *akasha*, or space.

Additionally, the Etheric Body is also where subtle prana exists and from which the ten pranas manifest in the Vital Body. Remember this is subtle prana, not the physical prana found in the Vital Body. Because it contains the subtle prana, the Etheric Body has the capacity for containing, holding, and balancing energy. Some healers can access this level of being by directing subtle prana into the Vital Body, which then heals the Physical and Emotional Bodies. By exploring and focusing on this body, you can gain access to more prana, more energy, for your daily life.

Balyogi states that the Etheric Body is where the majority of nadis or subtle nerve channels exist—approximately 3,500,000 of them. The nadis are the yoga equivalent of the Chinese medicine meridian system and are much less understood and utilized in the West than the acupuncture meridians.

Akashic Fields, Storehouse Consciousness, and the Etheric Body

The Etheric Body also contains the *akashic fields* and what's often referred to in Jungian psychology as the "collective unconscious." The akashic fields are similar if not the same as the classic Indian teaching of "storehouse consciousness," which is also located in the Etheric Level of Being. Storehouse consciousness has a variety of meanings, but in general, it is where all previous experience and knowledge are stored.[4] Some teachings say that storehouse consciousness is where the knowledge of past lives resides. To explain how the akashic fields or storehouse consciousness exists, Balyogi compares the akashic fields to a macrocosm, and your individual mind to a microcosm contained within the macrocosm. Therefore, the individual mind has the potential to access everything that is in the macrocosm, just as your personal computer can access all the information on the Web.

As with all the Bodies of the Subtle Level, gaining clarity regarding the Etheric Body can be a little daunting at first. Think of your first Three Bodies—the Physical, Vital, and Emotional—as comprising a container within a larger container. The Etheric Body is the larger container. Balyogi uses the analogy of a mother with a child in her womb. The child has a beating heart that is contained within the mother who also has a beating heart. The hearts are distinct but not separate; they are united in receiving nourishment from

---

4   For a reference to storehouse consciousness in the Buddhist tradition, see the *Trimsatika (Thirty Verses)* of *Vasubandhu.*

the same source. It is because the levels of being are nested within one another in this manner that movement among them is possible. As you become more aware that this is true, you become more fluid in moving among the bodies.

The longer you meditate, the more obvious it becomes that this mysterious level of being really does exist and that it affects you constantly. And you also recognize that it is most beneficial to be the recipient of energy flowing from someone who is accessing this Level of Being. Consciously or unconsciously, you most likely participate in many activities to nourish yourself in this realm, from yoga, meditation, breathing exercises, running, tai chi, aikido, and certain other martial arts, to psychotherapy, bodywork, and even hugs and smiles.

- **Corresponding kosha**: *Manomaya kosha*.
- **How it's nourished**: The Etheric Body needs all aspects of yoga to help clear the channel so that the five subtle elements can manifest and all the higher levels can flow into the three lower Bodies. The Etheric Body is constantly nourishing the three lower Bodies. When the energy is flowing from the Etheric Body, dullness, lethargy, and depression are dispelled.
- **How it expresses love**: It expresses love as a nourishing energy in the form of healing or caring energy.
- **Color**: Yellow.

5. Astral or Psychic Body *(Antehvahak Sharir)*

In some yoga systems, the Astral or Psychic Body is what is being referred to when the term Subtle Body is used. The Astral Body is the one that "travels" if you have an out-of-body experience or a near-death experience. When you dream, you are in the Astral Body, and this is true even for certain kinds of daydreaming.

When I first started teaching this material, I was surprised to discover how helpful identifying this Body was to some yogis whose meditation experience was characterized by an "absence of being present." For such people, recognizing that they were getting lost in the Astral Body and being able to label what was happening with clarity allowed them to return to being mindful in the moment in their meditation with a new ability to become concentrated.

When you have a remote seeing experience, you are accessing the Astral Body. If you take mind-altering drugs, according to Balyogi, you sometimes access the Astral Body, which might explain why the insights that arise from drug induced awareness often do not remain once the mind has left this body—it is not where you ordinarily exist in the human realm.

According to Balyogi, the Astral Body is where what remains after the death of the Physical Body resides. It is a nonmaterial realm that is not contingent on having a Physical Body to manifest. The devas and other celestial beings that are described in ancient Asian teachings are located in this realm of existence.

Becoming familiar with the Astral Body allows you to locate, ground, and orient yourself if you have meditation experiences that seem genuine but by ordinary reality standards could be interpreted as hallucinogenic or delusional in nature. Additionally, if in daily life you tend to have disorienting shifts in consciousness due to a trauma or chemical imbalances, you are able to recognize what is happening and hold yourself steady until the experience subsides. Likewise, when you encounter others who report such experiences, this teaching provides a way for you to understand and attend to their experience. This perspective can be particularly helpful with someone who is having a moment of genuine spiritual awakening and simultaneously being triggered by trauma, such as post-traumatic stress disorder (PTSD) or mental instability. Additionally, for people who are uncomfortable directly experiencing the Emotional Body (as opposed to emotions), there is a tendency to unconsciously take refuge in the Astral Body. In such cases people report feeling disassociated, out of their bodies, or not quite present.

The Astral Body also houses a vital bridge between the Subtle Level and the material world—what are known in traditional yogic philosophy as the *karmendriyas* (the five subtle sensory organs of actions) and the *jnanendriyas* (the five subtle sensory organs of knowledge). *Indriya* means "sense" and these five inner senses for knowing and action create the sense organs of knowing and action in the physical world. These are a central part of Balyogi's Nine Bodies map and will be explored in more detail in following chapters, particularly Chapter 9.

The five karmendriyas are the Subtle Level's initiators of doing. They manifest in the material world as the five action organs: the mouth, hands,

genitals, anus, and feet. The five jnanendriyas are the subtle sensory organs—
manifesting in the material world as the senses of touch, taste, smell, vision,
and hearing. Thus the Astral Body is not only the Level where you move out of
the body, it is also the Level that carries you into the physical realm.

- Corresponding kosha: *Manomaya kosha.*
- How it's nourished (what it needs): The Astral Body needs to rest in its own
  nature. You do not need to do anything specific to nourish it; just be in
  contact with it. Balyogi likens the process to the indirect way in which
  the body creates vitamin D from sunshine. The Astral Body is also
  nourished by the energetic potential of Bodies Seven, Eight, and Nine.
  Thus, your Astral Body is being nourished regardless of your actions.
  However, being in a conscious relationship to the Astral Body gives it
  more freshness, like smelling flowers that are still on the vine rather
  than those that have been cut. (If you have a strong interest in this
  Level, then pay careful attention to this analogy. It provides a vital clue
  to accessing the Astral Body that I can't describe directly.)
- How it expresses love: It expresses itself as the love for liberation.
- Color: Red.

6. Intuitional or Supra-Mental Body *(Vijnanamaya Sharir)*

The main characteristic of the Intuitional Body is *awakened awareness*, the
capacity of intuitional vision or insight described at the beginning of the
chapter. In the Vedic tradition, this capacity would be called "vijnana,"
meaning realized wisdom. Balyogi variously calls this Body the supra-mental
Level of Being or higher mind or "beyond mind"—because the knowledge
that is accessed is beyond the objective and subjective thinking capacities of
the lower or ordinary mind. In other words, intuitional seeing is a form of
knowing or insight that is beyond the ordinary cognition of the brain.

According to Balyogi, it is the Intuitional Body that is developed so effectively in Buddhist teachings and practices. The knowing of the Intuitional
Body is also called *buddhi*, meaning discriminating intelligence and intuitive
awareness. Buddhi has such an illuminating quality that when it is active the
ordinary mind and senses become still. In the Nine Bodies teachings, the
Intuitional Body is the key to spiritual growth; it is the Body for the realization of attainment. The "fruits" of intuitional seeing are called knowledge,
insight, or realization, and they bring full liberation from greed, aversion,

and delusion—the sources of the grasping mind that cause suffering.

The Etheric and Intuitional Bodies work together. The Etheric Body is like a radar that picks up subtle information about the nature of mind and reality, while the Intuitional Body interprets and understands the signals that the Etheric Body has picked up. Through the interactions of these two Levels of Being, you can recognize the meaning of premonitions, know things that you have no earthly reason to know, and can inexplicably become one with another.

When you access the Intuitional Body in conjunction with the Etheric Body, you sometimes experience exalted mind states that, while powerful, do not bring about true change in one's spiritual maturity. This is often confusing to meditation students. For example, when you experience "oneness," see perfection in the world just as it is, or feel no hindrances in the mind, it is easy to identify these mind states as being "final attainment." You mistakenly believe you have gone beyond the ego. But these exalted mind states always end, and you find yourself facing the same old ego challenges. They are valuable for creating inspiration and faith, but they are not the purpose of meditation practice in either the Buddhist or Patanjali tradition. Direct knowing, insight, and realization are what free the mind.

Intuitional insight arises like the flash of a camera; it is just suddenly there. However, in many instances, the insight has to be experienced repeatedly before it becomes an on-going part of your perceptual and decision-making capacities. Also, you may have a life-changing insight, the implications of which take years of practice and reflection for you to fully understand. Finally, you cannot actually practice having insights; instead, you practice cultivating the external and internal conditions that are most likely to lead to the arising of insight. As the Buddha and Patanjali explained, you release the mind from being at odds with itself through ethical behavior; you create a healthy body that has the energy to practice meditation; you cultivate restraint and renunciation to withstand greed and aversion; and you develop the mind and heart through meditation practices.

▌ Corresponding kosha: *Vijnanamaya kosha*

▌ How it's nourished (what it needs): The Intuitional Body needs contemplation, tranquility, light, intellectual unity, and a sense of attainment. It also needs time for wandering, meaning the mind needs time to just be, to not engage in any doing or even knowing activity, not even meditation. What this type of nourishment points to is an inner experience that cannot be put directly into words but is important for accessing the Intuitional Body. Ask yourself how you might do this wandering. This body needs good values and truthfulness so that the mind is not clouded by hindrances.

- **How it expresses love**: Like a flash of knowing, there is immediate excitement and inner elation. Love blossoms from the inside without any thinking.
- **Color**: Golden-orange, like the radiating sun.

Bodies Seven Through Nine:
The Spiritual, Divine, and Cosmic Bodies

The final three Bodies of the Nine Body system (which are refinements of what is known as the Causal Level in traditional yogic teachings) contain the most subtle and mysterious levels of consciousness. They are the seed of life, the root of all existence. Just as when you see smoke you know there is fire somewhere, so it is when you see life—you know it originates in this realm. This Level is invisible like the roots of trees, but all the visible Levels, such as the Physical Body, depend on the invisible. The great challenge is to maintain balance between the first three Bodies and the last three Bodies, for if the Spiritual Level is not attended to, the Physical, Emotional, and Vital Bodies do not thrive. The Spiritual, Divine, and Cosmic Bodies cannot be described anatomically.

Balyogi uses the words *avyakta*, meaning "invisible," and *vyakt*, meaning "the expressed," to explain the relationship between these refined layers and the first three Bodies. All that is manifest is vyakt, meaning it is expressed. But the source of all that is expressed is avyakta or invisible and originates from these mysterious refined Bodies. (See the *Eternal Journey* illustration in Chapter 6.)

The Spiritual, Divine, and Cosmic Bodies are invisible, not expressed. They are potential only. *The role of spiritual practice is to cultivate choice in what we manifest.* We practice in order to manifest our highest goodness and clarity. When you ask Balyogi how he is, he will say, "I am Divine," by which he means he is in touch with this sacred energy.

The consciousness of these refined Bodies is mysterious, a puzzle that is not meant to be solved. Although it is not understandable, you can feel its presence. In order for spiritual development to reach this level of consciousness, the ego must surrender its place as being the center of identity and become a subservient, cooperative ally to the heart on the journey to liberation.

Other teachers refer to these refined Bodies as the Divine Body, God's Body, and the universal soul body. They are also referred to as the *vajra* body, the rainbow light body, and the diamond heart body.

The Spiritual Body and the Divine Body are only slightly separate, but that slight separation makes a big difference, according to the Nine Bodies teachings. The Cosmic Body can only be treated as mysterious.

7. Spiritual Body *(Atmik Sharir)*

The Spiritual Body does not contain the five elements, either in their physical manifestation or in the form of the subtle elements. It is pure potential, but it can be felt energetically and cultivated through practices of generosity, service, ethical behavior, and caring. The Spiritual Body can be accessed through yoga, meditation, unconditional love, and other metaphysical practices.

The Spiritual Body is the Level of Being that contains all the light and dark possibilities of life. Everything at this Level is potential and manifests elsewhere. Whether your words and actions in the world are good or cause suffering depends on your activity in this Level of Being. If your intention in any given moment is pure or harmonious (sattvic), then the movement of mind is toward knowing or directly experiencing the exquisiteness of the Divine Body. If your focus is impure (tamasic), then the movement of mind is toward strengthening the ego and moving into worldly concerns. Even if your motives are wholesome, if the mind is fluctuating because it is overly impassioned and active (rajasic), then the strong vibrancy of that impassioned desire for liberation can block you from accessing the Divine Body.

The Gunas (Qualities of Existence) and the Spiritual Body

Anyone who can access subtle energetic changes in the body and mind is able to sense the effects of the different *gunas* (qualities or attributes of existence) in the Spiritual Body. In my experience, an impure (tamasic) motive feels heavy, dark, and cold, while an overly impassioned (rajasic) one feels thick, blinding, and overheated. A pure (sattvic) intention feels empty, bright, and cool. Oftentimes in daily life or even in meditation practice, we are unable to directly discern our intention because we are so caught up in an emotion. In a sense we are lost to ourselves, lost to being able to make choices based on our deepest values. Therefore, it is quite helpful to be able to tune into the energetic feeling that underlies whatever our mind state is at the moment because it allows us to know what is truly motivating us. (For more details about the gunas and their relationship to the Nine Bodies, see Appendix A.)

By cultivating the capacities of insight and intention while residing in the three Subtle Bodies, you develop the ability to locate, focus, and cultivate pure intention. As with so many other aspects of the inner journey, this requires patience and persistence because during our first years of practice we often career between discouragement, doubt, over-zealousness, and delusion regarding our capacities.

- Corresponding kosha: *Anandamaya kosha*.
- How it's nourished (what it needs): The Spiritual Body is nourished through being in connection with luminous consciousness. Moments of resting in luminous consciousness occur when there is no fluctuation in the mind because the mind is without thinking. Even the briefest of moments can be nourishing. The Spiritual Body needs self-respect but not ego respect. It benefits from witnessing and realizing oneness and unity through the surrender of the ego. The Spiritual Body requires nameless and formless love to overcome duality and experience the interdependent nature or "oneness" and emptiness of all things. But in order for the Spiritual Body to manifest in the plane of human existence, you must develop the capacity to separate from that oneness and make its enlightened qualities available in the world of duality.

The Spiritual Body has the capacity for and the need to wander, to be separate and not be identified with anything, and exclusively dwell in the emptiness. If the Spiritual Body stays in unity, which is sometimes called "one mind" or "pure mind," it does not manifest into the lower Bodies. This separation from the sense of oneness through wandering allows individual consciousness to occur. Our journey then is to come back to the unity but with the seeing vision or insight or awakened mind that we have gained in making our journey. One of the oldest spiritual arguments has to do with whether this separation from unity is a mistake in perception, meaning that individual consciousness never left the unity, or whether there truly is a duality that has to be overcome, meaning a literal transformation and transcendence into unity. Be cautious about getting caught in such speculative theory and concentrate on the actual experience of your practice moment-by-moment, day-to-day.

- **How it expresses love:** Manifests as love of spirit. It's felt as the light of love itself.
- **Color:** White.

8. Divine Body (*Divya Sharir*)

Realization of the Divine Body is the highest level of human experience. Balyogi explains that the distinction between the Spiritual Body and the Divine Body is like the distinction between fruit and root. Although the fruit and roots of a tree have different functions, when looked at closely, they are interdependent manifestations of one another. The realizations that occur in this body bring about liberation from suffering and free the heart from contraction. The Divine Body is the Level of Being where few people are willing to go because it means death to the ego. Death to the ego does not mean that the ego disappears but rather that it ceases to be your identity from which you make decisions. Another way of saying this is that when directly accessing the Divine Body, you are no longer seeking consciously or unconsciously personal advantage, and all your instincts including survival and sexual instincts are passive. You are literally "living in a divine state."

The Divine Body is mysterious and indescribable, yet it can also be *known* through intuition. We discover its existence through accessing the Intuitional Body in our meditation. Almost everyone has had some felt intuition of the Divine Body, although it may have been fleeting in nature, and many have been greatly inspired by this felt sense of presence. For example, a feeling of it can occur while being in nature, while witnessing the birth of a baby, in romantic love, in contemplative prayer, in silence and stillness, and in meditation. However, few people turn to meditation in order to directly realize it through the felt sense. To do so requires a genuine dedication to practice and inevitably involves a purification of the mind, which occurs while meditating. This purification results in a mind that is more sattvic in nature. Please keep in mind that the Divine Body is not a thing, nor a personality. It is not anything that is manifest; it is the generative capacity for all that comes to exist.

Emptiness and Wholeness in the Divine Body

To attain realization of the Divine Body, you must first experience its emptiness, just as the Buddha did. Paradoxically, once realized, you discover that this emptiness radiates with a benign potential that cannot be described in words. The closest approximation might be what the ancient Greeks called *agape* or impersonal love.

Part of what makes accessing this realization so challenging is the necessity of experiencing the two seemingly opposite realities of oneness and emptiness that are actually complementary in nature. Balyogi says, "The realization of oneness *radiates* (vibrates, generates) wholeness and the *emptiness* radiates (vibrates, generates) love." He describes these realizations as attained by meditating while being in the Intuitional Body.[5]

The Divine Body is the highest Body that we can directly realize through the intuitive felt experience. Through accessing the Spiritual Body and the Divine Body, we make choices that create karmas that influence our future. Karma means actions. Think of it as seeds we plant that blossom later when conditions are right for them to do so. The primary determinate of our karma is our intention, not what actually happens, which is often beyond our control.

Like the light of the sun that shines equally on the rose and the thorn, the tree and the weed, the Divine Body offers its generative capacity for the creation of conscious life that is free of judgment. In other words, whether you are acting skillfully or unskillfully, causing harm to yourself or another or not, you are the recipient of this amazing capacity of luminous consciousness. Since all people have this capacity regardless of merit, spiritual practice can be viewed as learning how to utilize consciousness to first create wholesome karma and, ultimately, to move beyond the creation of karma to full liberation of the mind and heart.

---

5   In Theravada Buddhism, there are various suttas that teach the Four Boundless, which are virtues or innately radiating qualities of kindness, compassion, sympathetic joy, and equanimity. These point to the same potential that manifests through intentional practice. For instance, see sutta 99 in the Majjhima Nikaya.

Karma and Liberation in the Divine Body

In the Buddha's teaching, the spiritual journey comprises an Eightfold Path. This path begins with two core areas of understanding—karma and the Noble Truths of the existence of suffering and the end of suffering. The Pali word for suffering is *dukkha,* and it has a larger meaning than "suffering." It includes dissatisfaction, tension, and stress. When Balyogi teaches how to work with karma through the letting go of identifying with sense-consciousness, he makes a distinction between the immediate benefit of ceasing attachment and the permanent letting go of the grasping and clinging that keeps the mind in a never-ending cycle of tension and unease. The first benefit he calls *freedom from dukkha*, by which he means the temporary ability to let go of being caught in dukkha. The second he calls *liberation from dukkha,* meaning the absolute end of all attachment, greed, hatred, and aversion in which even the possibility of dukkha no longer exists.

Balyogi teaches that the Buddha attained liberation. But he emphasizes that each of us has many opportunities to temporarily free the mind from suffering while making the long and difficult journey to permanent liberation from suffering. Balyogi's teachings in this regard are in accordance with those of Patanjali.[6]

- Corresponding kosha: *Anandamaya kosha*
- How it's nourished (what it needs): Nourishment for the Divine Body is ecstatic bliss. This requires sattvic states of consciousness, which come through a clear and stable mind that is able to stay concentrated. The Divine Body also needs realization of fulfillment (meaning consciousness needs to know itself as divine), transcendence (such that there is no longer identification with the ego), and the presence of the divine virtues of nonattachment and open-hearted generosity.
- How it expresses love: It manifests as a nondiscriminating, nonpreferential love. To "fall in divine love" is to be open to and feel the suffering of the world so fully that you transfigure the Subtle Body to enable you to help alleviate the pain and despair.
- Color: Like the Spiritual Body, the color of the Divine Body is white light, tinged with gold.

---

6   To understand Patanjali's view of the causes and end of suffering, start by reading Sutra 2, lines 1 though 8, although the entire Yoga Sutras are an explanation of how to achieve freedom and liberation.

9. Cosmic Body (*Karan Sharir*)

The Cosmic Body is transparent and empty, yet everything that can be expressed, animate and inanimate alike, comes into existence through it. But the Cosmic Body itself is not defined or limited by what exists. As is true for the Divine Body, the Cosmic Body is not a "something" or a "place" in the ordinary sense of those words. You cannot attain a felt sense of the Cosmic Body, however, you can *intuit* its mysterious existence through the felt sense of the other Bodies and the realizations that arise.

Balyogi states that people do not know that their heritage in consciousness is rooted in the Cosmic Body; therefore, few understand the possibility for realization that occurs when you liberate the mind at this Level of Being. Balyogi states, "This lack of understanding is the last veil that obscures liberation. When the Buddha attained this level of realization, he demonstrated what was possible for all others."

Balyogi says that when seeking to access the Cosmic Body, meditation practitioners mistakenly imagine it to be a specific point of light like a flashlight shining in the dark that would draw their attention when, actually, the light of the Divine Body is like the sun; it lights up everything. Thus, if you look for the single point of light, you are overlooking it. The ocean and the wave, the raindrops and the river, are all different forms of water, but they are not separate from water, nor does any single one of them define water or limit the scope of water. Similarly, when you focus on the Cosmic Body, there is no individual separateness, just oneness, which then generates the diversity of existence.

Cosmic Body as Love Itself

Balyogi says that the pure Level of Being of the Cosmic Body is love itself. When you seek love from another in your daily life or seek someone that will generate feelings of love within you, you are looking for what you already have. All love is already within you in its giving and receiving forms as pure love without attachment or expectation, but you have to discover its presence before you can rest your mind in its presence. You are love, so when you feel love from another, you are experiencing this innate presence of love encountering itself through you and the other person. Likewise, when you have love for another, you are simply remembering what you always were and always will be—love itself.

▌ **Corresponding kosha**: None; transcends the koshas.

▌ **How it's nourished (what it needs)**: The Cosmic Body needs living in its own nature, which is complete and fully nourished by its own existence. This is why it is referred to as the Absolute. Balyogi says nothing is missing in the Cosmic Body; all is within it, so it is beyond need of any sort. There is perfect satisfaction. This state is captured in the Bhagavad Gita when Lord Krishna reveals his Cosmic Body, and Arjuna sees that it contains not just the stars, planets, and space but something more that can't be expressed in words. In deep samadhi when you sit in absorptive wonder, you experience a hint of a hint of this Level of Being.

▌ **How it expresses love**: It manifests simply as itself.

▌ **Color**: The Cosmic Body can be any color or transparent; so it can be colorful or colorless. (Examine the *Flame of Consciousness* illustration in Chapter 8 to gain further understanding of this.)

4

CONNECTING TO THE NINE BODIES IN MEDITATION

Connecting to the Nine Bodies in Meditation

Just reading about and reflecting on the Nine Bodies can make a difference in your self-understanding and how skillfully you respond to various challenges in your life. However, it is through meditation practice that you will systematically learn to connect and explore each Body directly. Many of the meditation instructions I suggest in this chapter can only be fully implemented when you can sustain strong concentration for a period of time. Realistically though, most of the time you will not have such access; instead, your connection to any particular Body will be fleeting or unstable. In fact, you may never succeed in establishing unwavering access to the Bodies of the Subtle Level. Despite how frustrating that can be, you will nevertheless be able to recognize which of the Bodies most characterizes your consciousness at any moment and observe how it is affecting you.

Your mind already moves in and out of these different Bodies, and they are continually affecting your physical body, attitude, perception, and mental capabilities. So just having the ability to recognize the underlying energies of the various Bodies can bring equanimity to the mind. Moreover, at times in meditation and daily life you will "stumble into" or be "swept into" one of the more subtle Bodies. Therefore, if you have practiced meditating on that Body, even if you have never seemingly made any progress, you will still be prepared to work with it more wisely. Additionally, exploring the Nine Bodies may help you better understand other teachings regarding samadhi and its powers that you may have received.

Finally, through this exploration some of the more obscure and confusing teachings of various spiritual traditions may start to make more sense to you. Oftentimes, we can feel that there is something important in a spiritual teaching but it is so unclear, contradictory, or incomprehensible that we

either cease trying to understand it or we just accept what is said without reflection. The map of the Nine Bodies can provide a context for some of these teachings and can help account for what seems like conflicting descriptions of spiritual moments by revealing that they occur at different "Levels of Being." For all these reasons, it is worthwhile to spend at least some time meditating on the Nine Bodies, even if doing so does not become part of your regular practice.

One Totality with Nine Manifestations

Even though we are exploring the Nine Bodies in terms of their individual characteristics in this book, there is only *one totality of being*, which has nine discernible and accessible manifestations. This means your moment-to-moment daily life experiences already reflect an ever-changing, cascading manifestation of the different capacities of consciousness that manifest in each of the Nine Bodies. For instance, when you are experiencing life from the Physical Body, such as when you feel great pain, the Emotional Body becomes predominant almost instantly as fear or dread arises in the mind in reaction to the pain. Also, sometimes you may move quickly from the Emotional Body to the Etheric or Astral Body if the intensity of the pain elicits a stronger reaction in the mind. It is important that you not lose this perspective of the totality of being or else you may fall into the trap of thinking of parts of yourself as stored in separate silos, which can distort your self-perception.

Goals for Accessing the Nine Bodies

The first goal of these teachings is to help you recognize the aspects of being you are experiencing, particularly during meditation practice, and to learn how to work with it skillfully. One of the benefits of the Nine Bodies teachings is that it provides you with an overview of the interconnection and ultimate *oneness* of the various capabilities of consciousness, which enables you to use these various capacities to balance and develop your mind.

The second goal of the teachings is to assist you in developing the ability to direct your attention to each of the Nine Bodies because being able to include the totality of being in this manner is beneficial to any meditation practice, even if it is at a very superficial level.

To a large degree, the meditation exercises that follow are sequenced and progressive, meaning you should begin by meditating on a Body that you have previously accessed and use that Level as your starting point to access the next Body. You do not always have to follow this pattern, but if you do so initially it will help create consistency in your ability to direct attention to any meditative object. For instance, I have a natural ability to directly access the Etheric Body. I cannot always connect to it directly, but I can access it with some frequency. However, when the goal of my practice is to work on developing access to all the different Bodies, I choose to go through the longer step-by-step process to access the Etheric Body that I describe in the following paragraphs. I do not even attempt a shortcut because I want to deepen my ability to choose which Body I want to access, to be deliberate in my practice, and to develop my skill at accessing different Levels as best I am able.

Using meditation to access the three Bodies that constitute the Gross Level is relatively easy to do, and whatever level of meditation skill you have at present is probably sufficient. However, accessing the Subtle and Causal Levels requires ever-finer degrees of connection to your meditative object. The reason for this is that the objects you are meditating on become less and less coarse as they move from ordinary physical and mental experiences to energetic, vibrational, and then sublime in nature.

You may want to start your exploration of the Nine Bodies by repeatedly directing your attention to the traditional teachings of the Physical, Subtle, or Causal Levels. You initially learn to identify your experience in this more general way, then when that becomes easy to do you start to fine-tune how you are practicing. For instance, I will sometimes instruct meditation students to simply recognize that an experience they are having is primarily at the Subtle Level and to work with it at that Level rather than trying to identify whether it is within the Etheric or Astral Body. Nonstriving, patience, curiosity, and persistence are the qualities of mind that will lead you to access each of the Nine Bodies.

Utilizing Breath Meditation for Access

The method I use for systematically working with the Nine Bodies is meditating on the breath as an object. There are other possible methods, but the breath is a familiar meditation object to mindfulness and yoga students, and most people can easily locate it within the body. I refer to the breath as the *air* or *wind* element. Although I use both terms for the sake of variety, I prefer to call it the wind element because we have a tendency to associate air with breath and then think of the breath as "my breath," which blocks the mind from being able to stay with the impersonal nature of the wind element as a meditation object. By concentrating on your breath with patience and persistence, you gradually learn to detect ever-finer degrees of awareness of the wind element through this series of meditations.

Please note that I am teaching mindfulness of the breath in this specific and limited manner for the singular purpose of helping you locate and maintain attention in each of the Nine Bodies. Mindfulness is ordinarily taught for the purpose of creating the conditions for mind-liberating insights to arise. Once you learn to locate the Bodies in your meditation practice, you can then practice mindfulness for cultivating insight from each of the Bodies, if that is your form of practice. The meditations that follow will help bring you in touch with a number of the Nine Bodies, at least momentarily, but you need to practice them diligently and with a relaxed, nongrasping, nonjudging attitude. When appropriate, I also note the benefits for accessing a particular Body in daily life.

Accessing Bodies One through Three:

The Physical, Vital, and Emotional Bodies

Just as in the previous chapter, I have divided your meditative explorations of the Nine Bodies into three sets of three. Before you explore each Body, you may want to review the overview of that Body in Chapter 3. The instructions below serve as instructions for formal meditation practice. They are also general orientations to accessing and developing sensitivity to these Bodies in daily life.

Begin with Bodies One through Three: the Physical, Vital, and Emotional Bodies. These are the Bodies that comprise the Gross Level. It is important that you spend some weeks practicing mindfulness of each of these Bodies before you move on to exploring the Bodies of the Subtle Level (Four through Six), which are more challenging to access. Stay with these first three Bodies until you can access each with confidence during your daily life, as well as in your meditation practice. So often in our pursuit to have a "special" experience, we miss the incredible specialness of the ordinary. This is such a loss.

Moreover, if you do not practice accessing these three Bodies, you fail to build a solid foundation for directing attention to a specific experience and sustaining attention on that experience, which you will need in later meditative stages. You do not have to be able to be deeply concentrated in a manner that is unshakable, but the consistency of your attention staying on the object does have to be "good enough." By good enough, I mean that you need to be able to gather your attention around the characteristics of a particular Body until you gain access to that Body. Your attention may waver somewhat, but your attention needs to stay mostly where you direct it for at least ten minutes. Do not fret if at present you are only able to stay focused for just a few minutes or seconds. Over time your concentration will grow in stability such that the chosen object stays in the center of your attention.

To start out, even though you may feel that you already know the Physical Body, practice at least three meditation sessions focused on this Level to ensure that you can direct your attention to the Physical Body with ease and keep it there. Then do at least three sessions focused on the Vital Body, followed by at least three on the Emotional Body. Then spend a couple of weeks flowing back and forth between these three Bodies to develop ease and confidence in accessing and moving between them. Remember, you're not just learning about these specific Bodies—you're learning a new approach to practice that will help you as you explore the more subtle Bodies.

▶ MEDITATION 1: The Physical Body

Begin with simply practicing mindfulness of the wind element manifesting as breath in the Physical Body. Be mindful of any physical sensations that tell you that you are breathing; breath is occurring. You may feel the wind element as pressure, tingling, or vibration, or as an in-and-out or rising-and-falling movement. When you are able to consciously feel these body sensations directly without commenting on them or trying to control them through your thoughts, you are directly accessing the Physical Body. Confirm whether this is true for you. You will see that indeed consciousness *knows it knows* physical sensation. Instructing you to do this confirmation may seem unimportant, but the "knowing you know" aspect of consciousness builds strength and confidence of mind, which helps the mind develop its more subtle capacities for attention.

If for any reason you are not settled sufficiently to stay with the breath, use the earth and fire elements in the body along with the breath for locating the direct experience of the Physical Body. Feel your feet touching earth, feel your buttocks touching earth through your chair or cushion, feel your hands touching earth, notice two or three breaths as sensations, and then start over again with your feet. Be specific about what you are noticing with each body touch point. How do you know you have feet? Is it the hardness or softness, the warmth or coolness of the feet? How do you know you have hands? Is it a feeling of warmth or coolness, heaviness or lightness, pulsation, tingling, or stillness in the hands? These questions represent a relaxed inquiry that allows you to arrive at a direct experience of the Physical Body. When you find yourself commenting on your experience or appraising how well you are doing, stop and return to being conscious of the physical sensations of the wind, fire, and earth elements.

When you are more settled, drop everything but the movement of the breath as wind as your focus. Also, if other physical sensations start to fight for your attention, such as old injuries or feelings of discomfort from sitting, allow them to be temporary objects of meditation for they too are bringing you into the Physical Body. Just be sure to note as you meditate: "The Physical Body is like this."

One way to describe the felt sense of being in the Physical Body is as "embodied consciousness." Another is feeling "grounded in the body." As you become more mindful, it is easy to fall into the unrecognized habit of being a *removed observer* who is skillful at noting and conceptualizing but does not directly experience what is arising. To balance this "headiness" and develop embodied consciousness, you practice staying in your body as a felt sense as you experience the push-and-pull of emotions and thoughts. One way embodied consciousness is described traditionally is "knowing the breath within the breath" and "the body within the body," both of which refer to the immediacy of the felt sense rather than to our mental views about sensations. Moreover, from this embodied consciousness you can develop a felt sense for the nervous system based on the *principle* of being *grounded*. You will discover that your attention can be grounded in any conscious experience, not just the body, if you cultivate the intention to *rest attention* on that experience. Just as the nervous system has a parasympathetic relaxation response when it realizes it is safely resting on earth, which in turn calms and clears the mind, this calming relaxation response is generated when accessing each of the Bodies.

Once you learn to rest your attention, it becomes a useful tool for connecting to the more subtle Bodies. For instance, when you start to access the Etheric and Astral Bodies, you may notice that you have little body awareness in the one and maybe none in the other, yet you can maintain this inner sense of being grounded. Feeling grounded even in nonmaterial focused consciousness will help keep the mind calm and clear so that your attention can become more and more subtle. You can even feel grounded when your focus is bringing awareness to the activity of *knowing* or consciousness itself. At its most subtle level, being grounded in knowing creates the paradoxical feeling of a *groundless ground*, a phrase you may have heard in various spiritual teachings. You may have such a feeling at some points in your meditation practice.

From the practical perspective, it is very helpful to be able to access the Physical Body in daily life when the mind is racing and emotions are strong. I recommend that you repeatedly return to establishing mindfulness of the body within the body throughout your day. It provides a beneficial break for an overly active mind or a mind that is habitually tuning out.

▶ MEDITATION 2: Accessing the Vital or Prana Body

Experiencing the felt sense of the Vital or Prana Body requires more refined attention. You are switching from focusing on the physical sensations of the breath to the energetic feelings that arise with the movement of the breath. We can generally recognize vitality in others or ourselves, but in this meditation we are moving from that general awareness to a specific felt sense of the vitality.

To access the Vital Body, begin by focusing on the movement of the breath and then utilize reflection to consciously confirm that all movement represents the presence of energy. Movement simply cannot happen without energy—it is a scientific law. Once you've established your focus, move your attention away from the coarser level of matter represented by the skin, tissue, bones, etc., of the body and begin to note the feeling of energy in the body associated with the breath. At times, you may lose any sense of the breath and only feel the energetic pulsation as its own entity. Mentally instruct yourself to direct attention to this less coarse Level. It takes some experimentation and false starts to establish attention at this Level.

When you start to have a direct felt sense of the vitality of the physical realm, you are accessing the Vital Body. You can directly feel the qualities of arousal or stimulation that occur when you inhale and the quality of release of energy that happens when you exhale. Notice that the feeling of vitality is subtler than that of the air touching your nose or the movements of chest and belly. Can you feel directly the body being nourished and renewed? Remember that the Vital Body contains not only oxygen but also what Balyogi calls élan.

The Vital Body is the furnace of the Physical and Emotional Bodies. It needs fuel, prana, and rest to function properly. When the furnace goes out, you have no vitality. We call this "burnout." Or sometimes, something goes wrong with the fuel lines from the furnace to the Physical and Emotional Bodies and we cannot properly access the fuel. I point out these problems to emphasize that the Vital Body is its own Level of Being. I often encounter people who have little or no feeling for the Vital or Prana Body, despite how palpable it is with just a moderate amount of directed attention.

It is easy to doubt that you are accessing the Vital Body, and the doubt may stop you from relaxing more deeply into the direct experience of it. Or the doubt can be so large initially that you quit without putting in the time to learn how to access this Body. Not accessing the Vital Body is a real loss because it is something that everyone can learn to do and it creates physical and mental balance. If you persist, you eventually become *conscious* that you can indeed directly feel prana. And you feel how refreshing it is to do so. You may feel it as tingling or bursts of energy, or enhanced awareness, or countless other possibilities. But you *know you know* you are feeling it. The various forms of breath yoga called pranayama can also help you locate the Vital Body. I particularly like the alternate nostril breathing practice that is frequently taught in the yogic tradition. But for it to be most effective, it needs to be done as a meditation.

Mindfulness of the Vital Body is a great resource for feeling more alive, having more energy, and being more resilient in daily life. Some people are able to access it without ever consciously knowing they are. If you know someone who seems to have an amazing amount of energy, they are likely accessing the Vital Body directly. In daily life, the Vital Body signals to us when we are being skillful or unskillful in regard to it. The pranas respond well to gentle attention, while anxiousness, fearfulness, or neurotic attention depletes them or interferes with their function. If you learn to *stay grounded* in consciousness of the Vital Body, you will automatically be nourishing it.

▶ MEDITATION 3: Accessing the Emotional Body

To access the Emotional Body, continue to focus on the breath. After a short period of time, you will discover that various emotional thoughts arise and interrupt your focus on the breath. Rather than ignoring these thoughts as you did in the first two meditations, make each emotion your meditation object temporarily such that you are becoming conscious of the arising and passing of emotions. Of course the emotions will change, or your mind will sometimes stop having emotions—but don't worry, they will return!

Each emotion is expressed as a felt sense in the body and creates an observable movement of the mind. Watch what happens in the mind. Notice how easily it becomes discursive, or gets lost in thoughts and opinions regarding the emotion being felt, or becomes bored. Observe how the pleasantness or unpleasantness of the emotion affects the mind. Note that every emotion has a body component indicating the presence of that emotion, although sometimes it is quite subtle.

As you make these observations, you are accessing the Emotional Body as it is manifesting moment to moment. The trick to meditating on the Emotional Body in this manner is to not get fascinated or disturbed by the content of the thoughts that arise but rather to stay with the recognition that "Emotion is like this." If it is a particularly difficult emotion, you may not be able to resist being pulled into it. If that occurs, try naming the emotion, for example, "Regret is like this" or "Being excited is like this," until the mind is calm once more. If the mind does not return to calm, then focus again on the Physical Body as your object until it does. In meditation practice, two principles always apply: You must be willing to *start over* repeatedly, and you need to *start where you are*, that is, acknowledge what the mind is doing in the moment in order to redirect your attention to where you want it to be.

Just as accessing the Physical Body is beneficial to a peaceful and purposeful daily life, so too is the recognition that you are focusing on the Emotional Body. Oftentimes, just that recognition alone will calm the mind. If not, you can easily learn to move from consciousness of the Emotional Level to the Physical Level though directing your attention. You also learn not to trust the thoughts that emerge when you feel overwhelmed in the Emotional Body, and you learn to reorient your consciousness through attention to visual and audio stimuli. This skill is of particular use when emotions arise associated with past trauma, or if you are in an uncertain or high-pressure situation.

Accessing Bodies Four through Six:
The Etheric, Astral, and Intuitional Bodies

Once you begin to feel at ease accessing the first three Bodies such that you can direct and sustain your attention on whichever one you choose, you are ready to work with accessing the next three Bodies: the Etheric, Astral, and Intuitional. These are the three Bodies that are traditionally grouped together as the "Subtle Level" in the traditional yogic systems. You may find it useful to review the overview of these Bodies in the previous chapter before starting.

This work requires a higher degree of concentration than the work with the first three Bodies. If you do not have access to this degree of concentration, you may wish to first explore the meditation instructions I offer in Chapter 5 for working with Balyogi's illustrations, because those involve more reflection, contemplation, and open awareness than concentration.

Often you can't accurately identify which of these three Subtle Bodies you are accessing, but you can recognize that you are experiencing one of them in some form. For instance, you may not know if what you're experiencing belongs to the Etheric or the Intuitional Body, but you do know you are focused on what is occurring in one of the more Subtle Bodies in this layer. Fortunately, knowing just that much is enough; it keeps you going in your exploration, and over time you gain the clarity that allows you to be more discerning in your understanding. The trick is to hang out in a certain realm for a while. You will naturally start to differentiate between the Bodies and distinguish more details.

▶ MEDITATION 4: **The Etheric Body**

Start with the breath in the Physical Body and go through the same process you used for accessing the Vital Body by becoming conscious of the breath as the energy of the wind element. Patiently establish the realization that movement, by definition, is energy; therefore, the breath at the Subtle Level is really just an energetic experience. Reflect on this until you feel the movement of breath as energy so consistently and with such stability that you are able to switch from the breath to the energetic field of movement as the object of your meditation. At this more refined level of awareness, breath, body sensations, emotions, and thoughts arise and pass on their own as energetic flows and fluctuations.

Now that you have established attention in the Vital Body, you are ready to move to an even subtler level, becoming conscious of the Etheric Body. (Remember, there is a direct link between the Vital and Etheric Bodies.) Reflect and focus on the fact that in the Vital Body even energy itself is very physical and coarse. Invite the mind to become aware of the energy of luminous consciousness. You are shifting your focus from energy in the Vital Body to the *energy that powers consciousness*. As you stay with the energy of consciousness as the object of your meditation, the feeling of breath becomes faint and fades into the background, and the mind becomes absorbed into the energetic field.

It can also be helpful to say to yourself: "May the Etheric Body be experienced." Accessing the Etheric Body feels like a *surrendering of the activity* of consciousness that is involved in the knowing of objects in order to experience the *state* of consciousness itself. As you stay with this request to know the Etheric Body, maintain a stable one-pointed meditation and expect nothing special to occur as part of this knowing when it arises. Make sure that you are not demanding that something happen and avoid creating a concept of what it will feel like to experience this level of being directly and fully. Each person has his or her own unique experience of the Etheric Body. Please avoid judging yourself on your efforts and what you are experiencing.

Eventually, over the course of a meditation session, you may feel your mind is in a different realm, as though you had taken a mind-altering drug. The feeling may be of a "soft-eyed focus" in which the mind is bright and alert but not engaged in any of its usual activities. Do not be alarmed if this mind state brings feelings of uncertainty or unfamiliarity. Also, do not get attached to it if the mind feels blissfully relaxed or rapturous. Once this mind state has arisen, stay with the feeling of the *altered focus* or *mind space* as your object. You are accessing or becoming conscious of the *felt sense* of the Etheric Body. The mind may move in and out of this experience for a long time before it becomes truly stable. Be patient and continue to incline the mind toward the Etheric Body. By "incline" I mean the gentle use of intention along with the periodic request, "May the mind experience the Etheric Body."

Like the Vital Body, the Etheric Body has an energetic quality to it, but it feels lighter and more *dispersed, like a field of knowing,* in contrast to the contained feeling of *prana being embodied* that is associated with the Vital Body. It is as though your consciousness has assumed an expanded state like a radar or CT scanner and is able to directly feel and receive data from a wide array of subtle sources that are not directly visible. You are starting to reach a state of heightened awareness, but this heightened awareness is very different than when you are on high alert or are afraid in everyday life. It is characterized by an inward, receptive feeling as opposed to an outward orientation of increased alertness. In your meditation, stay with this feeling of heightened awareness until you feel yourself drop into this subtle mind state. In this state, you will still have reflective consciousness. You will *know you know* that you are having the experience. But you may well feel that some larger sense of consciousness is present and the consciousness that is aware of what is happening is much smaller and embodied locally in the body.

There is no single way in which to experience the Etheric Body, so I can only make a general statement about the experience. Whereas the energy of prana in the Vital Body feels solid and substantial, the energetic feeling of the subtle prana in the Etheric Body feels like something you might imagine at the quantum level of physics where light can be either a wave or a particle. You may not notice anything energetically. Or the feeling may be similar to when your leg has fallen asleep and as you start to move you feel little pinpricks. You may feel a tingling sensation or a wave of vibration or pulsation. Although the feeling of energy is present, the energy is not moving directionally, it is moving in place. It is the presence of *knowing* felt as energy.

The Etheric Body is an ideal place for the mind to rest while observing experiences arising and passing in consciousness. Two examples of this style of meditation are Big Sky and Big Mind meditations in which there is little identification with or interest in the thoughts and sensations that arise like clouds moving across in the sky. In daily life when you are feeling stressed or burned out, taking time to lie down and invite the knowing of the Etheric Body can be a source of renewal.

As I stated in the previous chapter, the Etheric Body is where the experience of kundalini rising occurs and is then felt in the Physical and Vital Bodies. Such intense energetic experiences are specifically developed in Tantric or Kundalini Yoga. But intense energetic experiences of all kinds, including shaking, heat, and spontaneous movement, are common occurrences for people meditating in a wide variety of forms. All such experiences have a connection to the Etheric Body. If you are a physician, therapist, or bodyworker, accessing this level of being while you care for another person adds dimensionality to your work. It is helpful to remind yourself that your patient also has an Etheric Body. You can invite the Etheric Body to help in the healing process in whatever Level of Being is ill or injured. If you are sufficiently skilled, you can assess if they are lacking a strong connection between their Physical and Etheric Bodies and guide them in nourishing the Etheric Body.

▶ MEDITATION 5: Accessing the Astral Body

To use meditation practice for accessing the Astral Level of Being, first go though the steps necessary to establish the mind in the Etheric Body. Then incline the mind to experience the Astral Body and request, "May I know the Astral Level of Being." You are shifting the mind from a feeling of being *grounded in a field of knowing* in the Etheric Body where there is still a sense of physicality to *nonlocal spacious awareness*. The mind is moving away from a focus on the here and now, and while you are still conscious of what you are experiencing you are not locating it in time. You may feel as though you are looking down at the body, or are no longer identified with the body, or that your mind can travel anywhere.

As this transition to the Astral Body occurs, your consciousness may flit back and forth rapidly, frequently, or both rapidly and frequently between body awareness and nonembodied consciousness. You may have sufficient consciousness *to know that you are knowing* what you are experiencing or you may be tuned out such that there is not a reflective, self-aware aspect to your consciousness.

It is not unusual for those who meditate to report falling into or passing through the neighborhood of the Astral Body in their practice. I have worked with a number of yogis who seem to spend much of their meditation time in this Body without realizing where they are. They report feeling spacey, spacious, vacant, tuned out, absent, or not present. Or they say their consciousness disappeared for a while. People who practice open awareness meditation or who are attempting to achieve *rigpa* in Tibetan meditation can rest attention in the Astral Body without realizing it and in doing so are not able to achieve the goal of their practice.

Access to the Astral Body can happen spontaneously in daily life, although such occurrence is usually somewhat chaotic and not very deep. This spontaneous accessing of the Astral Body may be due to an emotionally charged event, or a strong memory, or intense anticipation of the future. Few people are able to develop any mastery in reaching, staying with, and exploring the Astral Body through such spontaneous access.

Deep Absorptions and the Astral Body

In the Theravada tradition, there are a series of meditative absorptions or samadhi states called the *jhanas*. In traditional Buddhist teachings, a number of psychic powers are listed as being accessible in a particular state of absorption. (See Patanjali's Yoga Sutra III, 37–43 for similar powers.) The jhanas arise based on five factors being present in the mind: directed and sustained attention, rapture, joy, and one-pointed equanimity. When these five factors are present or when the mind is so deeply absorbed that many of them have dropped away, you can most easily choose to direct the mind to accessing the Astral Body in the deepest manner.

As with many of the other deep absorption states, accessing the Astral Body can be seductive, and it is easy to get lost in the various altered mind states that may arise. It is the Level of Being in which archetypal images arise, where visions occur, and the sense of your own body can change radically. You can *see* the cosmos, *hear* its beautiful sound as the spheres move, *know* endless spaciousness, and *experience* the vastness of consciousness. But all such experiences are temporary; they only represent a certain state of mind, not liberation from suffering. Once you leave that mind state, you are back in the realm of suffering. Beware of getting lost in the parlor tricks available in the Astral Body!

In your daily life, the Astral Body is where the subtle impulses of the mind to move toward action (karma) and knowledge (jnana) occur in the karmendriyas and jnanendriyas (see Chapter 3). If you develop the ability to recognize these impulses as they are occurring, you can get a feel for the way that sense-consciousness manifests as a series of discrete moments as well as a continuous flow. You may be surprised at how much disruption or disengagement is happening in your mind. Just bringing awareness to this phenomenon starts to smooth the flow of consciousness without you having to do anything to make a correction. In meditation retreats, because the mind is protected, not overly stimulated, and continually directed toward practice, it is often possible to observe this smoothing out of consciousness as it occurs. If you attend meditation retreats, you may have felt this and appreciated the feeling but not understood what was happening or why.

▶ MEDITATION 6: **Accessing the Intuitional Body**

The next step in refinement of consciousness is accessing the Intuitional Body. To do so, establish stable attention on the Etheric Body as a foundation. Request, "May the Etheric Body be known."

While the Etheric Body is accessed through the energetic field and the Astral Body through attuning to nonlocal spaciousness, the Intuitional Body is accessed through its *profound vibrant stillness*. The mind at this Level is bright and vibrant, but it is also calm and still. It is a mind that is not easily disturbed, even by strong pleasant and unpleasant sensations and mind states; it simply receives and absorbs any experience with equanimity and can easily isolate itself from sense gate stimuli. This is the felt sense of awareness that arises when you are accessing the Intuitional Body. The Intuitional Body is the most *energetically refined* of the three Bodies in this Level.

The direct feeling of the Intuitional Body is empty spaciousness, receptivity, clear seeing, and a quiet mind that is uninvolved in objects arising in consciousness. It can be described as the penultimate form of consciousness. You see things just as they are. At this Level of Being, the mind is alert, stable, flexible, and easily placed on any object of experience for purposes of samadhi or insight. The mind is filled with calm and a feeling of well-being and is isolated from any concern about the world. It is such a wholesome, satisfying feeling that when you access the Intuitional Body you easily recognize you are doing so.

Intuitional Body as Beyond Ordinary Consciousness

When you turn the mind to the practice of insight once you have accessed the Intuitional Body, you can experience direct awareness of luminous consciousness as a phenomenon, as I described in Chapter 2. Also, the Intuitional Body is where you are most likely to realize the true nature of mind—radiant, responsive, and empty.

My Buddhist teacher Ajahn Sumedho speaks of the necessity of "intuitive awareness" in meditation practice. It is also described simply as "that which knows." Only at the Intuitional Level of Being is such a capacity of mind possible. At this Level of Being, deep understanding comes as flashes of insight that bypass the ordinary consciousness. Balyogi teaches that the Buddha was a master at accessing and residing in the Intuitional Body where he gained direct insights that brought the attainment of liberation. By direct insights I mean nonordinary recognition or knowing that is not using inductive or deductive logic; it is a knowing that simply bursts into consciousness.

Because of its malleability at this level, the mind can be directed toward deeper concentration, if you choose. When Balyogi described in Chapter 3 his experience of a three-day, unbroken meditation in which he never left pure awareness, he was resting in the Intuitional Body. He then had his major insights regarding the illumination and illuminated aspects of consciousness upon coming out of this meditation while still accessing the Intuitional Body. This impersonal capacity of the mind utilizes the cognitive ability of ordinary consciousness but penetrates the nature of mind and reality in a manner that ordinary consciousness, observing, and thinking cannot do.

Ordinary consciousness is left behind in the most advanced concentration state. It is here that you can experience pure awareness as described in Chapter 2. You can become so absorbed that you only experience awareness; there is no consciousness of this awareness while in this mind state. Instead there is only an unmoving, nondoing awareness that is not conscious of its own existence. The knowledge that you are in that place of empty stillness comes only after you leave the state, and you rediscover it through remembering and reflecting. Balyogi says that at this level of refinement, you are getting a foretaste of enlightenment. Leaving this deep absorption and moving from pure awareness back into consciousness of subject and object provides you with liberating insights about your identity and how clinging in the mind causes suffering.

Attainment of Realization in the Intuitional Body

Through the knowing of the emptiness of mind, you come to the realization of enlightenment or *nibbana*, the ultimate mind state of awakening and freedom. It is the awakened mind moment described in Tibetan Buddhist teaching, "*Gate, gate, para gate, parasamgate, bodhi svaha*: gone, gone, gone far beyond, ah!"

The awakening experience is the ultimate stage of consciousness, and, therefore, is a step beyond the awareness of consciousness of the Intuitional Body. However, it is through resting your attention in the Intuitional Body that attainment of freedom occurs. I stress this distinction because sometimes people have very profound experiences through the combination of the Etheric and Intuitional Bodies and conclude that they are enlightened. It can seem so because the mind clearly sees suffering and the end of suffering. But full awakening, as best as I understand it from my teachers and my practice, is a step of consciousness beyond knowing into *realization as a phenomenon*, a movement into manifest being itself where not even the seeds from which future greed, aversion, or delusion might take root.

Remember that in the Nine Bodies teachings, enlightenment is presented as an attainment that arises due to practice. It is not an achievement of ego; it is beyond ego, which is why it is an attainment. The Intuitional Body is not an ego-centered Level of Being; it is represented by the awareness of the impersonal nature of luminous consciousness.

Accessing Bodies Seven through Nine:
Spiritual, Divine, and Cosmic Bodies

I have little to offer about accessing the three most subtle Bodies, which together comprise the Causal Level. In part, this is because their nature is *sublime*, which means from this realm they can be felt as ephemeral or illusionary. In Balyogi's language, they relate to the *illuminator*, the power source for the electricity or illumination of consciousness that I described in Chapter 2. You will simply come to know them by repeatedly accessing the Intuitional Body. With each of the Bodies in the Causal Level, you can request that a specific Body arise in consciousness, just as you did for the other Bodies.

Of the three, the most directly felt is the Spiritual Body because we can feel the wide range of thoughts, words, and actions that arise seemingly un-bidden in our minds. We can have the most terrible thoughts and impulses as well as loving and generous ones arising spontaneously, often seemingly from nowhere. The Spiritual Body contains all of these *potentials of the mind*. The Divine Body is subtler still and is closely related to the Spiritual Body. Balyogi describes the Divine Body as being like the root of the flower while the Spiritual Body is like the flower's bloom. Even more refined than the previous two Bodies, the Cosmic Body can only be known and felt as myste-rious. For me, the most important gain from accessing the three Bodies of the Causal Level is the felt sense that mind, however defined, is something larger than the brain or some emergent property of the brain's functions. This felt sense relates to pure awareness, to the unborn, uncreated, and un-manifest.

▶ MEDITATION 7: Accessing the Spiritual Body

To access the Spiritual Body, follow the same procedure you utilized for ac-cessing all the previous Bodies and first establish the mind in the Intuitional Body. You can make the request, "May the mind know the Spiritual Body," and then focus on the possibility of the Spiritual Body arising. The Spiritual Body is one of *potential* to manifest, not *actuality* of manifestation in the physical realm. This does not mean that the Spiritual Body does not exist but rather that it is even more subtle and sublime than the vibration and stillness of the Intuitional Body.

Access to the Spiritual Body occurs through the Intuitional and Etheric Bodies. Experiencing the Spiritual Body is like feeling the underlying power of the ocean. In some places the ocean is calm; in others it is rough. At times you can feel the effect of the wind on the ocean and the undertow of waves breaking onto shore. Imagine what it would be like if you could feel all of the different qualities of the ocean at one time as un-manifest energetic waves of possibility.

Similarly, in accessing the Spiritual Body, you can feel the "ocean of potential" in the mind, which can manifest as thoughts, emotions, words, and actions. The Spiritual Body is an energetic sense of possibility that is un-manifest, yet it can be felt directly and intuited. For the untrained mind, if access to the Spiritual Body occurs during meditation, the feeling can be overwhelming. In daily life, it can cause disorientation because it is so expansive and seemingly unstable. Once you experience the Spiritual Body, you have the insight that what arises in the mind in any moment is determined either by the causes and conditions that characterize that particular moment and your mental habits or by mindful cultivation of deliberate intention. This is why we practice meditation—to be able to have choice about what actually arises from this vast potential.

When you are accessing each of the three subtlest Bodies, you are at the shoreline where the manifest realm touches the edge of the un-manifest realm. Therefore, if your mind is still and stable, it is possible for you to feel the gravitational pull the ocean of possibility has on the Physical and Emotional Bodies. Even before any thoughts, words, or actions occur in the mind, the presence of possibilities affects you physically, emotionally, and psychically.

If you are able to feel the energetic pull of impulses and possible mind states the way you can feel the tide in the ocean, you are accessing the Spiritual Body. It is easy to conceptualize this Body and miss the direct experience because we are accustomed to theorizing as a mental activity. In my view, we have more access to the Spiritual Body than we care to admit. Its existence tells us that life has meaning, there is choice, and choice matters. For me, it indicates that transformation and transcendence are genuine possibilities, not just idealizations. However, our liberation does not come from believing in the existence of an ocean of possibility called the Spiritual Body but in the actual letting go of mental fluctuations caused by greed, hatred, and delusion.

▶ MEDITATION 8: Accessing the Divine Body

To access the Divine Body, again establish your attention on the Spiritual Body. Then note that there is a feeling of benevolence that underlies all the tides of possibility in the mind that can be detected when the mind is empty and still. The only way I know to describe this level of the Nine Bodies is as an energetic presence of well-being or benevolence. When you directly feel this, you are accessing the Divine Body. I am not describing an entity of some sort, nor any kind of personality, and certainly not a god. Rather the Divine Body seems to be an innate energy of benign presence that is necessary for existence to manifest. (In the language of physics, the energy of the Divine Body is why "something" exists rather than "nothing.") By this

I mean that the energy of the Divine Body is allowing all incarnate forms to be, and all incarnate forms have the limitations of the arising and passing. Thus, there is the continual dance between the un-manifest and the manifest, and in our brief moments of realization we have the great privilege of knowing it directly.

Remember this is a Level of Being that exists within each of us. It is so subtle that it can only be felt in its energetic presence and cannot be explored in the manner that the Subtle Bodies can be. The Divine Body is an uncreated harmony un-manifest in the worldly realm, but its benign energetic presence is something to which we can attune our minds and hearts. In Buddhism this benign energetic presence is called *bodhicitta*, the non-personal love of the Awakened Heart. In Patanjali's Yoga Sutras, it is *purusha* or *chit*, that which is beyond the physical realm and beyond ordinary mind functioning.

Regarding the realization of the Divine Body, there are various and contradictory teachings: some postulate the need for a "journey" of becoming, others claim that we are already awake—there is no journey, and no self to make a journey. These different descriptions arise because teachers are trying to describe the indescribable. Naturally they do so based on the manner in which they have accessed this Level of Being. Maybe when full awakening has occurred, one has continual direct access or oneness with the Divine Body. Maybe this is what the Buddha means when he says, "What needed to be done has been done." Maybe all blockages to this Level of Being have been removed.

❱ MEDITATION 9: **Accessing the Cosmic Body**

There is no way to directly access the Cosmic Body in the Nine Bodies map. It has energy, but the energy lacks any characteristics that can be felt directly, although it is an integral part of the Nine Bodies map, as can be seen in the three *Flame of Consciousness* illustrations. Balyogi refers to the energy of this Body as being *rahasyatmic* or mysterious energy. He says that the Cosmic Body lacks even a perfume; it has no whiff or hint of an essence that be directly detected. You can only infer its existence by the experience you have in accessing and working with the Divine Body. I cannot even speculate as to how a fully liberated mind experiences this Level of Being.

5

HOW TO WORK WITH BALYOGI'S
ILLUSTRATIONS

How to Work with Balyogi's Illustrations

Now that you have some understanding of the Nine Bodies, you are ready to journey into the *symbolic realm* of Balyogi's teachings about consciousness using the illustrations he created. As discussed in the introduction to this book, Balyogi created these illustrations during his time of intense exploration of samadhi or deep states of meditative absorption. They are both a reflection of his inner experience and a means of communicating that experience to other practitioners. You may not be accustomed to looking for the spiritual meaning in art, but it has been used for this purpose for almost as long as humans have existed, as evidenced by ancient cave paintings and hieroglyphs around the world.[7] To receive a teaching in this manner requires that you *allow understanding to emerge* over time rather than expect to understand it at first glance.

Journey into the Symbolic Realm

In the following chapters, I present twenty of Balyogi's illustrations and relate them to the Nine Bodies. Although Balyogi did not present his illustrations to me in any particular order, I have organized them into six chapters, reflecting the major themes in his teachings. More than likely, you will need to return repeatedly to the descriptions of the Nine Bodies in Chapter 3 while you're concentrating on the illustrations. You may also wish to return to the teachings on consciousness in Chapter 2. If you are to receive any depth of realization from these teachings, it's important to be patient and persistent. They contain a lot of subtle material that you will want to explore over a long period of time.

---

7   If you want to sample the symbolic in Native North American culture, read *Where the Two Came to Their Father* by Maud Oakes, Jeff King, and Joseph Campbell, which explores the symbol of the Twin Heroes.

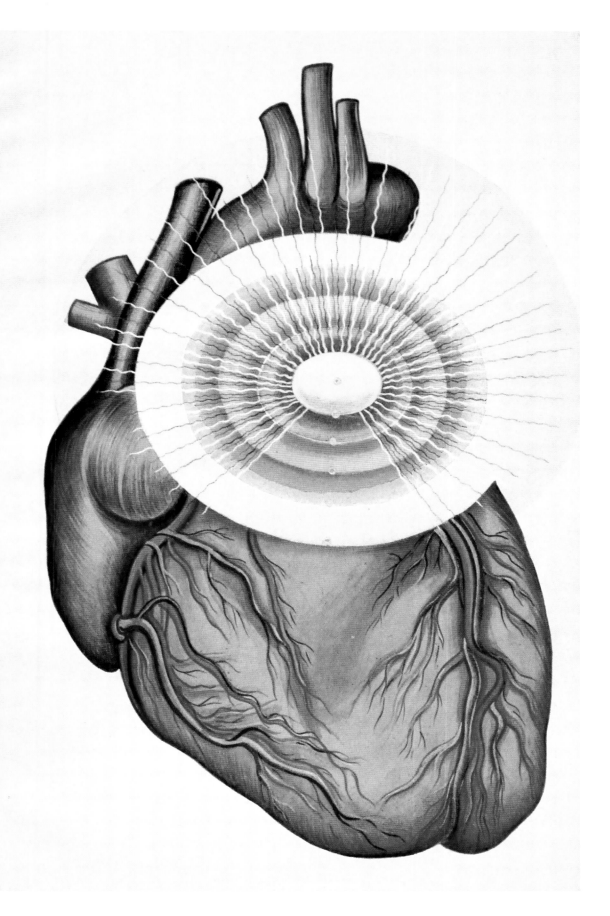

Each of the illustrations contains a teaching about the nature of mind and consciousness. I offer guidance from my own meditation experience to help you understand the symbolic meaning of each illustration and provide instructions for using each illustration as a meditation object. Additionally, I give instructions for contemplating each of the illustrations in a direct, discursive manner. The guidance I offer, although shaped by many hours of studying the illustrations with Balyogi, had to be narrowed to serve the purpose of this book and was chosen to reflect my own insights. Thus, the guidance is not meant in any way to be the definitive statement of interpretation.

Intuitive Understanding Has Its Own Rules

Exploring consciousness through imagery requires curiosity as well as trust in your capacity for *intuitively* understanding the symbolic. If you rush to conceptualize a symbol, you end up missing much of its content. For a period of time, you may feel as though you aren't "getting it" and you may conclude that there is nothing to this, but such thoughts are typical for anyone learning to interpret the symbolic. If you quit or rush through them, you not only fail to learn these teachings, you also fail *to learn how to learn in the intuitive mode*.

When you have studied the last drawing in a chapter, I suggest that you go back and look at each illustration in that chapter again. You will most likely need and want to revisit many of the drawings, particularly those that resonate with you. Therefore, do not expect to comprehend everything from the beginning. Rushing to comprehension in the symbolic realm often means settling for superficial understanding. If you succumb to such expectations of yourself, you will be denying yourself a genuine opportunity. As I keep stressing, patience and persistence are essential if you are going to engage in this type of practice.

Once you feel as though you have a personal relationship with the illustrations, it can be helpful and exciting to discuss them with others. However, beware of discussing them with others until this inner relationship has been established. You are engaging in the world of the symbolic, thus your psyche needs to develop its understanding at its own pace. Therefore, wait patiently for communication to grow between your thinking mind and the unconscious where your relationship to symbols resides. Yes, reflect on the illustrations, read the texts, and even speculate about possible meanings but mostly stay open to receiving *intuitions* regarding the symbols.

Each Illustration Is a Complete Teaching

I recommend that you approach each illustration as a complete teaching in itself. Before reading the corresponding text, spend at least three to five minutes staring at the illustration. Initially, just take in the entire image and then patiently notice as many details as possible. At first don't try to interpret what you are seeing; instead, just notice the feeling the image evokes in you, then observe any spontaneous thoughts you have about any part of the illustration or of the whole image. This is a meditation exercise in which you are allowing the meaning of the drawing to emerge from within you. You may well get restless doing this or decide that you could understand the illustration better by reading the text, but please try looking at it first. This will allow you to experience the image with a different part of your brain than the part that relies on language to interpret what you are seeing.

After you've gazed at an illustration long enough such that the details have registered in your mind and body, read the text. The purpose of the text is to help you deepen your relationship to the image. I am not attempting to tell you how you are supposed to see the image. The idea is for you to find your own meaning in the illustration, stimulated and aided by my experience with it.

You may need to read the text more than once and then go back and forth between the text and various parts of the image in order to fully understand them. In doing this you are allowing your relationship with the image to slowly emerge as you penetrate the depth of what it holds. It is still a meditative experience, but one that is being guided by the text. While doing this practice, you may have thoughts and observations about specific details or the overall impact of a particular illustration. Register these thoughts but don't get distracted by them. Use your meditative time for observing, not for conceptual thinking, making judgments, or forming opinions!

Once you have completed this meditation, ask yourself, "What is meaningful for me in the drawing? Why?" Pay particular attention when you feel as though you are recognizing a truth that is being revealed, but you have no words to describe what you are feeling. This style of learning from the symbolic is the most powerful means for allowing insights to arise within you. Sometimes, an important understanding comes much later. You may not even associate it directly with the illustration. Remember, you are awakening a capacity of knowing that is already inside you.

How the Descriptions of the Illustrations Are to Be Used

In most cases, the text includes an introduction to the illustration and offers suggestions for meditating on that particular illustration and a series of questions for your reflection, but I occasionally vary from this format. I often refer to previous drawings or drawings that appear later in the book, so you may find yourself looking ahead at an illustration or looking back at a previous one.

Sometimes I ask you questions for reflection about an illustration but don't provide an answer. You may find this frustrating at first, but I do it to help you have your own insights. Moreover, in subsequent drawings in the series, I often provide keys to the symbols used in previous drawings. These keys enable you to go back to earlier drawings and see them more clearly with their help, but in the meantime, until you encounter these keys, you will have developed your own understanding.

In general, each illustration helps you understand the others. Some illustrations provide a key realization for being able to read another illustration that shows up later in the book. If you allow your knowledge to build and your intuition to grow, your sense of finding meaning in these illustrations will become more robust. I realize that learning the language of symbols is somewhat slow and complex, and these illustrations represent a new language. But you will find that the accompanying descriptions provide a strong starting point for each illustration. Therefore, even brief contemplation will often yield inspiration and insight.

Learning to Take What Is Useful and Leave the Rest

What I find significant in each of Balyogi's illustrations and how I interpret their meaning is not always the same as what Balyogi shared with me. You too may arrive at different interpretations and have different insights from either of us. I celebrate you taking ownership in this manner. However, for this to be an authentic process, you need to continue relating to the symbols in the context in which they are presented, otherwise your interpretation may become a mere exercise in projection and ego justification and is worth little to you.

To engage in the symbolic is to go on an inner journey; therefore, you may find the symbols affecting your dreams, your relationships, your moods and emotions during waking life. Moreover, certain interactions in your daily life may take on symbolic meaning for you. Honor the symbolic as with reading poetry, but retain authority and responsibility for your speech and actions at all times.

6

BALYOGI'S COSMIC VIEW OF REALITY AND CONSCIOUSNESS

The Eternal Journey of the Transmigration
of Spirit and Consciousness

The Cosmos in Movement

The Cosmos in Repose

*This sequence of illustrations is a symbolic depiction of the ideas
described in Chapter 2 ("Insights Into Consciousness").
It gives an overview of the spiritual journey.*

The Eternal Journey of the Transmigration of Spirit and Consciousness

Before reading further, please take some time to meditate on this illustration using the instructions in the previous chapter. Then use the following suggestions to deepen your experience even further.

This illustration depicts Balyogi's tri-part vision of how reality is constituted, which he describes as "the ecology of reality." It shows the movement of luminous consciousness as it manifests in time, space, and ego identity. It also reveals how our relationship with luminous consciousness changes as we gain access to experiencing it in its highest and nonmanifest state.

Remember that as described in Chapter 2, the term "luminous consciousness" refers to the dimension of consciousness that is radiant and timeless. Just as electricity flows through a light bulb, luminous consciousness flows through the circuitry of our brains and nervous systems to create illumination.

The symbols in the *Eternal Journey* have many dimensions; therefore, they can be understood in various ways and are meant to inspire you to awaken to what is not visible about the reality of life. The sun-like symbol in the sky represents the radiance of pure awareness, which is not related to ordinary consciousness and not engaged in conscious activity. As described in Chapter 2, pure awareness is the transpersonal source that generates the electricity of luminous consciousness, which in turn illuminates the world and allows sense-consciousness to arise. Pure awareness itself cannot be described in words, nor compared or contrasted to anything else.

Represented by the black dots falling like rain from the clouds is the *dharma-megha*. Dharma-megha, meaning "clouds of dharma" (See Patanjali, 4:29), refers to the deep samadhi in which the meditating mind becomes temporarily aligned with pure awareness. The dots in Balyogi's illustration

symbolize the moments when the mind is in a nondual state of consciousness in meditation and free of all karmic imprints. When the dharma is showering on you, you are in a state of bliss that is referred to as *sat chit ananda*, meaning an elevated state of being, knowing, and bliss.

The mountain peaks represent exalted states of mind in which there is access to luminous consciousness. The mountain itself symbolizes the highest awareness possible in the worldly realm. It serves as an aerial for gathering the signals of spiritual insight, similar to how a collected mind focused on the dharma acts as an antenna in your life. Your Intuitional Body accesses the insights that are attainable here and that bring direct liberation (see Chapter 3).

Consciousness as Illumination and Illuminated

Linking this illustration back to Balyogi's teachings about consciousness in Chapter 2, pure awareness, represented by the highest sun-like figure, is the *illuminator* from which the *illumination capacity* of luminous consciousness arises. It is misleading to refer to this un-manifest consciousness as representing an "it" in any way, such as a god-like personality or an entity in the way that those words are usually used.

The second sun-like figure represents the highest manifestation of individual consciousness; it is directly connected to the dharma-megha state of meditation. It symbolizes the "electricity of consciousness"—the innate capacity of luminous consciousness to provide *illumination*, which in turn allows individual *moments of knowing* of objects to occur through the senses and mind (I call this sense-consciousness).

The third sun figure at the bottom of the page reflects how all mind moments are experienced through the arising of sense-consciousness. In all such moments, sense-consciousness occurs in the mind due to the pairing of the knowing capacity of consciousness with the electronics of the brain's various functions, including memory, association, and so forth. Thus, moment-to-moment experiences occurring in the mind are merely reflections of a reflection. This is why Buddhist and Hindu teachings describe everyday consciousness as having a dream-like nature.

Whether or not the physical, objective world exists independent of the mind or exists only in the mind is a perennial debate, but this illustration suggests that either way you only know and experience the world because you are imbued with consciousness. You simply cannot access the material world independent of consciousness. Thus, this depiction of reality accommodates both the dual and nondual interpretations of reality. It portrays a larger view of the process of consciousness that can accommodate and account for all such possibilities.

On its way down the mountain, the mind stream becomes more and more mixed with and characterized by the impurities of the mundane world that involve grasping and clinging to what is desired. The journey of the melting snow down the mountain can be viewed as a lifetime or just one mind moment, or it can represent the cycle of rebirth. Ultimately, consciousness has to shed those impurities through spiritual practice.

Symbols of Sattvic, Rajasic, and Tamasic Gunas (Qualities of Existence)

Symbolic illustrations simultaneously reflect many aspects or developments of spiritual growth and, therefore, can be applied to different teachings. For instance, in this drawing the highest sun-like figure also represents the sattvic (harmonious) guna—the refined, balanced quality of existence that is selfless in nature. The sun figure resting at the top of the mountains represents the rajasic (active) guna with its tendency to move into the material world unless the higher states of consciousness are accessed through meditation and renunciation. The sun figure in the water represents the tamasic (inert) guna, which is what needs the most purification to return to its true nature.

The Nine Bodies Reflected in the Three Sun-Like Figures

Balyogi also describes the three sun-like figures as representing the various Bodies. The highest one represents the three most refined of the Nine Bodies: the Spiritual, Divine, and Cosmic Bodies (the Causal Level).[8] The second symbolizes Bodies Four through Six: the Etheric, Astral, and Intuitional Bodies (the Subtle Level). The third represents Bodies One through Three: the Physical, Vital, and Emotional Bodies (the Gross Level). Balyogi states that the Cosmic Body must separate from "oneness" in order to come into the world of duality. The melting snow in this illustration captures the process of the one becoming the many, the arising of duality. As you can see, some of the snow is reabsorbed into the sky as water vapor and thus retains

---

8   Students of Patanjali may find it interesting to note that Balyogi also calls the highest sun-like figure *param cheta*, or "supreme spirit," and *param dhrista*, meaning "supreme seer."

a sattvic (harmonious) nature. But most of the snow has already melted and mixed with the less pure elements of the worldly realm of existence; therefore, much of consciousness is now rajasic (active) and tamasic (inert) and will have to undergo the journey of returning to its source.

So it is with our own inner journey. To attain purity, to let go of clinging, we must start where we are. This means becoming mindful of the stream of thoughts, emotions, and sensations that constitute our lives. Thus, our individual mind streams flow into the river of existence in both conscious and unconscious thoughts, words, feelings, and actions.[9] The ocean can be seen as the ocean of all life or as the great gathering of all conscious experience as it moves into death.

Finding Liberation for Mind and Heart

Examining the drawing closely, you will see that there is a dark gold line originating partway down the mountain and flowing directly back toward the first sun symbol. This line represents the direct path to awakening taken by the Buddha, who in his lifetime completely broke free of his entanglement with sense-consciousness.

The rainbow on the left side of the illustration represents another path, one that is gradual and progressive, and the one that most of us follow. The river of individual consciousness as its moves into the plain contains all the moments of sense-consciousness with its orientation to pleasure, avoidance of the unpleasant, and ego-centeredness. But through meditation and reflection, the mind begins to empty into the ocean of egoless consciousness and the emptiness of awareness itself. This process is greatly aided by generosity and blameless behavior. The more mature your practice, the more you are able to access the Intuitional Body in your meditation and travel more easily on this journey of returning to your true nature.

When the mind and heart are in this oceanic state of meditative concentration, they are sheltered from what are called the hindrances of mind—desire, aversion, and restlessness. A *filtration* process that leads to *purification* is shown as a dark mist arising and changing into a lighter form as the filtration does its work. Slowly, an energetic *transmutation* happens in the mind, as reflected by the rainbow body beginning to emerge. At this level of

---

9   In Jungian psychology, flowing water is often interpreted as the unconscious. Such an interpretation meshes well with Balyogi's vision. *Chiti* or consciousness as it flows into life becomes evermore unconscious of its true nature and less and less aware of what is motivating it in many instances.

purification, the feeling of divine radiance from the Cosmic Body is experienced. Identification with stimuli ceases and attention is drawn to dharma and away from ego self-reference. To reach the stage where our intention becomes organized around liberation requires a practitioner to develop the will and discipline to *sublimate* worldly desires so that the aspiration to attain awakening matures and becomes the highest priority of the mind and heart.

Transfiguration and Transmutation

The transmutation continues until a *transfiguration* of the mind has occurred in the process of return. The transfiguration occurs when you directly access insight into the nature of consciousness as reflected in the three *jyoti* or flames of consciousness (see Chapter 8). At this point, various extraordinary powers of mind such as the Buddha is said to have possessed become available. The ego loses its sense of being at the center of being and begins to function as an ally to the process of transcendence that is occurring.

The process continues until a state of *transcendence* is reached, which is reflected at the level of the second sun-like figure, but now consciousness knows itself, knows the nature of knowing. The ascension process continues as reflected in the lightning bolts into the bliss and knowing insight. Now the dharma-megha is known directly and felt as sat, chit, and ananda. The mind is filled with an awakened awareness and is finally capable of knowing its true nature. At this point the mind is in complete *tranquility*, extraordinarily still, and beyond time and space.

Reflecting the Journey in Life and at Death

There are various ways to interpret this illustration regarding what happens at death. You can view the illustration as depicting what happens to luminous consciousness at the time of your death. Luminous consciousness simply comes into being from a mysterious source and at death it returns to that mysterious source, which is unfathomable. There is nothing you can do to affect it. Or you can view it as symbolizing a process that occurs repeatedly in one's lifetime or in many lifetimes, and you can affect how it unfolds through meditating until the mind attains liberation. When the mind is fully liberated, you have a different relationship with luminous consciousness—you are not defined by your thoughts, words, or actions or controlled by anything that arises in any moment. The Buddha described this attainment as,

"What needed to be done had been done," meaning that the roots of greed, hatred, and delusion had been removed from the mind.

Through the ages, numerous mystics and meditation practitioners from various traditions have postulated different theories of what happens to luminous consciousness at death. What seems to be the most prevalent view is that *something* happens. It does not just end. But even if your view is that there isn't a connection between one life and the next, you are still faced with the question of how do you find meaning in *this* lifetime. You are a conscious being; you have the gift of being able to know that you know in any moment. So what are you going to do with this gift? This illustration suggests that within your lifetime you can radically change your personality and your ways of perceiving and acting from chaos (due to desire and aversion) to clarity, calmness, and kindness. To determine if this rings true for you, ask yourself how you feel when you see this illustration.

In my view, a specific interpretation of the journey is not nearly as important as recognizing that there is a journey and that you can awaken to its existence and participate in it consciously through practice. You are not simply a victim of predestination but rather an active cocreator of your future. And that future is determined by your actions in each moment. You are the heir to your own karma. The choices you make now matter greatly to your future well-being.

▶ Meditating on the Eternal Journey

This drawing most clearly illustrates the "illuminator, illuminating (illumination), and illuminated" teaching of Balyogi described in Chapter 2. Balyogi teaches that pure awareness is the generator that causes luminous consciousness to flow through the circuitry of our brains and nervous systems, enabling them to light up like a light bulb and illuminate our world for us through moments of sense-consciousness. His teachings about the importance of understanding illumination are subtle. The value of this illustration is that it allows the teaching to be "felt" or directly experienced. The illustration is pointing to how life continually cycles, and on some level we already understand this. Therefore, focus less on the conceptual level and focus more on your actual experience. For instance, in looking at this drawing, are you intrigued by the three suns and the three manifestations of consciousness? Does an "aha" feeling arise in you?

Examine the stream flowing down from the mountain and then connect it to the gold line that represents the Buddha's journey. Can you see that it forms an Om symbol? What do you feel is being expressed by this symbol? Once you have answered this question, do a meditation visualizing Om.

Reflecting on the Eternal Journey

Notice the lightning coming out of the clouds on the left side of the illustration and going toward the earth; how do you interpret this symbol? Notice that the first "sun" does not emanate rays, the second sun does, and the third sun has more rays than the second one. What might this be saying?

Notice the colors in the rainbow on the left. What is happening at this point in the eternal journey that is being represented by these colors? Why are there clouds all around the rainbow, and what do they represent?

What do you feel when you look at the three suns as a whole versus when you look at each sun individually? Notice that there are many inner rings or layers within the first sun. How do you respond to the effect of these layers?

As you examine Balyogi's other drawings in this chapter and then return to this one, how does it affect your understanding of this first sun? Be as still as possible in your mind and just absorb this drawing (you may or may not "see" movement when you do this). Is there a single feeling or intuition that stands out for you?

The Cosmos in Movement

In using the word "cosmos," Balyogi means the universe and all that is visible and nonvisible within it. This illustration is a vision of oneness in which all parts of the manifest universe are contained in an androgynous figure. The analogy is that of a great impersonal seer or mysterious capacity of knowing from which all material and nonmaterial existence is known. Balyogi says this image of the cosmos appeared to him in its entirety as a vision in meditation when he was accessing the vijnana chaksu (the "eye of awareness" described in more detail in Chapter 10). He sometimes calls this drawing *From the Tear to the Seer*, signifying the journey each of us makes from identifying with the manifest world of sorrow, dissatisfaction, and ego identity to resting the mind in awareness without clinging and grasping to what arises and passes. Keep in mind this journey is a description of the absolute; it is not an invalidation of the relative world where you care and take responsibility.

In the vast stillness, all the movement of the cosmos is held in a unified oneness. Ajahn Sumedho describes this vast ocean of one-pointed awareness as "the one point that includes everything," meaning that the liberated mind can see both emptiness and endless forms and experience the unity of awareness itself. The awareness does not move with all that arises and passes due to its illumination. It is simply empty and still.

The bright star embedded in the figure's hair at the top of the illustration is the polestar; scattered throughout the hair are the Milky Way and other galaxies. The hair symbolizes the dark, empty stillness of the one-pointed mind that allows you to see what is ordinarily not seen, in the same way that a moonless night reveals the brightness of the stars. The third eye in the center of the figure's forehead is the divine or spiritual eye, which Balyogi also

refers to as "the eye of the seer." From the third eye is radiating what Balyogi calls *rahasyatmic* energy—the mysterious energy, un-manifest, that empowers all consciousness to unfold. The sun at the center of the eye represents the vijnana chaksu (eye of awareness). This visioning capacity represents impersonal awareness; it is not personal ego-identity. Insight and realization arise on our inner journey when we access this impersonal awareness. If the ego starts to identify with this awareness as "me and mine," we start to lose our way in the journey.

The journey to oneness starts in the mountains with coming into this physical realm. You must travel through the river of temporal existence until you gain the knowledge to start the journey to freedom. The bolts of lightning on the left side of the drawing represent cosmic kundalini, the universal energy of transcendence that is available to each of us. This impersonal energy is called *chiti-shakti*, and it plays an important part in transformation when the spiritual journey is viewed on the energetic level rather than in terms of insight and realization. It appears repeatedly in Balyogi's illustrations. The clouds surrounding the lightning represent imbalanced human emotions that are being transformed. The clouds at the eyebrows represent the transfiguration of those imbalanced emotions into balance, order and harmony. The eyebrow clouds are the dharma-megha described in the previous drawing.

On the left side of the drawing is a green forest representing where yogis and other spiritual practitioners dwell. On the right side is the city where materiality prevails. Notice that there is no bridge between the two. Below the forest is a lake of serenity representing the equanimity of meditation practice. Balyogi says that this drawing represents only half of the cosmos, and that the illustration that follows this represents the other half.

▶ Meditating on the Cosmos in Movement

Looking at this illustration, notice that there is an inner realm of stars flowing down into the mountain that has a lighter blue background than the darker outer realm of stars. The stars in this inner realm represent the personal, individual aspect of the cosmos. We have our individual karma or life situation to work through. Also notice on the left the rainbow body of the tanmatras—the five subtle elements of earth, water, fire, air, and space that originate in the Etheric Body and then manifest in the physical world as the five material elements (see Chapter 3). This rainbow represents the effect of the Etheric Body. Then look closely at the swirl of water on the right, which represents a kind of container that defines temporal existence. Gaze steadily at this illustration for a few minutes before beginning your meditation. Then, in your meditation, notice how all sense experiences including mental activity come and go endlessly while the knowing capacity that registers each of them maintains continuity. The coming and going is *anicca* or impermanence, the ever-changing, always-in-motion nature of all manifest things as represented by the swirling water.

The stillness of the image as a whole represents the empty awareness that contains all the movement without itself being part of the movement. After your meditation, look at the illustration again and see if it is more alive to you. Do you see more detail? Does it feel more personal?

Do you see that there is a hidden sun that is lighting up the mountains? This light is coming from the second sun of the previous illustration and symbolizes how chit is the illumination for all that is manifest. In your next meditation, focus on luminous consciousness as an object of meditation. Use the image of the sunlight on the mountains as your object of meditation and observe what arises. Deeply appreciate the gift of consciousness and state your gratitude.

The third eye on the figure's forehead is the divine or spiritual eye. Notice that it is the same as the eye that appears in the first sun in the *Eternal Journey* illustration. Look back and forth between the third eyes in these two illustrations, and then meditate on them and notice what arises.

For Your Reflection

Can you spot the profile of a woman's face in the green forest? What does she represent to you? To me she is Gaia or Mother Earth, representing the immediate container for all that is manifest in a benign and beautiful form.

Notice the rays emanating from the third eye and flowing down to the left side from the bottom of the face and reaching all the way into the water. How do you understand these rays? What do they represent?

Can you discern the Om symbol that is made by the shape of the river and the rainbow? What might Balyogi be suggesting by containing the Om symbol within the human experience?

The Cosmos in Repose

In *The Cosmos in Repose* illustration, Balyogi completes the vision he started in the previous drawing. Here the movement from the *Tear* to the *Seer* has been completed; the journey is over. As you can see, there are no tears, meaning no dukkha or suffering, no clinging, no un-satisfactoriness. There is only calm. Greed, aversion, and delusions have been released. This is the state of nonattachment to worldly concerns. It is not a state of non-caring but rather caring without grasping. If you have reached this state, you have attained full realization. In nondual language, this repose already exists, and what we call development and practice are simply remembering our true nature.

On the left side of the illustration below the green forest, there are lotuses floating in the serene lake. On the right side, the city is well developed and there is now a bridge between the two, which illustrates a balance between the inner and outer life (or the un-manifest and the manifest). All the opposites of duality are resting in oneness. Notice that the stars still flow through the stream of existence. Also notice the fullness of the Cosmic Body, which is clearly visible when the woman is viewed as a whole. This illustration also captures Balyogi's teaching that everything that is *manifest* arises from mysterious or rahasyatmic energy, which is *un-manifest*.

▶ Meditating on the Cosmic Body in Repose

First focus on the third eye of the figure, the energy center just above and between the eyebrows. Then close your eyes and see if your own third eye resonates with what you just focused on. Also notice that it is similar to the eye in the first sun in the *Eternal Journey* illustration. Next, use "soft eyes"—let your eyes relax and softly focus—to absorb this drawing as move-

ment. Notice how the movement within the figure's body is contained by the larger stillness of the illustration. This points to the relationship between stillness and movement in meditation. In your next meditation, watch the movement of the mind and then notice there is also stillness. What is the nature of that stillness? This illustration is providing you with a clue for understanding the stillness.

For Your Reflection

Focus on the container of the figure's body, which holds earth elements, a city, and a concealed face. Can you feel the completeness that is being illustrated? What is the container of your own awareness that could hold all that you experience in a similar manner?

Notice the face of the figure and the concealed face. Is their serenity similar to yours or different? How do you interpret the halo behind the figure's head?

Balyogi teaches that the plains, the hills, and the mountains in this illustration represent different aspects of consciousness. What might each one stand for? Balyogi gives more than one answer to this question. The point is to awaken to the different levels of experience such that you can see each as it is and move your attention skillfully among them.

Flip back and forth among the three drawings in this section. What have you learned? Which one inspires you the most? Which is the least inspiring? Which do you feel you understand best and which one the least? Does each add a distinct quality to your feeling of the journey into wholeness and unity? Listen to your heart and intuition for answers to these questions, not your thinking mind.

7

THREE LEVELS AND NINE BODIES

Three Levels Teachings of Liberation

Auras of the Three Levels

The Three Centers Awakened

Nine Bodies

The illustrations in this chapter are a powerful way to explore experientially the Three Levels and the Nine Bodies as described in Chapters 3 and 4.

Three Levels Teachings of Liberation

This illustration presents Balyogi's view of the classical teaching of liberation and the Three Levels as described in Chapter 3. The human figure in front represents the Gross Level containing the Physical, Vital, and Emotional Bodies. The figure on the right represents the Subtle Level, which contains the Etheric, Astral, and Intuitional Bodies. The light blue body on the left represents the Causal Level, which contains the Spiritual, Divine, and Cosmic Bodies. The Causal and Subtle Levels work together. For instance, Balyogi teaches that the Tibetan mantra *om mani padme hum* first resonates in the Causal Level and from there spreads to the Subtle Level, which conveys it as resonance to the Physical Level.

It is through the Causal Level that a meditator accesses pure awareness. This state is ultimately mysterious and not fully comprehensible even when accessed.

The Buddha or swami figure sitting with the lotus at the navel area symbolizes the Awakened Self, the *inherent potential* that is within each of us. Balyogi refers to this seated symbol, which also appears in the next two illustrations, as the *mahakarana sharir*. It stands for both the Divine Body and the Spiritual Body, two of the bodies in the Causal Level as described in Chapter 3. (Note that the mahakarana sharir is represented at the navel of the figure representing the Physical Level, illustrating the idea that it is through the manifest realm that we contact these more refined dimensions of consciousness.) He says that you cannot make it a meditation object. Rather, it is emblematic of an attainment that comes through meditation practice.

The lotus flower above the navel area represents the spiritual heart that has been awakened. Flowing out of the navel area is the *sukshma or*

subtle prana that enlivens all Three Levels. We gain access to awareness of all Three Levels by purifying and awakening them through mindfulness and samadhi meditation, and by adhering to the yamas and niyamas (the yoga code of ethical behavior that Patanjali describes).

▶ Meditating on the Three Levels Teaching:

Once the mind is settled in meditation, start to notice how each moment is different from the one before it, if only slightly. Notice that this stream of changes occurs constantly. Given this steady stream of change, ask yourself repeatedly: Who am I? Alternatively, ask: Who is having these thoughts? Notice if these questions make your mind tight, restless, or frightened. If so, reassure yourself of the existence of your body, thoughts, and emotions before continuing with the meditation. If you reach a point where your mind feels spacious and has let go of a fixed view of itself, can you start to notice a hint of the energy of the Subtle Level? For instance, you may feel enhanced energy flowing through your body, or a sense of amplified clarity, or an ability to direct energy to the object of your attention. If you are able to notice such energy, can you also notice the emptiness underlying this subtle energy?

Alternatively, stare at this illustration until it becomes imprinted on your mind such that you can still see it with your eyes closed. At this point, start to feel the elements of the Physical Level—earth, air, water, fire, and space. Keep your attention on the Physical Level until you distinctly feel it. Then do the same with the Subtle Level, which you will feel as an energetic experience. You may have to stare again at the illustration in order to re-establish the image internally before focusing on the Subtle Level. Finally, with the image fixed in your mind, invite yourself to imagine the existence of a mysterious third Level. Keep your attention fully focused on this imagination and observe what happens after twenty or thirty minutes.

For Your Reflection

Can you imagine the existence of these three Levels of Being? Can you see why it's useful to access them separately? Which do you accept as referring to genuine reality? For instance, some traditions treat the Physical Level as an illusion, but you may feel that it is the only body you are absolutely sure exists. Based on your experiences, you may be willing to acknowledge the possibility of the Subtle Level but may not be sure it points to something; or you may totally believe this level of being exists. The purpose of this reflection is to discover where you are starting from in terms of your conceptual thinking or fixed views. The goal is to be open to the possibility of different levels of existence without forsaking common sense or your ultimate authority for determining the nature of existence for yourself.

Auras of the Three Levels

This illustration is another depiction of the Three Levels. Here awakening or realization has occurred and is reflected in the aura that emanates from each of the three Bodies. The body in front symbolizes the Causal Level. The small circle in the middle represents the mahakarana (the seated figure symbolizing the Divine and Spiritual Bodies, which was described in the previous illustration). Balyogi sometimes refers to the mahakarana as the "center of the center," and it is what unites or creates a through line from the physical plane of existence to the most sublime plane. As you can see, the color and form of the mahakarana is the same as the aura around the head of the small figure.

The figure in the middle represents the Subtle Level. Notice that the aura of the second figure is the same color and form as that in the first figure, but it is larger and the aura is more fully radiating as indicated by the small red lines at the edge of the aura. The Subtle Level is energetic in nature, and these red lines reflect this energy.

The figure in back represents the Physical Level in a moment of meditative attainment of the mahakarana. The golden, sun-like orb in the center represents the awakened mind manifesting at this moment. Note that the Physical Level has the same silver aura as the other two figures surrounded by a larger red aura and strong radiating lines that are barely visible in the other two auras. This fuller aura represents pure consciousness radiating the electricity of luminous consciousness as described in Chapter 2, which allows for moments of sense-consciousness to be illuminated or known.

This illustration, as well as the illustrations that precede and succeed it, offers an important teaching about realization. Yes, in meditation you can discover that there really are three Levels (or Nine Bodies), but the reality

is that the three (and the nine) are one. This paradoxical truth requires that your mind open to holding truths that are "opposites" but not exclusive of one another. This "three being one" is a common motif in spiritual traditions. It reflects the insights of unity, that ultimately there is only the "one," but it can manifest as seemingly contradictory truths of oneness or separateness, depending on the perspective that is being accessed. This teaching will be more dramatically presented in the *Nine Bodies* illustration that follows.

One other important aspect regarding "the three and the one" is that when the mind attains the ability to *simultaneously* experience both the truth of separateness and the truth of unity, a new maturity of mind becomes possible. When the three and one are realized as insights together, they constitute a *fourth* psychological insight—the realization of *wholeness* on the spiritual journey that completes the freeing of the heart.

Yes, pure awareness with its emptiness and radiance as described in Chapter 2 is the ultimate truth. But as we have so often seen throughout history, genuine spiritual insight does not automatically manifest in nonharming ways. The fourth realization points to a stage of development in which you are dwelling in a mind that is free while at the same time responding appropriately to any suffering you encounter. In my own practice, I express my aspiration to realize this fourth stage of development in these terms: "May I attain wholeness and unity." Wholeness is paying attention twenty-four hours, seven days a week to all 360 degrees of your life with the intention of not causing harm. It brings together the relative truths of ordinary mind states with the absolute truths of the mind-heart's inherent freedom. Similarly, when the Buddha teaches wise understanding as the first step of the Eightfold Path in the Four Noble Truths, he teaches that the absolute and the relative are distinct but both are vital insights for liberation. To me a true "master," in contrast to a "person of knowledge," is a teacher whose moment-to-moment existence is seamless between the absolute and the relative and who has mastered wholeness as well as unity.

▶ Meditating on the Auras of the Three Levels

Spend some time focusing on the figure in the back with the golden halo and the serene expression. Focus on him until you can close your eyes and still visualize his face. Once this is possible, invite your mind to become one with his serenity. After a few minutes, shift your attention to the second figure and repeat this process. Next, shift your attention to the figure in the front and go through the same process. Finally, envision each of these figures within you.

In another meditation session, focus on the heart area of the smallest figure in front until you feel you are making contact with your own heart center. Close your eyes and allow this to be your meditation object. A few words of caution: Do not use your heartbeat as your meditation object. It is not the object of this meditation and it is simply not a skillful object to use without advanced training.

For Your Reflection

Reflect on the feeling of serenity shown in this image and ask yourself how much serenity you experience. What would you need to do to have more serenity? Think of the times you have felt grounded in something larger than yourself. Did it bring serenity? If you were going to create more serenity in your life, what would need to change?

The Three Centers Awakened

When I first saw this illustration, I felt a sense of calm and well-being, and it felt totally familiar to me. The illustration depicts all Three Levels as well as many of the distinctions of the Nine Bodies teaching. The drawing evokes the felt sense that comes when awakening occurs. The Gross Level, represented by the figure as a whole, is being bathed in prana, symbolized by the golden lines flowing throughout the body. This flowing prana signifies the Vital Body, as well as the Etheric Body (located in the Subtle Level) from which prana flows through to the Gross Level.

On the forehead is a seated figure bathed in gold, representing a yogi who is awake and aware in the Subtle Level. At the top of the forehead just above the seated figure is a small dot or star, symbolizing the *bindu*—a point or dot where power or energy converges and can be accessed. In this illustration, the bindu point has been accessed and the spiritual or wisdom eye is fully open to realization (this "eye of awareness" will be explored in Chapter 10). A blue circle surrounds the bindu point and symbolizes realization of emptiness. Many teachings from other illustrations are also reflected in this illustration; here, however, all the work that needed to be done has been done, and realization is complete.

The globe in the chest area represents the Causal Level. The figure inside emanates light in all directions and symbolizes the realization of liberation and the knowing of the Spiritual and Divine Bodies. This light emanating from the Causal Level is the ultimate source of the prana that flows first into the Etheric Body and then into the Vital Body.

The seated figure inside the blue globe in the navel area is a symbol of the mahakarana, the symbol of the Divine and Spiritual Bodies that was described in the two previous drawings. The blue globe itself is a symbol of

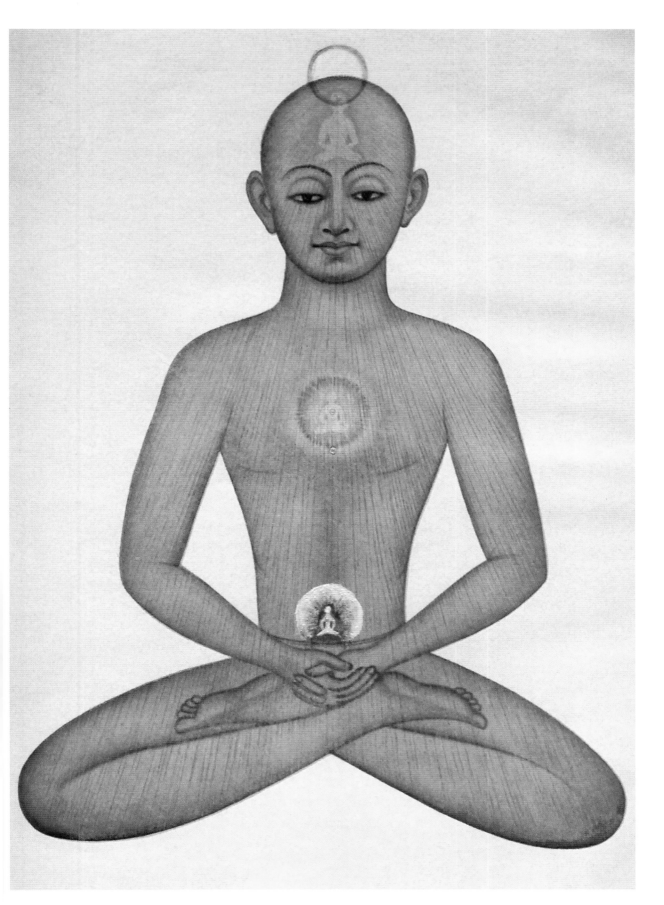

the Intuitional Body (located in the Subtle Level). Since it cannot be accessed directly as an object of meditation, the mahakarana is attained through the mind resting in the Intuitional Body.

Balyogi says that when this state of awakening is starting to occur in meditation, physical and emotional healing can occur just by touching the navel area with your finger or by touching the *kurma nadyam* (described in the *Tortoise* illustration in Chapter 9). He also says that when this state of awakening is starting to occur, the energy from the navel area may spontaneously start to touch the spine and that the feeling of kundalini energy may arise.

Although such a description of energy may sound foreign to you, I had just such an experience with the spine and kundalini while sitting in meditation twenty-five years before encountering Balyogi and his Nine Bodies teaching. I was just beginning my practice and was at a complete loss as to how to skillfully respond to this altered state, which lasted some hours.

The purpose of including Balyogi's remarks about healing and reporting my own experience is to point out that on the path of liberation many altered states of mind and seemingly inexplicable energetic experiences may occur in your practice. It is worth remembering that these teachings are not instructions for liberation but are a description or map for recognizing these unusual mind states and energetic phenomena and responding wisely to them so they can be used to support your journey toward awakening rather than distracting from it.

❱ Meditating on the Three Centers

Start your meditation with focusing on a point a couple of inches below your navel and about one-and-a-quarter inches inside the body. Place your index finger over this point and notice any sensations that arise during your meditation. Next place your finger slightly inside the navel, either directly or on top of your clothes. Keep it there during your meditation and observe what you experience.

Next, focus on your heart center, not the physical heart but rather closer to the center of your chest. Place your fingers there, and when you feel you have made a connection close your eyes and allow this area to be the object of your meditation. Again, notice the felt sense in this area of the body and how your well-being is affected.

For the next meditation, move your attention to the center of the skull. You can locate this point by first focusing on the third eye area and then drawing an imaginary line through the brain to the back of the skull. The point of focus is about half way toward the back of the skull. Be careful not to tense the face and scalp as you are focusing on this area. Signs that you are tensing include tightness in the jaw, your breath becoming jagged, or starting to have a headache. Relax for a few minutes and try again. If you continue to have difficulty finding the focus point in the skull or you continue to have tension, abandon this practice. It is not skillful to struggle to access this point. Instead, switch your focal point to the openings of your nostrils, and when a sense of calm appears let it bathe the skull entirely. If you're utilizing the breath to create this focus, don't focus on the breath inside the nostrils but rather keep your attention on the nostril openings. Once you've established your attention using one of these methods, go through the same steps of noticing what's arising, the emotional effects, and how your well-being is affected. You may have to do a number of meditations on each of the three centers in order to achieve stable concentration.

For Your Reflection

Can you feel all three centers of the body? It's not unusual to feel numb or vacant in one of them, so be patient in your exploration. As you become familiar with them, you will learn how to activate awareness of each. In the course of your day, start to notice what creates imbalance or causes you to go numb in your body, heart, or head center. Is there a pattern to your thoughts, emotions, or energy that might be causing this to occur repeatedly?

Reflect on a time when you felt all three centers were in harmony. What could you do to create the conditions for this to happen more often?

Nine Bodies

The *Nine Bodies* illustration demonstrates how each of the Nine Bodies is contained within the others. In other words, there are Nine Bodies, but there is also just one Body. The nine are interconnected and are manifesting as one in any given mind moment, which is why Balyogi uses the terms "layer," "level of being," and "body" interchangeably. Thus, purification or caring for any Body benefits all of them. Moreover, with patience and knowledge, you can begin in any Body and connect to each of the others and to the whole. Balyogi says that the way to unfold and realize the Nine Bodies or nine Layers of Being is through the Vipassana technique of watchful awareness or mindfulness. He says the unfolding is similar to the way a bud opens up into a flower. (Note that in this illustration, Balyogi depicts the Nine Bodies with the Physical Body being the largest and the others nested within. In other illustrations or descriptions he depicts them the other way. One reason for depicting the subtler Bodies as smaller is to illustrate the fact that they are more difficult to access.)

The large, purple-gray figure is the Physical Body that exists in the material world. The next largest, blue figure is the Vital Body. The green figure represents the Emotional Body and completes the three Bodies of the Gross Level in the traditional teachings. The red figure represents the Etheric Body. The orange body symbolizes the Astral Body, and the yellow-gold figure stands for the Intuitional Body. These three together are the Bodies of the Subtle Level in traditional teaching.

The seventh, eighth, and ninth Bodies are not as clearly distinguishable. The white figure represents the Spiritual Body and the hard-to-see figure within it stands for the Divine Body. It is presented more like an image of the flame of consciousness (which will be described in Chapter 8) than

an actual body. The Cosmic Body is not directly accessible, so its existence is implied by the first two Bodies. It is to be intuitively felt or seen with the Spiritual Eye. These last three Bodies compose the Causal Level. Remember that these three Bodies do not manifest directly as physical phenomena, thus are not so visible.

▶ Meditating on the *Nine Bodies* Illustration

Focus on this illustration until you begin to have a feeling for what it conveys. Then, in your meditation, start to visualize and differentiate among the first six Bodies. Begin by starting to distinguish between your Physical Body and Emotional Body until the two become easily identified in your mind. Next, utilizing the breath, start to feel the Vital Body that energizes both the Physical and Emotional Bodies. Work with this until you can separate the felt sense of these three Bodies. Gaining the ability to access and separate the next three Bodies is going to take much longer. This process is described in detail in Chapter 4. You can use this illustration to support those instructions for accessing each Body.

For Your Reflection

How would it feel to have a multilayered experience of any moment of your life? Does it make you uneasy or excited? Thinking back over your life, have you ever experienced the different Levels of Being?

8

THE FLAME OF CONSCIOUSNESS

Flame of Consciousness with Nine Bodies

Flame of Individual Consciousness

Details of the Flame of Individual Consciousness

*This chapter integrates the previous two chapters into one integrated symbolic
presentation. It illustrates the manifestation of luminous consciousness
in the physical realm and how the mystery of luminous consciousness
shows up in the mundane moments of daily life.*

Flame of Consciousness with Nine Bodies

The *Flame of Consciousness* illustration is the most comprehensive presentation of Balyogi's vision of the connection between consciousness, energetic experience, and spiritual reality. It is as close as he comes to illustrating the full map of the Nine Bodies Teaching in one drawing. The *Flame of Consciousness* shows the multiplicity and interconnectedness of all spiritual, mental, emotional, and physical experience. The entire journey of manifest awareness is symbolically presented here. The drawing illustrates that everything in the manifest world is interdependent, co-arising, and far more magnificent and inspiring than the surface levels of the material and emotional realms of existence that we usually identify with a self. We are freed by our newfound awareness that our essence is not our ego identity with its stresses, anxieties, and endless wants. Instead, we are part of this great mystery of luminous consciousness and pure awareness.

With the help of this drawing, you can track how the un-manifest energetic potential of the Spiritual and Divine Bodies becomes a physical and emotional reality by manifesting through the Subtle or Energetic Bodies. It also shows how you can start with being mindful of any physical or emotional mind moment and trace it back to its energetic basis and then to its origin as un-manifest potential. Most importantly, the drawing points to the mystery of consciousness by revealing the different aspects of consciousness itself. As with all of these illustrations, it is leading you to a felt sense of luminous consciousness. It is not a textbook drawing of the brain's neuro-circuitry.

The ideas and details contained in the imagery of the *Flame of Consciousness* are so rich in meaning that it can overwhelm comprehension. To address this problem, I have included this illustration three times, each with

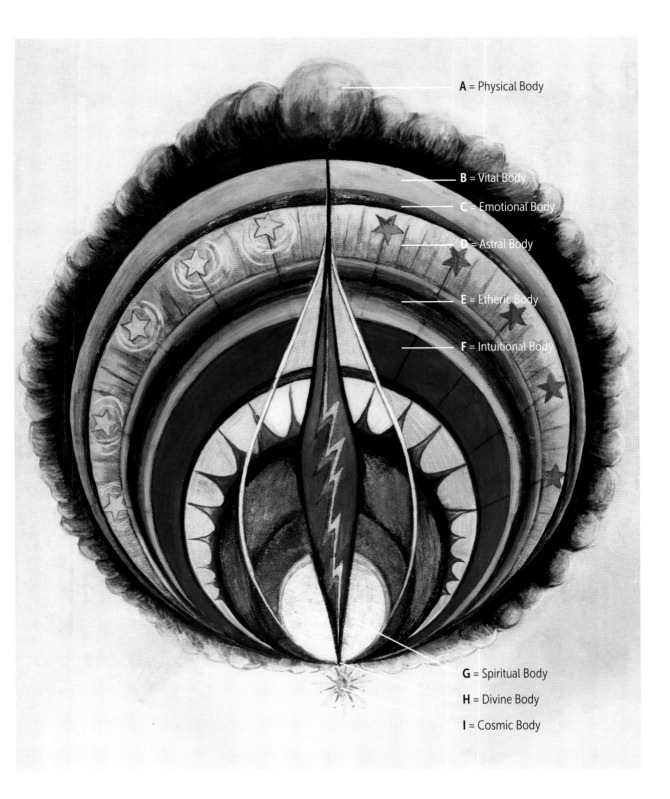

A = Physical Body

B = Vital Body

C = Emotional Body

D = Astral Body

E = Etheric Body

F = Intuitional Body

G = Spiritual Body

H = Divine Body

I = Cosmic Body

a distinct set of teachings. Each of the illustrations is labeled according to the particular aspect of the teaching that is being highlighted. This approach to the vast material in the drawing will allow you to more easily penetrate the powerful symbolism it contains.

As with the previous illustrations, stay oriented to the feelings of familiarity, recognition, and deep connection to the mystery of consciousness. You are being led into your own felt sense of what it is like to be conscious and to be grounded in an awareness that knows itself to be conscious (luminous consciousness). When you access this felt sense of luminous consciousness, you will likely experience awe, aspiration, and a sense of residing in something much larger than the ego's self-referential thinking.

In this first iteration of the illustration, the focus is on locating the Nine Bodies within the *Flame of Consciousness*. Once you've located these Levels of Being, it becomes easier to see the central symbols of consciousness and, subsequently, the finer details contained within each Body. Additionally, by first concentrating on the Nine Bodies themselves, you get the chance to integrate all the earlier teachings of the Nine Bodies through imagery.

The Bodies in the Causal Level

The diamond-like crystal (I) at the bottom of the illustration symbolizes the unfathomable realm of the Cosmic Body. This is the point of unity or oneness; it is similar to a hologram in which everything is contained in the one point. For now, just remember that the point of unity is un-manifest in this realm.

The Divine Body (H) is symbolized by a point just below the diamond-like crystal on the periphery of the circle. This is the point of entry for the mysterious energy that brings illuminating awareness into the manifest realm. The Spiritual Body (G) then appears as colorless infinite space. Although it is empty, it is the portal for all that arises in the material world.

In this illustration, the three Bodies of the Causal Level are revealed to be empty of mental and physical substance. For some yogis this unfathomable emptiness is inspiring; for others it is confusing and frightening. Balyogi teaches that chit—the source or illuminator of chiti or consciousness—is associated with the Causal Level, in particular the Cosmic Body (I).

The Bodies of the Subtle Level

The Intuitional Body (F) is symbolized by the wide red ring and the red rays emanating from it. Notice that the Intuitional Body is directly in touch with the Divine Body (H). In subsequent illustrations, you will see how this leads to inner knowing, insight, and realization. Adjacent to the Intuitional Body (F) are five rings of color symbolizing the Etheric Body (E). These are the five tanmatras (subtle elements), which aren't described here but will be highlighted in a subsequent illustration. Finally, the wide multicolored ring containing ten stars is the Astral Body (D). Each star represents one of the five karmendriyas and jnanendriyas (the subtle organs of action and knowing described in Chapter 3, which manifest as the organs of action and knowing in the material world).

The Bodies of the Gross Level

Immediately next to the Astral Body (F) is the Emotional Body (C), which is visible as a narrow green ring. The Astral and Emotional Bodies often interact. The light blue ring adjacent to the Emotional Body symbolizes the Vital Body (B). The Physical Body (A), which is the most readily visible and most easily felt, is represented by the dark blue cloud-like ring surrounding the entire image. Luminous consciousness originates in the Cosmic Body (I) and then flows through each of the seven Bodies in between to manifest as the Physical Body (A).

▶ Meditating on the Flame of Consciousness with Nine Bodies

If you wish to use an unlabeled version of this illustration for your meditation practice, turn to page 39.

Gaze at the drawing without thinking about the individual bodies until the illustration feels alive to you. Practice letting go of your ordinary mind's need to know what you're looking at and cultivate "don't know mind." Observe the drawing without knowing or needing to know what any part of the illustration or the illustration as a whole means.

Once you've been able to do this, continue staring at the illustration for a while and then close your eyes and observe what happens. Be receptive to a feeling of movement, or becoming, or depth in the drawing that you may recognize as part of your own experience in meditation. Previously, you may not have had a name for it or a way to describe it, but ask yourself if the illustration accurately reflects some aspect of awareness that you have felt.

Review the descriptions of the Nine Bodies in your mind numerous times as you contemplate the illustration. Then close your eyes and evoke each of the Nine Bodies, starting with the Physical Body, as best as you're able. Next, turn to Chapter 4 and follow the meditation instructions for gaining access to each of the Nine Bodies. This will require several meditation sessions, as you need to limit yourself to working with what you can access and what is just beyond it. For instance, you may easily access the Physical (A) and Vital (B) Bodies, but struggle to access the Emotional Body (C) at times. If this is your range of access, then limit your practice to these three bodies initially, but see if you can access the Etheric Body (E) occasionally.

For Your Reflection

If Balyogi's teachings of the Nine Bodies point to something that is true about reality, what is the implication for your life? Go back and look at the *Eternal Journey* and the *Cosmos in Movement* illustrations in Chapter 6. What do those two drawings and the *Flame of Consciousness* have in common?

Flame of Individual Consciousness

You have now reached the essence of Balyogi's vision of the illuminating capacity of consciousness. This illustration captures a moment of consciousness manifesting in time-space. First focus on the area defined by the light bluish-white teardrop shape (E), which symbolizes sense-consciousness. Note that within the teardrop there are many elements, which will be described in more detail below. It is the combination of all these elements that allows you to be conscious of a sense experience, thought, or emotion and to know that you are conscious of what you are experiencing. On a grander scale, the illustration is saying that it is the mysterious energy of pure awareness that fuels the luminous consciousness that lights up your experience of the universe.

The mysterious rahasyatmic energy (A) that empowers all consciousness to unfold flows from the Divine Body where it meets the Spiritual Body, encounters the inherent potential (or what some modern mind researchers might call the ever-changing *probability curves* of thoughts and actions residing in the mind), and then, based on causes and conditions, manifests in the Subtle Level, which in all three of its Bodies is energetic in nature. From the Subtle Level, it moves all the way to the Physical Body. The cloud-like structure surrounding the drawing symbolizes the Physical Body. (See the details of the Nine Bodies in the previous illustration. More specific details of consciousness will be presented in the next illustration.)

It is through this process of the "electricity" of luminous consciousness that you have the capacity for sense consciousness of all stimuli in every sense gate, including body movement and body function, as well as touch, sound, smell, sight, taste, and mental activity while also having access to insight and realization. Moreover, you can know you are having these

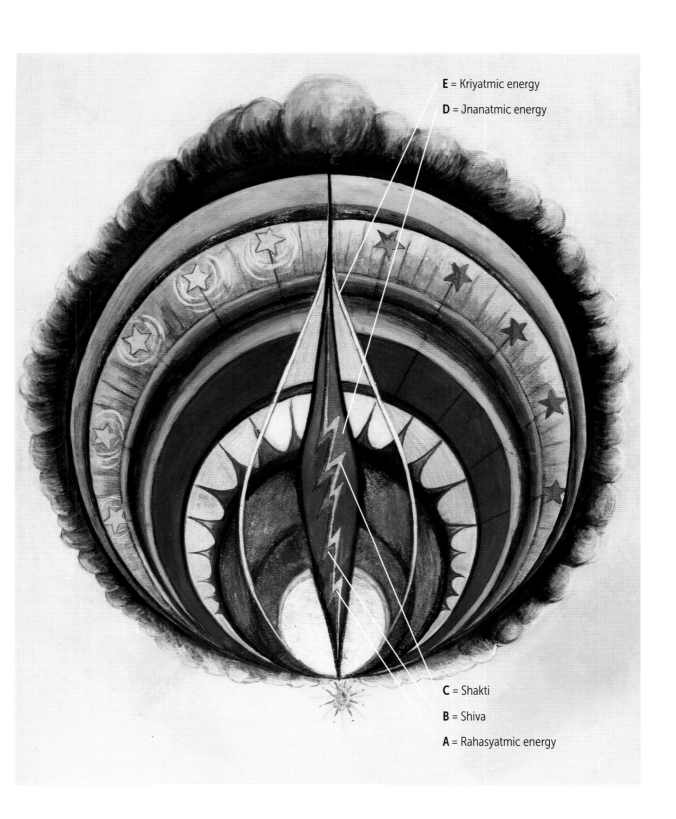

E = Kriyatmic energy

D = Jnanatmic energy

C = Shakti

B = Shiva

A = Rahasyatmic energy

experiences and can reflect on them in order to determine their meaning and how you wish to respond to what is being known.

When you look closely at the *Flame of Consciousness* illustration, you can see that it is actually composed of the three forms or "flames" of consciousness. Balyogi calls these forms flames because each moment of consciousness of any sort is like the sudden illumination of a match being struck in the dark or a bolt of lighting in the night sky providing sudden illumination. Looking at the three, you can see there is consciousness manifesting as *doing (kriyatmic),* shown in the blue teardrop image. Next is consciousness manifesting as *knowing (jnanatmic),* symbolized by the red, candle-flame shape with the lightning inside it (D). (I will explain the importance of this particular symbol as a sacred image below.) Finally, there is consciousness manifesting as *being,* which is related to luminous consciousness and is symbolized by a transparent line (A) that runs between the two aspects of the kundalini lightning image that are explained below.

Since the Subtle Level is solely energetic in nature, you can understand that all three manifestations of consciousness represented by the three flames manifest as energy in the Intuitional, Astral, and Etheric Bodies. Yet, as the drawing reveals, all three flames of consciousness extend into the Vital, Emotional, and Physical Bodies as well. How could it be otherwise? The more embodied and connected you are in the first three Bodies, the more attuned you become to the subtler Bodies. Paradoxically, though, if you become *caught up and identified* with the Bodies of the Gross Level, you will be less aware of the more subtle levels of experience and have less access to intuition.

All doing activity requires the energy of the Subtle Level. Consciousness involved in doing is termed *kriyatmic.* The consciousness of doing occurs with the help of manas (mind) and the ego. As you may recall, manas and ego are two of the four elements that make up the antah-karana, the four instruments of inner knowing described in Chapter 2. The ego inspires or signals the mind through the karmendriyas or subtle senses (residing in the Subtle Level) that motivate the organs of action, such as hands, feet, genitals, anus, and mouth. As you can see, this flame is quite large and prominent because so much of consciousness has to do with activity. Notice that it flows all the way into the Physical Body.

The red flame in the center of the drawing (D) is consciousness manifesting as *knowing.* Knowing occurs through the jnanendriyas, the subtle senses that motivate the organs of knowing such as taste, smell, sight, hearing, touch. The *jnanatman* also resides in the Subtle Level. It is consciousness that ignites knowing. Subjective knowing occurs with the help of buddhi (intellect) and chitta (memory, emotions, habits, mental conditioning, and past impressions), which are the remaining two parts of the antah-karana (the four instruments of inner knowing). The subjective consciousness of knowing is the process through which you acquire knowledge, reflect, make decisions, search for meaning, balance your life, and decide your core values. The Intuitional Body utilizes the jnanatmic flame of consciousness in meditation and in seeking wisdom through study and reflection.

To repeat the analogy that was presented in Chapter 2, the *illumination* power of consciousness *illuminates* the intellect and the chitta, in a process similar to the way electricity empowers a light bulb. The intellect and chitta then have the capacity to illuminate each moment of subjective knowing in your life, all of which are *illuminated* at the various sense gates through sense consciousness, which everyone experiences.

Now, notice the lightning bolt (C) that originates in the Cosmic Body and extends all the way to the Physical Body. The lightning itself represents the explosive movement of energy in the Subtle Level associated with kundalini awakening. Balyogi says that the lightning represents male and female energy. The gold lightning (B) is male energy or Shiva, the energy of the consciousness of knowing; the silver lightning (C) is feminine energy or Shakti, the energy of the consciousness of doing. This illustration helps explain what may be the true goal of kundalini yoga—to unite these separate energies in order to enable flowering of the full potential of consciousness such that you directly access the realm of rahasyatmic energy. The arising of kundalini is not the only way to access this realm of pure consciousness. Various schools of Buddhism use a combination of samadhi and insight practices to arrive at the same destination. The rising of kundalini is an energetic experience originating in the Subtle Level but felt in the Physical Body. For this reason there is much confusion about what kundalini is, how one achieves it, and why some people experience mind-body disturbances when it occurs.

Between the gold and silver lightning bolts is the transparent third flame (A) that represents the energy of pure awareness, which is neither the consciousness of doing nor of knowing but is what allows both to exist.

We get a taste of this pure awareness when we rest in luminous consciousness. We experience the felt sense of it as one of *being* rather than doing or knowing. Pure awareness does not utilize any part of the antah-karana (meaning that it exists independent of our perception of it). It is independent of ego, intellect, all mind stuff, and activity. Yet, it is this third flame of pure awareness radiating through luminous consciousness that allows what arises during a moment of sense-consciousness to be known, whether it is a moment of action or knowing.

There are many conflicting views and teachings regarding it and disagreement as to whether it even exists. Its manifestation in the Subtle Level as energy is called rahasyatmic because it is indeed mysterious, yet in deep samadhi its presence can definitely be felt and intuited.

The *Flame of Consciousness* is useful in providing context for the never-ending debate about whether physical reality has any independent "realness" or if all reality is "mind-only." And is there a complete separation between nature and pure awareness or are they two aspects of one unity? The context provided by the illustration points to the interconnectedness of consciousness and physical reality. For meditation practitioners, this interconnectedness can be directly felt and explored such that insight will arise.

❯ Meditating on the Three Flames of Individual Consciousness

If you wish to use an unlabeled version of this illustration for your meditation practice, turn to page 39.

Gaze steadily at this illustration until you can see it as multidimensional and full of movement. Notice that from one perspective the three flames are in front but from another perspective the Physical Body is in front, emanating out of the three flames. This symbolizes the eternal dance between the manifest and the un-manifest. Notice your body's reaction as you continue to stare at the illustration. Be interested in the felt sense of your experience. Close your eyes and let your attention be wide and spacious and invite that same felt sense that you experienced when looking at the drawing.

Do a three-part meditation. First, picture the three flames of consciousness and hold it as an inner image with your eyes closed. Second, reflect on chitta and then on your ego and just observe what you experience. Finally, as best you are able, empty your mind of thoughts and hold your attention steady on consciousness itself. When you are not looking at objects or identifying with being a subject who looks at objects, what is the nature of consciousness?

For Your Reflection

Notice if your mind tries to grab hold of all the labels in the drawing. Beware of thinking, "If I could just know all the labels, then I could really understand it."

What is your emotional relationship to this drawing? The *Flame of Consciousness* is an illustration of something that cannot really be described. How might you let the impact of the illustration register more fully in your mind and heart?

Can you start to separate the consciousness of knowing and doing in your daily life? Why is wisdom sometimes present in your doing, and why is it absent at other times? Can you detect when the consciousness of knowing has an agenda and when it does not?

Look again at the red flame (D) with the lightning in the center. The shape of the red flame is a *vesica pisces*, and its shape is derived from an overlapping of two spheres. When you overlap two spheres you get this kind of shape in the common area. Spheres were used in ancient times to represent wholeness. The vesica pisces is one of most profound geometrical images in spiritual traditions. It has been used as a symbol of Christ (the fish drawing), as an overlay on the tree of life image, and as a symbol of the vagina of the female goddess. It has also been used as a symbol of the god and goddess coming together to create new life, which relates to the male and female kundalini energies contained within the image. One other implication is that of two becoming one, or the oneness that is implicit in all duality. As far as I know, Balyogi is not aware that he was utilizing an ancient symbol so appropriately in the illustration he created more than fifty years ago.

Details of the Flame of Individual Consciousness

This version of the *Flame of Consciousness* shows the details of Balyogi's vision of how consciousness works, as described in Chapter 2. The light blue circle stands for the Causal Level and the anandamaya kosha (for more about the classical understanding of the koshas, see Appendix A). Notice the thin light blue ring (A) at the edge of the Causal Level that is slightly darker than the blue-white space inside it. This ring is the periphery of pure awareness. This is the area that is being accessed in meditation when you completely free yourself of the manifest world and all that exists in the mind is awareness without any object or subject that knows there is only awareness. This pure awareness is related to what Balyogi refers to as *chit-akasha*, or the inner subtle space of consciousness. A key part of spiritual practice is purifying the mind, at least temporarily, of various hindrances that cause it to contract and grasp. When the mind is completely free of grasping and resting in luminous consciousness, you start to get a foretaste of pure awareness.

The large brownish-gold ring (B) represents chitta, the mind stuff of memories, associations, emotional impressions, and habits of mind that constitute one of the four parts of the antah-karana (the four instruments of inner knowing). When the illuminating power of luminous consciousness moves into the realm of knowing through the Subtle Level, it lights up mind stuff such that it can be known.

Adjacent to that gold ring is the large green ring of the ego (C). When I was first able to understand this illustration, I was surprised to discover that the ego had such prominence, and I questioned Balyogi about it. He explained that the ego is necessary for human functioning and that it accompanies even the more subtle forms of consciousness, pictured here as ex-

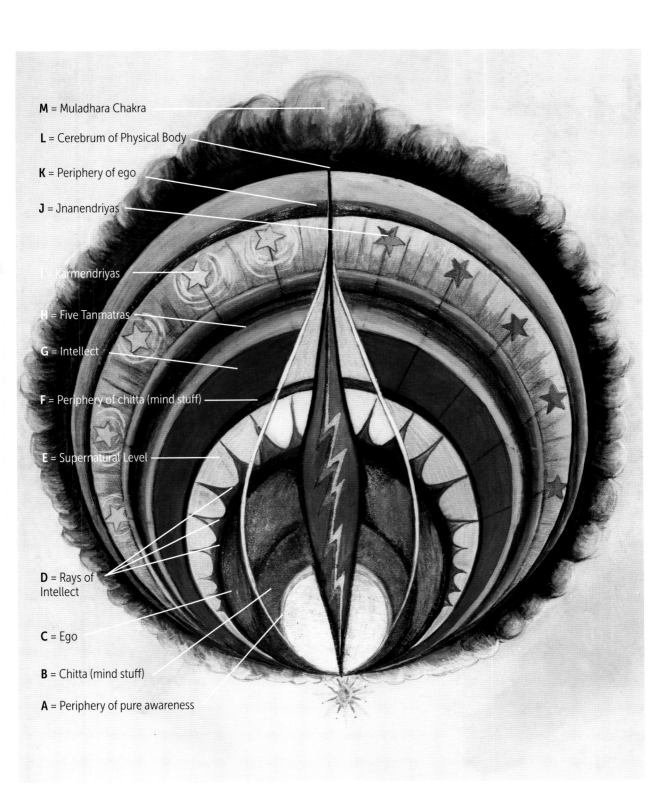

M = Muladhara Chakra

L = Cerebrum of Physical Body

K = Periphery of ego

J = Jnanendriyas

I = Karmendriyas

H = Five Tanmatras

G = Intellect

F = Periphery of chitta (mind stuff)

E = Supernatural Level

D = Rays of Intellect

C = Ego

B = Chitta (mind stuff)

A = Periphery of pure awareness

tending to the edge of physical existence (K). He described the ego as being the "complex of identity" and stressed its vital role in having the strength to undertake inner exploration at the subtle levels. As part of your spiritual journey, you are first creating a healthier ego and then transcending the ego. Because it is so central, if you fail to include the ego in your practice, it can corrupt any insight you have.[10]

Surrounding the ego is a thin red circle (D), which represents the intellect, the source of reasoning. The intellect is what is meant by the "higher mind." The tan-colored ring is "the supernatural" level of mind (E), which is penetrated by flashes of intuitional knowing (also D). By supernatural, I understand Balyogi to mean those capacities of the mind that are not considered possible by conventional thinking. These activities occur in the Subtle Body through the capacities of the Etheric, Astral, and Intuitional Bodies. This realm includes all paranormal activity such as knowing the future, seeing at a distance, knowing the mind of another, and telepathy.

When the mental attributes of memory, association, and so forth of chitta connect to the jnanendriyas (the organs for knowing) (J) by passing through the intellect (G), cognition occurs. The intellect resides in the Intuitional Body. In this illustration, the large red ring (G) stands for both the Intuitional Body and the vijnanamaya kosha. The Intuitional Body contains the Buddhi (the higher mind) and it is directly connected to chiti, which is shown at the bottom of the page where the Subtle Body first emerges from the Causal Body. The higher mind is not a "doer," rather it makes decisions, reflects, creates, helps you stay connected to your intention, and provides the capacity of knowing. The manas or lower mind functions with the senses; it is reactive in nature and conditioned by your habits and emotions.

Balyogi highlights this distinction between the higher and lower mind by illustrating that unlike the jnanendriyas, the karmendriyas (I), the organs of action, connect only through the manas or lower mind. Thus, Balyogi is using symbols to indicate that the act of knowing is a more complex and subtle process than taking action.

The five subtle elements (tanmatras) (H) are located in the Subtle Body. These five subtle energies are the basis of the material world's five elements as has been previously described. Notice that all three flames of conscious-

---

10   In the Theravada Buddhist tradition it is taught that the conceit of "I" is not finally extinguished until the fourth or final level of realization has occurred. To understand the role of the ego better, I recommend reading Jack Kornfield's book *After the Ecstasy the Laundry: How the Heart Grows Wise on the Spiritual Path* (New York: Bantam, 2001).

ness extend through the tanmatras. These flames of consciousness provide the energy for the Etheric Body to affect materiality through the tanmatras. Next to the tanmatras are the karmendriyas (I) and jnanendriyas (J), the subtle organs of knowing and action that are located in the Astral Body, as shown in the first of the *Flame of Consciousness* illustrations. Surrounding them is the periphery of the ego (K), as described earlier. Can you see how interwoven all experience is? It is a web of various capacities and levels of mind activity.

The wide, light-blue ring most prominent at the top of the illustration symbolizes the Vital Body; this same ring also represents the pranamaya kosha. In this illustration, Balyogi includes the cerebrum of the Physical Body (L). At this level, illuminating power of the flame of consciousness is fully extended into the Physical Body, which is illuminated by it—meaning that it is alive with all its particular characteristics. Sitting at the top of the illustration is the *muladhara chakra* (M), which ties the chakras into the flames of consciousness. Although it is not possible to simply overlay the chakras onto the *Flame of Consciousness* illustration, there is clearly a relationship, and you can see how a refined chakra practice can increase consciousness. The gross body of (L) also represents the annamaya kosha. Thus, all five of the koshas or sheaths are presented in this illustration.

▶ Meditating on a Moment of Consciousness Manifesting

If you wish to use an unlabeled version of this illustration for your meditation practice, turn to page 39.

This drawing contains an immense amount of information; therefore, it is easy to retreat into conceptualization when studying it. Utilize your meditations to counterbalance this tendency to conceptualize. Start with gazing at the illustration until you feel the dimensionality of the image as though it were a layer cake. Then go into your meditation with this layer effect as your object and observe what you experience. Next, focus on the three flames of consciousness as you did for the previous illustration. Hold each of them in your mind as the object of meditation and again observe your felt experience in doing this.

Also, focus steadily on the light blue circle (A) representing the periphery of pure awareness until the image is stable in your mind. Invite the knowing of this pure awareness. You may eventually get a hint of a feeling for the existence of awareness without objects, or with repeated practice and strong samadhi you may actually get a direct experience of it.

For Your Reflection

Balyogi is presenting a full and complex view of reality. If you wish to learn from it, you will need to review it repeatedly. Before doing any other reflecting, go back and reread the text for all three of the flame drawings, and then see if you can locate the Nine Bodies on the two drawings where they are not labeled.

When you read that emptiness is characteristic of the Spiritual and Divine Bodies, what is your reaction? Does it affect your perception of what comprises the world? What do you find true or possible regarding pure consciousness? If you believe it is part of reality, is it really necessary to experience it yourself?

Similarly, Balyogi postulates the realm of the supernatural. How might the supernatural realm exist in a manner that is compatible with science? If you do not believe that any type of extraordinary capacity exists, how does that affect your relationship with the rest of these teachings?

9

AWAKENING IN THE SUBTLE LEVEL

Explosive Awakening

Side View of the Nine Chakras

Back View of the Nine Chakras

The Tortoise Channel

Thousand Petals of Consciousness

The illustrations in this chapter all point to different ways that working consciously with the Bodies in the Subtle Level can support awakening. In particular, the illustrations of the chakras help place yogic teachings on chakras and energy systems in the context of the Nine Bodies work.

Explosive Awakening

In the *Explosive Awakening* illustration, Balyogi is showing what he calls the state of "supreme yoga," meaning that the mind and heart have awakened. Supreme yoga can be understood as referring to any genuine stage of awakening that is occurring or to the final moment of total realization, but it is not referring simply to a mind state of extreme bliss. States of bliss are relatively common occurrences in meditation practice; experiencing stages of awakening is not. Final attainment of the stage that Buddha described as "what needed to be done, has been done" is very rare.

The explosive, lightning-like nature of awakening that is often described by masters in many spiritual traditions is clearly visible in this illustration. The yogi is meditating by accessing the Intuitional Body (Body Six) and the insight of realization has occurred. Above the person's head, the colorless globe surrounded by the multicolor aura represents the *shunya chakra* (the eighth one in Balyogi's system) where emptiness is being realized in the moment. The blue space on the forehead and part of the person's skull represents the Etheric Body being fully active. This means there is full access to the knowing that is available in the akashic field, the subtle space of the Etheric Body. (For a full description of the akashic field, see Chapter 3.) The tan area above the blue forehead symbolizes the vijnana-chaksu, the eye of wisdom where ignorance and delusion are being removed. (The vijnana-chaksu is described more fully in the *Eye of Awareness* illustration in Chapter 10.)

The crescent moon and the smaller colorless globe located on the man's head symbolizes the *nada bindu* being accessed. The nada bindu, a point in the center of the forehead just above the third eye, is the juncture between the un-manifest and the manifest world. It is sometimes described as being

the subtlest point of the Intuitional Body, just short of dissolving into the Spiritual Body (Body Seven). According to Balyogi, the nada bindu is where the advanced yogi focuses the mind for realization of the three subtlest Bodies that comprise the Causal Level. A yogi accesses this point by meditating in the Intuitional Body.

Balyogi will sometimes refer to the nada bindu as the "the eye of enlightenment." In Tantric teaching, the nada is the mystical sound or vibration that created the manifest world. It manifests through the nada bindu. It is through this "eye of enlightenment" during deep meditation when you are resting in the Intuitional Body that you obtain supreme knowledge and supreme consciousness. The nada bindu is the gateway to that which is beyond the mind. It is also where differentiation and separation from unity occurs when the un-manifest comes into manifest existence as subtle energy and then flows into the physical world. As we saw in the *Eternal Journey* illustration at the beginning of Chapter 6, the manifest ultimately lets loose of its tamasic and rajasic qualities and returns to unity in an eternal cycle.

Below the nada bindu on the man's forehead is the third eye, and it too is fully open. However, it's noteworthy that Balyogi says that the third eye can only "see" up through the Astral Body and is not able to "see" the more subtle levels of the Nine Bodies. Seeing or realizing these more subtle bodies is possible only when the Intuitional Body is being accessed.

In the man's chest is the *anahata chakra* where the spiritual heart symbol is fully open (upcoming illustrations in this chapter will show details of the chakra system). Balyogi says the Buddha experienced the spiritual heart opening. The spiritual heart's opening occurs in the Intuitional Body and is symbolized by the five arches, which represent the blossoming of awakening in the five koshas or sheaths of the traditional teachings (see Appendix A for a description of these koshas). The heart awakening is occurring in the anandamaya kosha and spreads to the other koshas. Flowing from the heart into the Emotional Body is the "living electricity of consciousness" represented by the lightning image at the navel level. (Refer to Chapter 2 to refresh your understanding of how the enabling aspect of luminous consciousness allows each moment of sense-consciousness to arise.) Flowing upward from the lowest chakra is the snake-like kundalini energy rising from the muladhara chakra. The word *mula* means root; notice how the man's first chakra, the muladhara, appears to be rooted in earth. Balyogi says that the upward flow represents feminine energy in the man while the downward flow represents the masculine energy; when they join together, they become the creative force of awakening. (The reconciling and merging of these two creative forces appears repeatedly in these illustrations.)

◗ Meditating on the Explosive Awakening

This is a very powerful illustration for meditation purposes because in Balyogi's teachings, the nada bindu is the gateway to the Absolute or Deathless. In your meditation, first focus on the root chakra and the feeling of being grounded—first in the illustration, then in your own embodied experience. One way you can enhance this experience is by identifying the earth element in your own body and inviting it to rest on Earth. In Zen practice this is referred to as "sitting in the bones." After you have established the feeling of being grounded, you can then start to focus on the Etheric Body, following the descriptions presented Chapter 4. Once you readily access this level of experience, follow the instructions that allow you to focus on the Intuitional Body.

In this illustration, mind (manas), higher intelligence or intuition (buddhi), ego (ahamkara), and memory or mind stuff (chitta) are fully blossoming. In Vedic literature these four capacities are said to comprise the internal organs that generate the psychological processes from which both emotions and intentions are created. (They will be described further in relation to the following illustration.) Using your capacity of knowing as your object of meditation, see if it is possible to distinguish these four different capacities for yourself. This may take numerous meditation sessions.

For Your Reflection

The bindu point can also be symbolized by a triangle to indicate where the three forces of mind—action, knowing, and being—come together. Some yoga traditions teach that the triangle exists at the base of the spine, while others teach that it occurs in the forehead or on top of the head. Balyogi incorporates it in both places in his teachings. He reports that he is presenting both the Tantric view of kundalini and his "scientific" view of the Nine Bodies. He does so to capture both the dynamic aspect of awakening as movement (base of the spine) and the more static aspect of awakening as realization (top of the head).

Reflect on the dynamic aspect of your practice in which you are moving the mind to a higher state of consciousness and the more static aspect of your practice in which you are surrendering any doing; just be available for the unfolding of understanding to occur.

Which aspects of this illustration appeal to you? Do you find focusing on the "electricity" of awareness useful or not? Have you learned to establish the feeling of being grounded in the root chakra in your own meditation? If not, is it because you don't think it's important or have you simply not learned how to yet?

Side View of the Nine Chakras

This is one of three illustrations by Balyogi of the chakra system. In traditional yogic philosophy, the chakra system (along the energetic pathways or nadis that connect the chakras) is described as a map of the energy systems in the body and mind. The word chakra—which literally means wheel—is used in a variety of ways in meditative practices. On a physical level, each chakra can be said to correspond to a nerve plexus in the body at a particular location. On an energetic level, it refers to the rotation of feminine Shakti energy in the body at the same location. Balyogi teaches that all the chakras actually exist in the mind but have resonance in a particular area of the body.

In the Nine Bodies System, the chakras and the nadis are considered part of the Etheric Body. The energy that resides in the chakras vitalizes the Physical and Emotional Bodies. The main practice of some yoga systems is to open and balance the chakras. Balyogi teaches that pranic energy (associated with the Vital Body) and psychic energy (associated with the Emotional Body) can be partially or completely blocked and that by balancing the chakras it can be released.

Many traditional yogic systems teach that there are seven chakras. Balyogi, however, teaches that there are nine chakras as shown in this illustration. He teaches that the seventh chakra is actually composed of three chakras, two of which are of a transpersonal nature and are known only through insight or realization. Balyogi says that the Buddha was the first yogi to have realization of the *shunya* or eighth chakra, which reveals the emptiness of all things. (In this illustration, the eighth chakra sits above the Om symbol at the top of the head.) Balyogi says that the ninth chakra is

known through the realization *of sat-chit-ananda,* an elevated state of being, knowing, and bliss that he calls the Seer of Emptiness.[11]

This illustration reveals Balyogi's vision of the nine major chakras.

1. The first or *muladhara* chakra at the base of the spine (pictured as a red lotus) is associated with *bhumi,* the earth element. It is linked with survival instincts and the fight, flight, or freeze response.

2. The second or *svadhishthana* chakra in the sacrum area is correlated with the sexual organs and energy. It is associated with water and the adrenal glands, as well as emotions and creativity.

3. The third or *manipura* chakra at the navel level of the spine is characterized by *agni* or the fire element. In Balyogi's illustration, it is represented by a triangle pointing upward. This chakra is linked with digestion and personal power, the capacity for individual assertion and growth. An imbalance of energy in this chakra can manifest as fear, anxiety, and being compulsively opinionated or having fixed views.

4. The fourth or *anahata* chakra at the heart level is associated with *vayu* or the air element. Its symbol contains an upward and a downward facing triangle encircled by twelve lotus petals. The anahata chakra affects the thymus and the immune system in general. When the heart chakra is in balance, the mind is filled with compassion and gratitude and can stay open to life's uncertainty and not be fearful or resentful. When not in balance, it manifests as lust, indecision, and arrogance. The heart chakra is also where the subtle emotions occur that can contain the opposites of life such as birth and death, pain and pleasure. Unlike the lower chakras, which are closely associated with karma, the heart chakra represents freedom of choice for the individual. A fully opened heart chakra is sometimes described as unconditional love.

5. The fifth or *vishuddha* chakra at the throat level is associated with the etheric or space element. Sixteen lotus petals surround the symbol. The vishuddha chakra is linked to the thyroid gland. It is related to the ability to think clearly and communicate well and, in psychological terms, to having one's own "voice." When it is balanced you are able to make distinctions based on values you have chosen rather than mirrored from your family or culture.

6. The sixth or *ajna* chakra at the level of the "third eye" between the

---

11   For experienced practitioners of Insight Meditation, the distinction between the realizations of the eighth and ninth chakras is similar to the distinction between the realization of final *path moment* and the *fruit realization* that follows. It is not an exact parallel, but it points to a similar distinction.

eyebrows is related to mind, ego, and individual nature. The symbol rests between two lotus petals. The ajna chakra is energetically connected to the pineal gland. When it is open, one has access to intuition and intuitive knowing, meaning the knowing that occurs is nonconceptual in nature. Nonconceptual means that there is a felt sense to it; your recognition is direct and palpable, as though your entire being is experiencing the understanding.

7, 8, and 9. The traditional seventh or *sahasrara* chakra is located at the top of the head and is associated with the pituitary gland and the thymus. It is linked to transcendence, and it is here that liberating insight arises. It is pictured as a thousand-petal lotus and is associated with consciousness itself and pure awareness, as described in Chapter 2. There is disagreement among traditional yoga teachings as to whether this chakra is *in* the head, *on top of* the head, or even whether it is a chakra at all. This is the most unique of the chakras; it represents overcoming clinging and attachment. In Balyogi's system, the other two "transcendent" chakras (the eighth and ninth chakras) are realized through awakening in this chakra.

Balyogi refers to the silver and gold symbols at the front of the person's body in this illustration as moon and sun icons, not chakras. (Other teachers refer to them as being a minor chakra called the *surya* or *hrita* chakra.) However they are labeled, they represent the unification of the feminine energy of the silver moon and the masculine energy of the golden sun which, once united, can be transcended and can empower spiritual manifestation.[12] These images of the sun and moon will show up in later illustrations.

▶ Meditating on the Side View of the Nine Chakras

Notice the upward triangle in the symbol of the third chakra and then notice the downward triangle in the sixth chakra. These triangles represent the flow of energy from below and from above. Take each of these chakras as meditation objects—first by contemplating them in the illustrations, then by turning your focus inside into your own direct experience.

Focus again on the sixth chakra. At the front, the third eye radiates out in all directions. Behind it is a downward facing triangle. This represents the vijnana chaksu, the "eye of awareness," or what I call "that which knows" or

---

12   In *Splendor Solis*, the medieval alchemy text that so influenced the psychologist C. G. Jung, there is an illustration of a half man, half woman that represents this same idea that unification of the masculine and feminine is the key to freeing oneself from attachment to this realm and realizing higher states. See Joseph Henderson's book, *Transformation of the Psyche*.

"the source of knowing." Balyogi's description of it can be found in Chapter 10. In my understanding, the vijnana chaksu does not belong to the personality; it is not "me or mine." Rather it is the capacity of awareness itself. To connect with the vijnana chaksu, when you have reached deep concentration in your meditation, place your attention in the very middle of the skull behind the third eye.

Notice the half-dark, half-light symbol at the back of the sixth chakra. This dot represents the nada bindu point described in the previous illustration. Notice that it appears again but in a darker state at the fifth or throat chakra along with an image of a drop of some kind of liquid. (The bindu point will be discussed in more detail in a later illustration.) This liquid is the sacred nectar of immortality or the deathless. It is described as being a kind of ambrosia and is called *amrita*. It flows from the pituitary gland down into the throat. When you have established strong concentration in your meditation, place your attention on this point in the back of your own skull. Notice how the mind responds to using this spot as a focal point in meditation. If it brings stability and sensitivity to your meditation practice, then use it as a focal point in other meditation sessions when your concentration is particularly strong.

For Your Reflection

Look closely at the anahata or heart chakra and notice that the symbol contains both upward and downward-facing triangles. These triangles constitute a key teaching regarding the role of the heart chakra as it relates to freedom of choice in life. How do you understand this teaching?

If you have previously studied the chakras in a different system, what is your reaction to the possibility of there being nine rather than seven? What do you find to be of genuine use in exploring chakras?

Chakras can be either open and balanced or blocked and out of balance with the other chakras. Thus, just as overcoming clinging and attachment are necessary to realize the seventh chakra, what might you need in order to achieve openness and balance in other chakras?

Back View of the Nine Chakras

In this back view of the chakras, Balyogi is illustrating the flow of energy through the spiraling circles of each chakra. The first chakra at the bottom of the spine is represented by a triangle containing fire. In Tantric teachings, the fire symbolizes the heat of *kundalini* (the latent energy coiled at the base of the spine) that is awakened and moves up the spine through the central channel of the sushumna. The white spiral moving up from the bottom of the spine symbolizes energy flowing upward as the kundalini moves through the sushumna, becoming ever more pure or sattvic in nature. The colored spiral (which is most visible in the second and third chakras) symbolizes energy moving downward from the highest chakra. Thus, energy is moving in two directions. Balyogi teaches that the white energy is the energy of luminous consciousness returning to its natural form as we saw in the *Eternal Journey* illustration in Chapter 6. The energy of the colored spiral reflects the effect of luminous consciousness moving into materiality and enabling the arising of sense consciousness. During this process, the mind becomes more rajasic (active and passionate) or tamasic (inert and lethargic). (This same theme of luminous consciousness being mixed with materiality was reflected in all three drawings in Chapter 6 by the water flowing down from the mountains.)

The sixth chakra is symbolized by the green downward-spiraling circles. The red lines are the 1,000 petals of the lotus, which represents the seventh chakra. (Note that the seventh chakra here is depicted as being more toward the interior of the skull, rather than at the crown of the head as in the previous illustration. This kind of variation is common in these teachings.) The eighth chakra is presented by a white halo. The outer gold halo symbolizes the ninth chakra. "The Buddha attained the opening of the

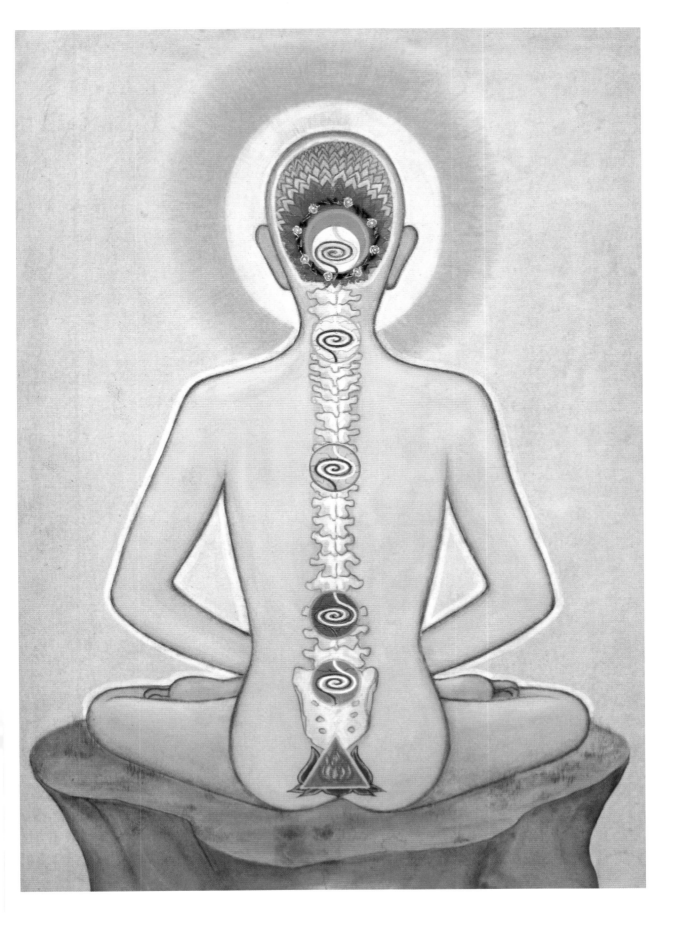

thousand-petal lotus and, therefore, became free from all dukkha forever," Balyogi says. To explain how this purity occurs, he offers two analogies. Just as coal can be transformed into a diamond, but a diamond cannot be transformed into coal—or as ghee can be made from milk, but milk cannot be made from ghee—tamasic energy and the ego once transformed through deep meditative practice can no longer exist. The impure elements simply are not there. Balyogi calls this "ego therapy." Once this transformation has occurred, what follows is the realization of emptiness in the eighth chakra and the knowing of the nature of all things in the ninth chakra. Referring to long-term practitioners who have attained a significant degree of liberation but are not yet fully awakened, Balyogi reports that he can "smell the ego" residing in such persons. He says that while they may have attained freedom from identification with ego activity, they are not free from "that which did the removing of the ego." This distinction between regular ego identification and a subtle sense of self can be helpful when encountering teachers who clearly have had deep realizations but do not resonate as being fully liberated. For instance in Theravada Buddhism, it is only at the fourth level of realization that this subtle sense of self is released.

This drawing illustrates the balancing of the masculine and feminine energies that were seen in the previous side view of the chakras illustration. The moon or feminine energy is represented by the white globe at the back of the skull in which the green circle spirals downwards. The sun or masculine energy is represented by the yellow or golden globe, which encircles the moon energy.

▶ Meditating on the Back View of the Chakras

Notice the petals at the top of the skull. These represent the sahasrara chakra. Contained within the sahasrara is a series of diamond-like shapes. These are the five karmendriyas (subtle organs of action) and five jnanendriyas (subtle organs of knowing) located in the Astral Body that were described in Chapter 3.

Also notice that the indriyas encircle a center that is gold (only part of the gold is visible), which in turn encircles a white ball. These white and gold balls within the head represent the personal manifestations of the universal qualities represented by the halos that surround the head. Balyogi is showing how luminous consciousness flows into each person through the sahasrara and manifests into personal material reality through the indriyas. This is a key realization in his teaching as it ties into the emptiness of sat-chit-ananda and resolves the paradox of the personal and impersonal.

First meditate on the triangle and visualize the heat at the bottom of the spine; notice how that feels. Then visualize the upward and downward energy in your meditation; notice how that feels. Finally, meditate on the sahasrara and Balyogi's image of luminous consciousness being both without and within. What does this evoke in you?

For Your Reflection

Focus your attention on the triangle containing the heat. Many people have reported the experience of energy rising through the spine as a strong pleasurable sensation of heat flowing upward to the back of the neck or to the top of the skull or to the third eye area. If this is literally true, how does this affect your view of the body-mind? Can you imagine the possibility that the movement of subtle energies through the body is a genuine experience and that if movement becomes blocked, it could cause painful physical sensations or mental confusion depending on where the blockage occurs?

The Tortoise Channel

Looking closely at this image as a whole, you will notice that the first chakra, the muladhara, represented by an upward pointing triangle, is now contained within an icon. Balyogi teaches that this icon is the *kurma* and says that it has the seed mantra "*kum.*" The kurma represents the *kaccha* or tortoise. The tortoise is a symbol for deep samadhi, the state of resting in awareness.

In verse 32 of the third chapter of the Yoga Sutra, Patanjali says that by focusing on the tortoise channel one can cultivate steadiness of mind. Called the *kurma nadyam,* Balyogi describes this channel as being a tortoise-shaped tube that is located in the area below the throat (not pictured). It is said that when you are fully focused on this nadi, you are free from thirst, hunger, and body consciousness and can stay perfectly immobile. You can go without food and water and be totally self-contained, like the turtle in its shell. Going into absorption on the kurma nadyam also strengthens the immune system and aids in healing. A technique Balyogi teaches for achieving this experience is to follow the vibration of the sound of *kum* in order to become still, centered, and concentrated.

Balyogi likens kurma meditation to dialing a phone number. Just as a phone number helps you reach someone, kurma meditation helps you reach or *dial into* stillness. Once you reach your destination, you then conduct the task that motivated you. On the phone, you talk with the person you dialed; in meditation, you investigate the mind after attaining steadiness of mind. Here again, Balyogi is making a key distinction for those practicing meditation. There are techniques for arriving at a destination or state of mind that empowers a certain capability. Once there, how you got there is not important. Oftentimes, yogis fail to understand this, particularly when bliss

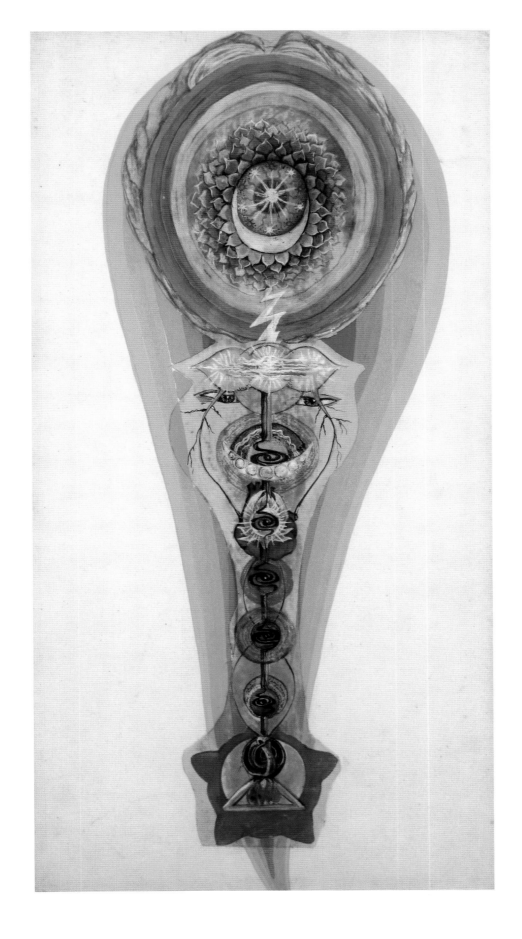

states arise on the way to reaching the intended mind state. The yogi gets distracted and becomes attached to the mind state, forgetting to do the hard work of practicing toward liberation. In Buddhism there is a phrase, "false nibbana," that captures the danger of becoming distracted by or attached to blissful states. Continuing with Balyogi's analogy, it's like being so thrilled with dialing the phone and reaching someone that you keep dialing repeatedly without ever speaking to the person and finding out the information that motivated you to call them in the first place!

In the sahasrara chakra at the top of the head in the illustration, the lotus petals representing the nerve endings or nadis appear as they did in the previous illustration. Also, notice the silver globe (white or colorless in the drawing), which sits at the locus of the third eye in the center of the sahasrara; this is mind or *manas*. The ten spokes emanating from the globe represent the five jnanendriyas and five karmendriyas that were also seen in the previous illustration. Remember, as described in Chapter 3, *indriya* means "sense" and there are five inner senses each for knowing and action in the Astral Body that create the sense organs of knowing and action in the physical world. They are activities of the manas or lower mind, in contrast to the buddhi or higher mind that knows through intuition or direct knowing.

In his teachings Balyogi refers to *bindus*, meaning points of access to powers or forces, which are also part of the Tantric yoga tradition. (The nada bindu that has been discussed in previous illustrations is one such point.) The triangle resting on the kurma at the base of the spine in this illustration is formed by three bindus that arise from three nadis, or subtle energy channels. Kundalini awakening is the process in which active or worldly energy rises with the help of these three energy channels (*ida*, *pingala*, and *sushumna*) into the *nada bindu*, as depicted as the sun and the moon in Balyogi's *Explosive Awakening* illustration. According to Balyogi, as you gain steadiness of mind, you access these energies.

▶ Meditating on the Tortoise Channel

Notice the bolt of lightning flowing from the kurma behind the chakras to the sahasrara chakra at the top of the head. In Tantra, this correlates to kundalini; however, in Balyogi's teachings it also represents the rahasyatmic or mysterious energy, which flows down from pure consciousness. Meditate on how this awareness flows into the third eye energy. Focus your eyes on this part of the drawing, noticing the globe at the center of the third eye and all the movement in the drawing. Then close your eyes and focus on your own third eye and observe what happens.

Next, notice the upward flow of kundalini in the sixth or throat chakra in the form of the blue spiral contained within the larger blue ring. Stare at this until it becomes a steady image, then close your eyes and focus on your throat chakra.

Now look at the two vines spiraling from right to left and crossing over within the chakras. These are the ida and pingala nadis of traditional Tantric teachings; the kundalini moves through the central channel or sushumna in the illustration. These are the three energy channels referred to in the previous section.

For Your Reflection

Notice that there are nine chakras represented in this drawing and then imagine and locate each of them within yourself. The relationship between the seventh, eighth, and ninth chakras is captured beautifully in this illustration. If you meditate or reflect on just this part of the drawing, it might be possible for you to get a direct experience of the levels of *awareness* as a felt sense of presence. (Remember that these illustrations are symbols through which you reach direct experience.) The seventh chakra is generally located where the lightning is first visible. The eighth chakra is generally located at the sahasrara (the thousand-petaled lotus), and the ninth is located in the shunya at the very top where the *vijnana jyoti* (light or flame of knowing) resides, as symbolized by the emanating light. (This is in a slightly different place than in the previous illustration.)

Notice that a pair of eyes looks out at you between the sixth and seventh chakras, and right above them is the third eye. Access to this third eye is available only when you are in the Etheric, Astral, and Intuitional Bodies (traditionally known as the Subtle Level). Mysterious energy in the form of lightning appears directly above the seventh chakra. Does this affect how you experience the illustration versus viewing it as kundalini rising, which it also represents? Does it help you feel the three-dimensionality of the drawing? Can you feel the sense of energetic movement in this illustration? It may seem as though you are seeing straight down the center of each chakra or looking from the top of the skull into the Subtle Level.

Reflecting on all three chakra drawings in this chapter, do you get a felt sense of the way you experience energy? Notice that the shape Balyogi uses to represent the kurma is similar to the pelvic cavity with its sitting bones and the heads of the femurs. If you focus on your pelvic area during meditation, do you feel any support of an energetic nature?

Thousand Petals of Consciousness

The *Thousand Petals of Consciousness* illustration completes the teachings on the chakras. This drawing is a cross-sectional view of the brain showing the alignment of the Subtle Level (the Etheric, Astral, and Intuitional Bodies) with the Gross Level (the Physical, Vital, and Emotional Bodies). You can consider this drawing to be a close-up view of the top section of the previous illustration, *The Tortoise Channel*. With this teaching, Balyogi reveals yet another level in the interaction between the Subtle and Gross Levels. The value of this drawing is that it can add to your felt sense of the existence of a Subtle Level and the practical, "scientific anatomical manner" that the Subtle Level energies interact with those of the Gross Level. You may want to flip back and forth between this drawing and the previous one.

At the very center of the drawing is a white globe. This globe is the *manas* or lower mind and flowing out of it are the five jnanendriyas and five karmendriyas. (Remember, as discussed in Chapter 3, indriya means "sense" and these are the five inner senses of knowing and action. These indriyas represent the subtle organs in the Astral Body that guide the organs of knowing and action to manifest in the material world.) The dark brown layer (which was originally orange before the colors faded) around the mind represents the intellect. The light brown layer (originally a golden color) symbolizes chitta (the mind-stuff or contents of the mind) and the Intuitional Body. "In the lap of the chitta is the intellect," Balyogi says.

Outside the indriyas is a silver circle (putty color in this rendering) of which only the top part and edges are visible. This symbolizes the ego, according to Balyogi's vision. At the periphery of the ego are the thousand petals of the sahasrara chakra shown as differently colored leaves. Each petal connects to the Physical Body at a particular point. According to Balyogi,

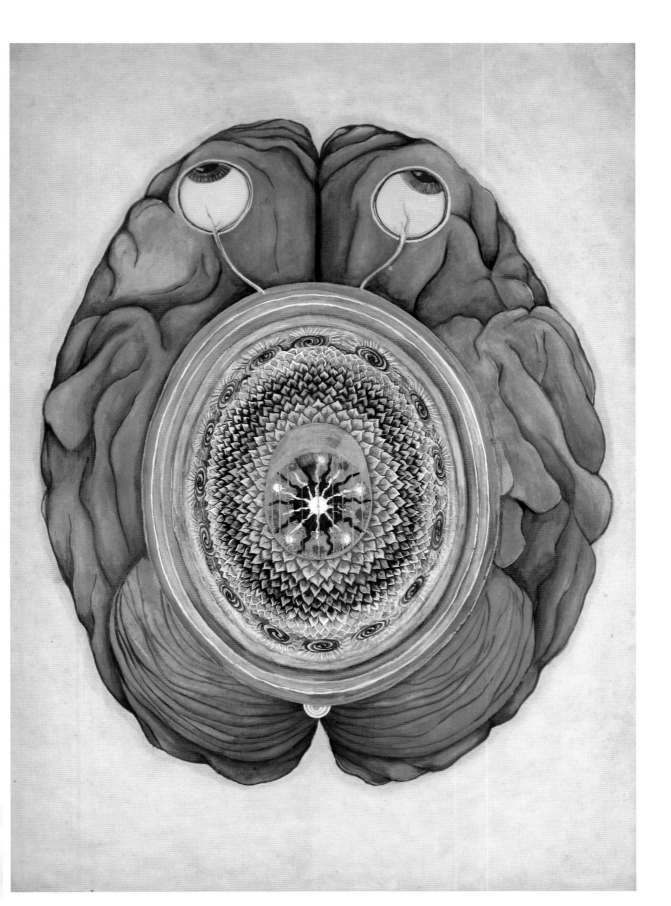

these petals communicate through the Etheric Body, which is the interface between the Subtle and Gross Levels. Maintain your focus on this illustration for an extended time in order to allow time for the feeling of the interaction between the Subtle and Gross Levels to be awakened in your imagination.

In the immediate border of the sahasrara is a band of purple spirals that represent tanmatric (subtle elemental) energy flowing. Immediately outside this energy band are five circles of various colors that represent the five subtle elements themselves. At the crevice at the very bottom of the drawing is a small opening that represents the nervous system of the Subtle Level and is the connection between the Subtle and the Gross Levels.

This is the opening of the sushumna, and it is through this opening that kundalini energy rises as it moves up from the base of the spine. Beyond the tanmatras (subtle elements) in the darker brown area is the physical brain itself with all of its folds.

▶ Meditating on the Thousand Petals of Consciousness

This drawing is a two-dimensional representation of a multidimensional image. Focus on the center of this drawing until you start to feel the depth or height that provides the dimension. Once you start to feel its dimensionality, close your eyes and notice your felt sense of these multiple dimensions. This drawing can also show movement despite its static form. Once again focus on the center of the illustration until you experience not only its dimensionality but also a sense of vibration or aliveness. Continue with this meditative exercise until you feel your body being affected by this combination of dimensionality and movement. It may be helpful to switch between staring at the drawing and gazing at it with soft eyes. You may experience various body-mind effects as you do this.

For Your Reflection

Balyogi's drawings and descriptions of the anatomy of the Subtle Level in relationship to the Gross Level are an analogy that points to the extra dimensions of consciousness. Do you find yourself wanting to quarrel with the specifics of his anatomy rather than opening your mind to the possibilities his illustrations point to?

The ultimate purpose of these illustrations is to inspire and awaken you such that you can start to explore the more subtle aspects of conscious-

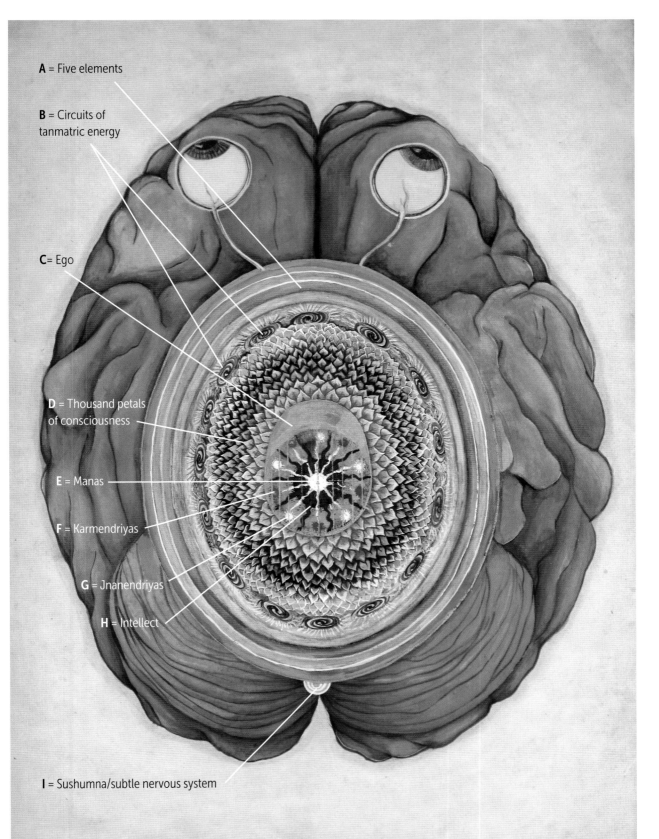

A = Five elements

B = Circuits of tanmatric energy

C = Ego

D = Thousand petals of consciousness

E = Manas

F = Karmendriyas

G = Jnanendriyas

H = Intellect

I = Sushumna/subtle nervous system

ness yourself. As you look at each drawing, this is what you are doing. One key insight that comes out of this work is the realization that what you understand to be you and what you understand to be physical reality are an ever-changing flow of arising and passing moments in your mind that are coming about largely because of unseen dimensions of consciousness. Is the way you are working with these drawings leading you to these kinds of reflections? Or are you more fascinated by the exotic nature of the material?

Go back and review all four drawings in this chapter. What do they arouse in the way of recognition or questions in your mind? These illustrations may have ignited numerous levels of recognition or knowledge. One is simply a stirring of recognition that you are in a territory of reality that you have felt in your own experience but has not been mirrored back to you previously. Another level is that you have felt certain energies in your body in the past, and these illustrations provide a context for understanding them, even though you may not comprehend or may even be doubtful of some of Balyogi's teachings. Another level is that the illustrations awaken a strong sense in you that the Subtle Level really exists, and you wish to be more open to experiencing it. Finally, you may feel that these four drawings have affected your interest in the nature of pure awareness and its mysterious energy—what it is, where it resides, what its relationship is to all the mind moments you experience in a day.

10

THE AWAKENED HEART

Luminous Consciousness in the Spiritual Heart

Three Hearts

The Radiating Heart

The Eye of Awareness

This series of illustrations focuses on the heart aspect of awakening.
The illustrations clearly reveal that this is a journey that brings us to
the true nature of the heart as it already exists within us.

Luminous Consciousness in the Spiritual Heart

The *Luminous Consciousness in the Spiritual Heart* illustration is an abstract representation of how, once you commit fully to the meditative path, your mind ultimately blossoms into awakening—meaning the mind is able to see clearly what leads to suffering and what does not and has the ability to choose the latter. In full awakening the causes of suffering are uprooted such that there is no longer any possibility of consciously or unconsciously choosing suffering out of desire, aversion, or delusion.

Examine the lower half of the drawing where the green and white spirals that were in the previous illustration are presented in more detail. The green spiral represents sense-consciousness flowing downward into materiality and worldly concerns. This downward spiral was presented as nature in the *Eternal Journey* drawing in Chapter 6. Balyogi sometimes refers to this downward movement as the "dark energy of consciousness" spiraling us into the realm of lust for and attachment to worldly pleasures and materiality.

The white spiral of luminous consciousness is flowing upward toward oneness and full awakening. Both of these flows of consciousness are occurring in the Subtle Level. The white spiral of psychic energy is sometimes called the "pure light of consciousness," meaning that the yogi's awareness is returning to its spiritual home—its essence or true nature. (The return or upward flow also appeared in the *Eternal Journey* illustration.) This movement comes through the mind resting in the Intuitional Body during meditation such that intuitive knowing or realized awareness (vijnana) arises as insight. The mind elements of the antah-karana (the four instruments of knowing described in Chapters 2, 8, and 11) are then utilized for insight, and deep understanding blossoms. Anytime this upward movement of the mind toward purification occurs, it has a renewing effect on the Gross and

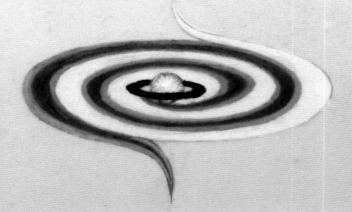

Subtle Levels. It is for this reason that meditation, when done wisely, can be so healing physically, emotionally, and energetically.

Now focus your attention on the upper part of the illustration, which is an enlargement of the golden-brown globe at the center of the lower part of the drawing. This globe is also at the center of the spirals in the following *Three Hearts* illustration, but more implied than visible.

The sphere at the very center represents all-pervading pure awareness. In the previous chapter, I described the realization of emptiness (shunya) that occurs when the seventh chakra opens in realization. The white globe in this drawing represents what comes after emptiness has been realized. It is indescribable, not based on thinking or concept; it can only be realized by practice. Yet words are necessary to point out the existence of this level of mind. For instance, in Tibetan Dzogchen practice, this pure awareness is called *rigpa* and is described as having three aspects: its *essence* is emptiness, its *nature* is radiance or luminosity, and its *manifestation* is responsiveness. In the Yogacara school in India, pure awareness is called Buddha nature and has three aspects that are inseparable: emptiness, radiance, and responsiveness. In Patanjali's teachings, it is called the Supreme Self, but to my understanding Self does not imply a personality or great being, rather it is a *not self* and is not personal. Balyogi refers to the white globe as chit, purusha, or the Supreme Self, and calls it pure awareness. In the Pali texts of Theravada Buddhism, this pure awareness has been referred to as the unborn, uncreated, and unmanifest. Of course there are large metaphysical differences in how these traditions interpret and understand this mystery of pure awareness. Even within each tradition there are disputes as to what is attained. However, there is general agreement that some fundamental change occurs that is markedly different from what characterizes the ordinary mind. In the Heart Sutra in the Tibetan tradition, this awakening is referred to in the following mantra:

> *Gate, gate,*
> *paragate,*
> *parasamgate,*
> *bodhi svaha.*
> Gone, Gone,
> gone beyond,
> unfathomably further than gone beyond,
> into awakened mind, ah.

Balyogi says the dark silver around the edges of the white circular globe is the jivamukti or individual purusha (soul). In Buddhism there is no individual soul, so it can be understood as the radiance of pure awareness. Although various traditions interpret consciousness differently, aspects of pure awareness are viewed similarly. The golden-brown ring around the globe represents luminous consciousness as described in Chapter 2. This golden-brown ring signifies responsiveness or cognizance, which in Dzogchen is described as "unobstructed, compassionate activity." The responsiveness of mind illuminates what is before it. In its essence, pure awareness is still and empty, but it empowers all mundane and divine moments of illuminated knowing in every person's mind. Consciousness that is not engaged with an object is without movement. It exists as a potential of knowing but at the moment is not engaged with any object; it is simply a knowing potential resting in itself. It is not cognizing. I realize that this is a puzzling statement, but many people who engage in meditation and contemplative prayer report accessing this stillness and marvel at the peace they feel.

As described in Chapter 2, what distinguishes luminous consciousness from pure awareness it that luminous consciousness is conscious of its own existence. It has consciousness itself as an object while pure awareness has no objects, no subject. There is no self, no entity to experience any subject or object; the awareness simply is. The luminous consciousness becomes associated with movement in the mind as the mind moves toward knowing objects of the sense gates (vijnana consciousness) or toward mindfulness of the knowing or consciousness of objects (*sati* in Pali). When consciousness starts moving with the objects of mind, we start to identify with the experiences of consciousness around internal and external experiences and mistakenly take ourselves to be the one experiencing our body or memories, or to be the "me" that is experiencing a thought or emotion. In Raja yoga, this misperception is mitigated through the use of the chant, "*Neti neti*," meaning "Not this, not that."

Western thought has also reflected on the mystery of emptiness and stillness of mind versus the movement of mind. For instance, the poet T. S. Eliot in *Four Quartets* captures this mystery and paradox of the relationship between pure awareness and individual moments of sense-consciousness: "At the still point of the turning world ... there the dance is.... And do not call it fixity...." Look at the top image and then the bottom image. Can you feel the truth of Eliot's words? Can you feel the stillness of the white globe? This pure awareness is not moving, but neither is it fixed; it simply does not live in the time-space of ordinary mind moments. Eliot goes on to say, "Except for the point, the still point, there would be no dance, and there is only the dance." This means that out of stillness, movement occurs, and individual moments of sense-consciousness arise, are illuminated, and are known. You know sounds, sights, feelings, tastes, body sensations, emotions, and states of mind because of this illuminating capacity. But any sense of permanence of these sensory-based moments would be illusionary; they arise from stillness and then pass. Therefore, finding peace and a sense of well-being in their arising and passing is impossible. However, when the movement of mind is known in the context of the stillness, then it is seen clearly for the temporary phenomenon it is, and the mind does not fall into greed, hatred, or delusion regarding it. In the next chapter, we will study the *Flame of Consciousness* drawing, and through that illustration the illuminating aspect of consciousness will become clearer.

▶ Meditating on Luminous Consciousness in the Spiritual Heart

In your meditation, watch the movement of your mind toward various objects. Observe how quickly the mind moves as sense stimuli, including thoughts and emotions, arise and pass. Do not try to stop this movement, just watch it with relaxed, accepting curiosity. Notice what happens to your mind after a while when you cultivate such a spacious meditation. Does the mind become more settled?

After practicing like this for a while, see if you can expand your meditation to make the constancy and commonality of "knowing" or cognizing your object of meditation. Thoughts, emotions, and body sensations will still arise, but you are seeing through them to the phenomenon of knowing them. Practice in this manner until you have regular access to this experience of knowing and then see if you can start to access it in your everyday activities. Being aware of knowing that experiences are constantly arising and passing is mindfulness meditation. As you learn to carry mindfulness into your daily life, it will provide a sense of being present and provide more "space" around experience.

During all your meditation practices, if the mind spontaneously becomes still or is not registering any experience other than something regular like the breath, allow that stillness to become the focus of your meditation.

Be careful not to grasp at it or attempt to make it last, just settle back into it the way you might relax your body into a chair.

For Your Reflection

You can start to explore the paradox of stillness and movement by observing the mind more closely in daily life. You can easily start to see how it moves toward an object in order to know it. More challenging is to see that a kind of "participating observer" can be cultivated. Although you are participating in whatever is occurring in your mind, some other aspect of you knows that it is occurring, and that aspect is not caught up in the experience. At this stage of development, you begin to have more choice in what you say and do and to a more limited degree in the kind of thoughts you have. But what about the pure awareness described above? Can you start to intuit it? Do you have some innate feel for its existence? Maybe opening to the idea is frustrating, confusing, or irritating to you or brings out skepticism. Just keep reflecting on the nature of awareness without trying to force any conclusions. Watch how just observing can bring about a different feeling state in the body and/or mind. What are the implications if in fact there is pure awareness? Does it affect what you believe to be the purpose of your life?

Three Hearts

The Nine Bodies teachings describe the existence of three hearts: the physical heart, which manifests as matter; the psychic heart, which manifests as energy in the Subtle Level (the Etheric, Astral, and Intuitional Bodies); and the spiritual heart, which resides in the Causal Level (the Spiritual, Divine, and Cosmic Bodies) and manifests in the Subtle Level as illuminating consciousness. This illustration represents the realization that can only be known from accessing the refined Bodies of the Causal Level. The physical heart is visible at the top and bottom of the drawing. The lotus flowers symbolize the psychic heart. The presence of the spiritual heart is barely visible as it lies at the very center of the spiral. The spiral itself represents luminous consciousness and it is moving both upward and downward through the lotus flower in the Subtle Level in the form of a green and white strand. (The spiral of luminous consciousness is drawn in greater detail in the previous illustration. You may want to look at it now before reading further.)

Balyogi says when the psychic heart awakens, its thousand lotus petals open. Each petal symbolizes purity and openness. (This is not found in any book, he says.) For this reason, the psychic heart is the seat of unconditional love, meaning *agape*—the love of the Bodhisattva and what is called "Christ consciousness." It is also the source of energy and of emotions; therefore, it is where "spiritual emergencies" can arise if your ego is overwhelmed by what it is accessing. Balyogi teaches that there is a major difference between spiritual emergencies (which more often happen on meditation retreats, but can happen in daily life) versus psychological emergencies when someone becomes disoriented or disassociated due to overwhelming emotions. Psychological emergencies happen in the ego; the ego is not part of the psychic heart.

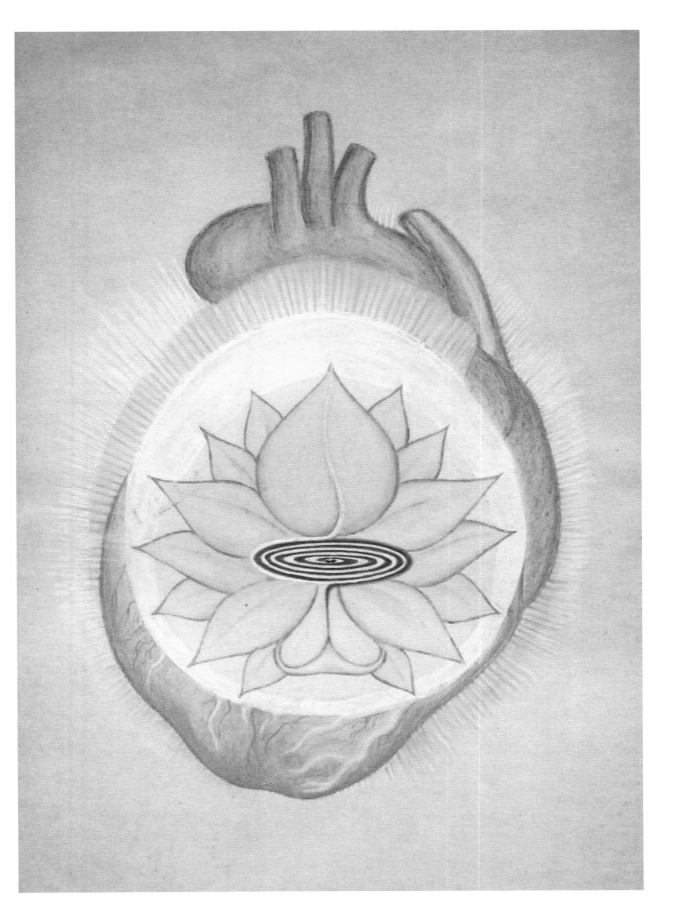

The radiating aura surrounding the edges of the physical heart represents luminous consciousness manifesting. In other words, consciousness illuminates all of the Etheric, Astral, and Intuitional Bodies, which in turn illuminate the Physical, Vital, and Emotional Bodies. Balyogi says that chiti (the Sanskrit word he uses for what I call luminous consciousness) receives its illuminating capacity from the spiritual heart, which is located in the Causal Level, even though it exists in the Subtle Level and nourishes the psychic heart.

Notice the green spiral flowing downward in the drawing. It symbolizes luminous consciousness in the form of energy moving into the world. Balyogi describes this downward movement as the energy of consciousness moving toward sense-consciousness. If you look more closely, you will see there is also a white spiral flowing upward. This white spiral represents a situation where the mind and the energy of consciousness are moving toward spiritual awakening. In an earlier drawing, *Explosive Awakening* (Chapter 9), this movement of the mind has been completed, and awakening is the result. The awakening of the heart occurred in the Intuitional Body.

The psychic heart directly affects the physical heart. The psychic heart contains the antah-karana—the "electronics of the mind" introduced in Chapter 2. (We tend to think of mind as happening in the head, whereas yogis think of it in the heart.) In Balyogi's analogy of the difference between the electricity and the light bulb, the antah-karana is comparable to the filament in the light bulb that allows the electricity of consciousness to manifest "here and now."

These electronics include both buddhi, meaning intuitive knowing and often referred to as intellect, and manas, ordinary mental thinking. The antah-karana also contains the "mental continuity factors" of association and memory, and the executive functions of the mind. (Some teachings say that the antah-karana provides the linkage between births, as shown in *The Mandalas of the Subtle Body* illustration in Chapter 11.) In Vedantic literature, the antah-karana includes chitta (meaning storehouse, memory, or "mind stuff") and the ahamkara (ego) as the mental continuity factors. Balyogi's teaching of antah-karana includes all four (buddhi, manas, chitta, and ahamkara) and he calls them "the four inner instruments of knowing."

The grouping of these four mental aspects can be helpful in modern therapeutic work as well as meditation in that it allows patients to see their mental afflictions not as a "self" with problems but as a series of process-es whose behaviors are determined by causes and conditions that can be changed. Also, these four inner instruments of knowing are involved in the purification of consciousness into pure awareness, as we will see in the fol-lowing illustration.

Luminous consciousness is associated with the spiritual heart, while both buddhi and manas are directly associated with the psychic heart. Psy-chological healing happens through the psychic heart. The various *kleshas* (afflictions) reside in the psychic heart. The psychic heart works through manas and buddhi to help release afflictions of the mind. For this reason go-ing to a silent meditation retreat is a healing or purifying experience for the ego. It is as though you are putting your psychic heart into a cooking vessel in order to build pressure and heat such that the psychic heart becomes pu-rified. You sit mindfully and compassionately with the afflictions that arise as mind states or physical sensations. The hours of sitting heat the vessel to a point where the afflictions are purified and released.

When someone hurts you, you feel it in the psychic heart. If you experi-ence an emotional shock or trauma, it goes into the psychic heart and causes psychological problems, which in turn may show up in some manner in the Physical Body. It is through *viveka samadhi* or meditation practice (called insight practice in Buddhism) that nonjudging yet discriminatory mindful-ness arises, which helps purify the mind of afflictions.

▶ Meditating on the Three Hearts

This illustration can serve as an awakening image for your heart connection. Begin by simply gazing steadily at the image and noticing the multicolored rays that seem to be radiating from the glowing center. Do not try to under-stand it, but rather focus on it as a felt experience in your body and mind. Now focus on the lotus petals as though they represent your highest aspira-tions and purest thoughts. Notice the softness and the feeling of bountiful-ness they reflect.

For Your Reflection

Notice that there are two prominent lotus petals, one at the top, unfolding straight up, and one pointing down. What does this symbolize? What does it say about the choices that exist in the Spiritual Body as described in Chapter

3? For some people the realization will arise during spiritual practice that everything is already perfect just as it is. Could this illustration be capturing this realization?

Reflect on your personal afflictions of mind. Can you distinguish between ordinary mind activity (manas) from which afflictions arise and the impersonal cognition (buddhi) that can see these mental hindrances as being based on conditions and not representing you? Can you observe your ego's current relationship to each affliction and see that this relationship is also simply based on conditioning that resides in the mind (chitta) in the form of memory, habitual associations, and conditioned perceptions, and therefore subject to change?

The Radiating Heart

This drawing illustrates how the spiritual heart is the ultimate source of the physical heart. Mysterious energy emanating from the spiritual heart—represented by the central white or "colorless color" orb—works through the Etheric Body to energize or illuminate the physical heart. The colored circles symbolize the antah-karana, the four instruments of inner knowing. As described in Chapter 2, the antah-karana is composed of *manas* (mind), *buddhi* (intuitive intelligence), *chitta* (contents of consciousness or "mind-stuff") and *ahamkara* (ego). The antah-karana is viewed as being the link between spirit and body. Thus this illustration is a more elaborate teaching regarding the heart than was presented in the previous illustration.

▶ Meditating on the Radiating Heart

Try meditating with the ego and buddhi (intuitive intelligence) as your objects. Observe the difference when you use your ego as the object versus the buddhi. Now see if you can make chitta itself the object of your meditation.

For Your Reflection

Can you easily identify when you are utilizing the manas or the capacity of mind that directs the senses versus when you are experiencing the buddhi? Can you see that chitta plays a role in both manas and buddhi? Can you see how the ego thinks it controls buddhi?

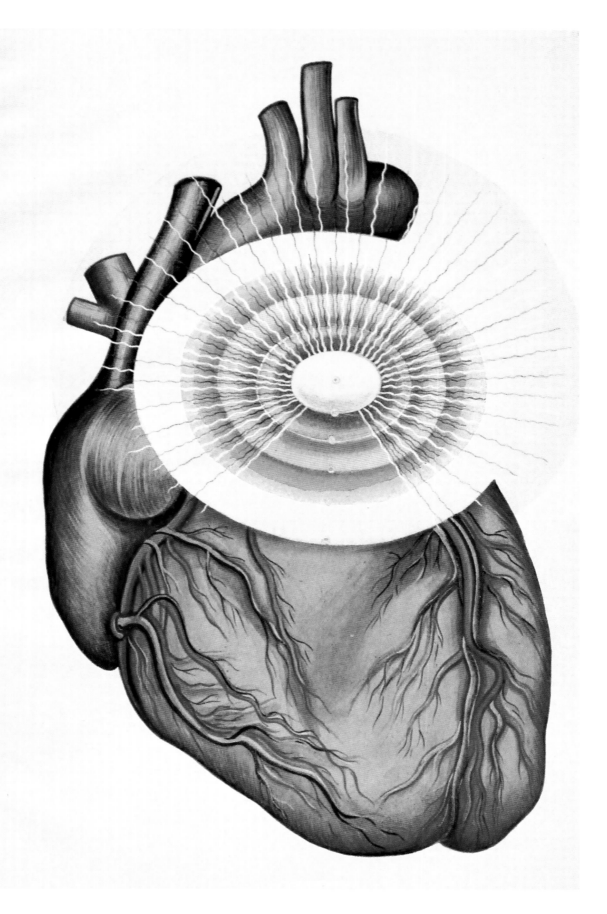

The Eye of Awareness

The *Eye of Awareness* illustration is a teaching about the vijnana chaksu. The vijnana chaksu, which Balyogi calls the "eye of awareness," and which I sometimes think of as "the eye of knowing," refers to a location in the Subtle Level associated with a refined state of mind in which an extraordinary type of liberative *knowing* is accessed. This state isn't deep sleep, waking, or dreaming—the three ordinary states of being. It is accessible through a combination of meditation, reflection, inquiry, and selfless service.

This type of knowing is *realized* or intuited in contrast to ordinary wisdom about how to live more effectively and skillfully. This state of consciousness occurs when the heart is fully open and awake. In Chapter 9, the *energetic* feeling of awakening was presented in the illustration *Explosive Awakening*, and earlier in Chapter 10 an *abstraction* of the awakened state was depicted in the drawing of *Luminous Consciousness*. This illustration is intended to capture the *transcendent* or cosmic feeling of being in the awakened state. This cosmic feeling is one of harmony, balance, and oneness.

When the eye of awareness is awake, the mind is not caught in self-reference; the heart is filled with radiating love that is so free from attachment that it experiences oneness even when dealing with the dual nature of ordinary reality. This illustration is not presenting a philosophical statement or pointing to a belief, rather it is describing what occurs at a genuine and realizable stage of spiritual maturity. All the illustrations in this chapter invite recognition of and inspiration for reaching this stage of consciousness that frees the mind.

In this drawing, a blue stream representing luminous consciousness flows from the eye of awareness and wraps around the rainbow heart. The rainbow heart is the awakened heart in which the awareness is all from love.

The flow from the eye to the heart Balyogi calls the "divine journey of life." The illustration represents a magnification of the eye of awareness and reveals what is actually occurring in the eye of awareness when you access this capacity of knowing.

At the center of the heart is a figure of the sun and moon kissing. Balyogi says this is not an ordinary kiss but rather the kiss of the opposites uniting and becoming one. In this unity and harmony, access to the eye of awareness becomes available.[13] The sun and moon kissing represent Shiva and Shakti, the full integration and balancing of the masculine and feminine energies, which occurs at this stage of spiritual growth. The heart is full of love and light and the emotions called forth are the *brahma-viharas*, the dwelling place of the Gods. In Buddhism there are four such mind states: *metta* or loving-kindness, *karuna* or compassion, *mudita* or sympathetic joy, and *upekkha* or equanimity. They are stated somewhat differently in various yoga traditions, but they have parallels nevertheless.

▶ Meditating on the Eye of Awareness

Look closely at the *Eye of Awareness* and notice that it contains a six-pointed star pointing in all directions. This indicates that all is in balance—the material world and the nonmaterial; the past, present, and future; and the pleasant and the unpleasant. Now picture that your mind, just as it is, has this capacity to be balanced. Begin your meditation in a relaxed manner, assuming it will become balanced on its own. Do not over-effort, just keep relaxing into knowing your breath and see what happens. Once your attention is stable, invite the knowing of this capacity to be present during meditation. You can utilize the image of the drawing in your meditation. In doing this meditation, you are not likely to drop into the eye of awareness until you have practiced extensively, but you may be able to sense the presence of this capacity.

During another meditation session, focus on the sun and the moon images enclosed by the heart. Invite this feeling of harmony, of deep acceptance of whatever arises, into your meditation. Repeat the mantra, "This too, this too," or "This, but not only this," in order to cultivate reconciliation of the opposites that are always present somewhere in the mind. The moment you become aware that your mind has wandered or gotten lost, pause and

---

13   This same stage of spiritual growth can be found in one of the drawings of alchemical text of the *Splendor Solis* (Plate I-9) in which the figure has both a female and a male head.

notice that the knowing creates harmony in the mind. In meditation, the mind ordinarily jumps so fast to judging, comparing, or controlling based on the emotions and conditions of that moment that the natural harmony of the eye of awareness is overlooked.

For Your Reflection

Reflect on your own experiences of masculine and feminine energies. Do they feel balanced in you? Balanced does not mean that they appear equally strong in your experience of yourself, but rather that each is available to arise with ease when conditions are appropriate. Remember, I am referring to energies, not male and female characteristics. In meditation practice, these opposites may be experienced as the ability to stay focused on the chosen object of meditation such that the knowing of it has continuity and the ability to soften into the object such that there is a *felt sense* of the object, whether it is the breath, body awareness, emotions, or thoughts.

You may have already noticed the heart image can be observed in the eye itself, even though the image is small. As mentioned above, the rest of the illustration is a magnification of what is occurring in the eye of awareness. In the same manner, your feelings of connectedness and of an open heart can be magnified by cultivating continuity of mindfulness of the heart space. This feeling of the heart being open to a "fourth dimension" may already have happened to you during meditation, while walking in nature, or while reading spiritual literature or poetry. For instance, the poems of Rumi or Hafiz are often used for inspiring the heart in this manner. Such a heart opening is sometimes referred to as the *bhakti* or the devotional aspect of spiritual practice.

This *Eye of Awareness* illustration completes the journey that we started with the *Spiritual Heart* illustration. Please return to the first illustration and take time to focus on each of the illustrations again. In what ways has your understanding deepened? In what way has your own felt sense of the journey been affected?

11

MANDALAS OF AWAKENING

Mandala of Antah-Karana

The Mandalas of the Subtle Body

Shri Yantra and Om Mandala

A mandala is a geometrical figure used for meditation that symbolizes some aspect of the spiritual or metaphysical world. The illustrations in this chapter are all mandalas that depict some aspect of the Subtle Level and its relationship to awakening.

Mandala of Antah-Karana

This illustration is an abstract model of the antah-karana—the four instruments of inner knowing first introduced in Chapter 2. At the bottom of this image is the subtle prana radiating through all four instruments. Next is the orange-colored chitta (mind-stuff), followed by the red-colored buddhi or intuitional intelligence. Next is the mind (manas) represented by different shades of green; the light green represents the higher or more refined mind functions while the dark green represents the lower mind, which is utilized for activity or doing. Finally, there is the ahamkara or ego in blue. Notice that the rays of subtle prana are much thicker close to the source, becoming increasingly thinner as they move into the less subtle forms of knowing.

▶ Meditating on the Mandala of Antah-Karana

Because it is abstract, this drawing is less of a mandala for meditation than most of the other illustrations in this book. It is included here for you to familiarize yourself with the different instruments of knowing so that you can better understand some of the other drawings, such as *The Flame of Consciousness*. However, if you focus on this illustration, it is possible for you to develop an intuitive feeling for how as the mind moves into the material plane the coarser it becomes. You may realize this as a very subtle kind of knowing in which it feels as though you are realizing something important, but you are not sure what it is.

For Your Reflection

Start to be aware of and attempt to identify these four instruments both in your meditation and in your daily life.

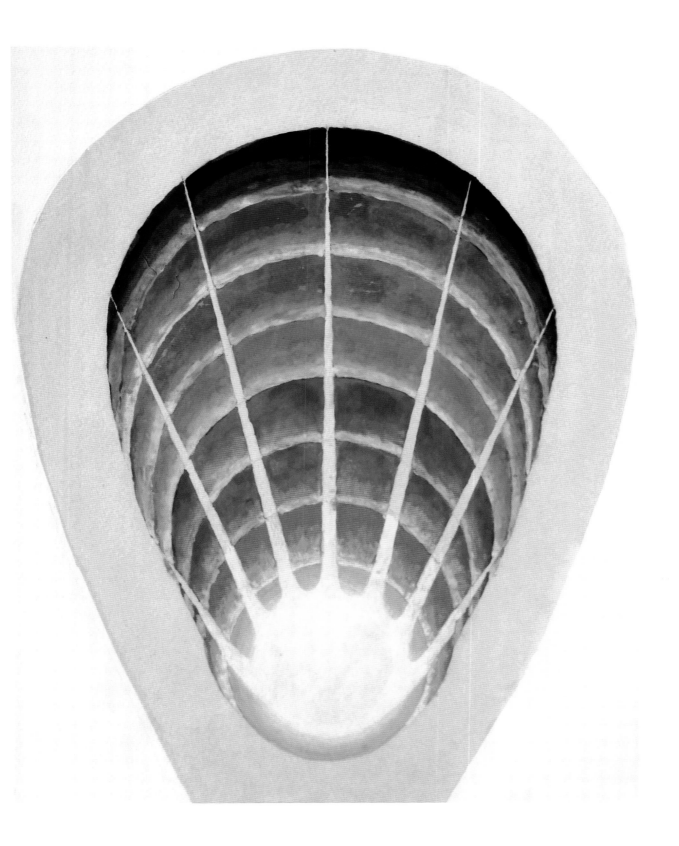

The Mandalas of the Subtle Body

In this illustration, Balyogi offers a different perspective of the Subtle Level. Thus far the Subtle Level has been presented in terms of its three Bodies—Etheric, Astral, and Intuitional. But in this teaching he is describing what he calls "mandalas" or "energetic zones" of activity that you can come into a conscious relationship with. This drawing was originally black and white, but Balyogi later colorized it to make it clearer.

Balyogi describes the Subtle Level as, "Shaped like a conch, and it grows in that shape in the etheric or akasha space surrounded by radiance." He likens it to the perfume of a flower in contrast to the actual flower. "The flower is physical, the perfume of the flower is subtle, and it can only be known by the sense of smell. The Subtle Level is to the Gross Level what the perfume is to the flower," he says. The intellect cannot access the Subtle Level, he says, "But there is a pulse, a vibration that can be felt." When I asked him if you smell a sweet, ambrosia-like fragrance when you are in direct contact with it, he replied, "Yes, so you have experienced it!"

"The Subtle Level is finite in contrast to the Causal Level, which is vast and infinite," Balyogi says. He describes the three states of being in the Subtle Level using the analogy of the mind: "The first state is when the Subtle Level is relaxing in the Spiritual Heart. Then it is in a state like the mind in dreamless sleep. When the Subtle Level is using the brain as a computer for thinking, it is like the act of dreaming in the mind during sleep. When the Subtle Level is in deep meditation, it is like being awake." Furthermore, he says that enlightenment happens in the Subtle Level; self-realization happens in the Causal Level. (Actually, when describing all of this, Balyogi used the traditional term "Body" for "Level"—however, for the sake of clarity and consistency within this book I have changed this to "Level" as previously discussed.)

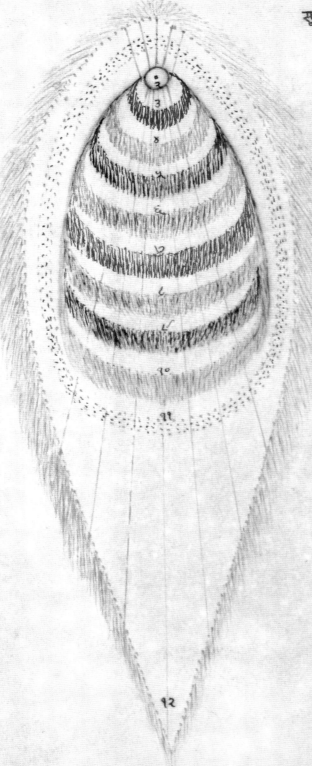

सूक्ष्म शरीर

१— जीवात्मा.

२— अन्तःकरण.

३— सूक्ष्म प्राण-मण्डल

२-४— चित्त-मण्डल.

५— अहंकार-मण्डल.

६— बुद्धिमण्डल.

७— मनो मण्डल.

८— ज्ञानेन्द्रिय-मण्डल.

८— कर्मेन्द्रिय मण्डल.

१०— सूक्ष्मप्रकृति-मण्डल.

११— पंचतन्मात्रा-मण्डल.

१२— **प्राणमय कोश.**

Written on the right side of the drawing are the names of the mandalas of the Subtle Level. The red dot in the center of the small blue circle represents *jivatman*, which is where individual chiti manifests in time and space. The area enclosed by the blue circle is the first mandala, which Balyogi identifies as representing the totality of the antah-karana (the inner instruments of knowing). To my mind, it makes more sense to view it as the energy of luminous consciousness that illuminates the antah-karana.

The remaining nine mandalas are represented by the spaces within the concentric crescents. The second mandala is subtle prana or the *sukshma prana mandala*. It represents the energy of the subtle prana that flows into and invigorates the Vital Body. The third through sixth mandalas are the four instruments of knowing found in the antah-karana: the third is chitta (the energy zones of the mind stuff such as memories and habitual views); the fourth is the ahamkara (ego); the fifth is buddhi (intellect); and the sixth is manas (mind).

Mandalas seven and eight are the jnanendriyas and the karmendriyas, the subtle organs of knowing and doing. Following these mandalas is the *sukshma prakriti*. Balyogi says that it is not a mandala itself but represents factors that affect the energy zones. The factors are the subtle energies arising from tendencies, habits, and all sorts of energetic vibrations.

Following the sukshma prakriti is the ninth, the *pancha tanmatra mandala* representing the energy zones of the five subtle tanmatras (subtle elements) that are found in the Etheric Body. The pancha tanmantra mandala is shown as a red, dotted, elliptical band that surrounds all that has preceded it. Finally, the tenth mandala is presented as a large, yellow, teardrop-shaped band that extends toward the bottom of the page. This is the energy zone of the pranamaya kosha. In meditation, some people get a felt experience of this energy zone and tend to view it as the energy body. They describe it as feeling like an egg or aura surrounding or else emanating from the Physical Body.

"When your Physical Body is dead, all that is left after physical death collects into the Astral Body," Balyogi says. "But it is only the jivatman and the antah-karana that go into the Astral Body. Together, they comprise the entire anatomy of the Subtle Level after death." This means that all other zones of life energy generated by consciousness are extinguished and are no longer present. According to these teachings about death, it is as though the

1. **Jivatman** = individual soul
2. **Antah-karana** = internal organs made up of ahamkara (ego), buddhi (intellect), manas (mind), chitta (mental content)
3. **Sukshma prana mandala** = subtle vital energy/ force ring/circle
4. **Chitta mandala** = ring of mental content
5. **Ahamkara mandala** = ring of the ego
6. **Buddhi mandala** = ring of the intellect/ discriminative faculty
7. **Manas mandala** = ring of the mind
8. **Jnanendriya mandala** = ring of organs of knowledge = ears, skin, eyes, nose, tongue
9. **Karmendriya mandala** = ring of organs of action = speech, hands, legs, genitals, anus
10. **Sukshma prakriti mandala** = ring of subtle nature (subtle aspect of manifest universe)
11. **Pancha tanmatra mandala** = ring of five elements = earth, water, fire, air, ether

12. **Pranamaya kosha** = vital energy sheath

light bulb of illumination for individual moments of consciousness of both objective and subjective nature are burned out, but the existence of illuminating consciousness is not necessarily affected.

▶ Meditating on the Subtle Body and the Mandalas

In order to do these meditative inquiries, it is necessary that you practice meditation until you have a strong degree of stillness of mind. When you're able to achieve one-pointed equanimity and no thoughts are arising, you can invite the Subtle Level to be known. Then simply observe what you experience as direct knowing.

Once you have some mastery of experiencing the Subtle Level, you can invite the Etheric, Astral, and Intuitional Bodies to be directly experienced. When you have some access to each of these aspects of the Subtle Level, then take luminous consciousness as your meditation object. Do not be interested in anything that arises in the mind whether they are body sensations, thoughts, or emotions—these are chitta or mind stuff. Stay interested only in the knowing itself as a phenomenon. (This is a very advanced meditation technique and will only be available after much practice.)

For Your Reflection

Balyogi says this about chiti (which I have been calling luminous consciousness): "Its very nature is to be pure, like the nature of cotton is to be white, even though it may be dyed other colors. There are different kinds of consciousness colored by obsession about money and power or pleasure and so forth, but Lord Buddha's chiti was directed within. It was *chiti sattva*, pure chit (pure awareness). This pure chit naturally wants to unfold. It is likewise with all people; you are already Buddha nature, you are not acquiring it. So all efforts of *sadhana* (spiritual practice) are to purify the chiti." The movement toward purity depends on three things: destiny (I understand this to mean your karma); *chanda*, strong motivation toward finding peace; and right intention, the intention to find freedom in just this moment." (See my book *Dancing with Life* for a thorough explanation of intention.)

You might reflect on your feelings about rebirth and how you understand it. There are many different interpretations and descriptions of what is reborn and how rebirth is conditioned. Some teachings suggest there is a "you" or "self" that is reincarnated, while other teachings suggest that only the capacity of consciousness is reborn. Other traditions say that there is not a self that is reborn, but rather consciousness with some continuity of memory and tendencies. Balyogi's teachings possibly fit into the later category.

What if it is only the habit and tendencies of your mind that affect what happens to consciousness at death? What does that suggest about practice and preparing for death? What if there is an interim period of time immediately after death of the brain where luminous consciousness can remain intact? How would that affect the way you prepare yourself for that moment?

Shri Yantra and Om Mandala

This final illustration presents an integrated view of the awakened state of awareness and incorporates Balyogi's teaching of the flame of consciousness (from Raja yoga) with the classic teachings of the Shri Yantra and Om mandala.

Balyogi says the Shri Yantra mandala represents the feminine aspect of "divine consciousness." The Om mandala symbolizes the masculine aspect. This composite of the two mandalas shows the union of feminine and masculine energies in spiritual awakening. In this illustration both aspects are fully awake and in balance, a harmony of mind and heart. This balance is happening in the awakened spiritual heart located in the Causal Level. "In the spiritual heart, we are never apart," Balyogi says.

The Shri Yantra mandala appears in the lower half of the drawing. The green leaves are the leaves of the pipal or bodhi tree, the tree that Buddha sat under the night of his enlightenment. These leaves represent the physical lungs and what Balyogi calls "the principle of two in one," meaning that just as each lung is separate yet they function together, so it is with duality and oneness, with both having their own truth. Overlaying the leaves is a red heart symbolizing the physical heart. At the base of the heart is the Shri Yantra mandala. The lotus petals above the Shri Yantra represent the flowering of the spiritual heart, although the spiritual heart itself is not visible in the illustration.

Flowing between and connecting the Shri Yantra and the Om symbol is the flame of consciousness. The flame of consciousness is the unifying image in the teachings of the Nine Bodies. The luminous consciousness is flowing into the brain in the form of three different flames. Each of these flames represents a different kind of consciousness. The red flame represents the

jnanatmic consciousness, which empowers the four inner instruments for knowing, the antah-karana, which was described earlier in this chapter. The green flame represents *kriyatmic* consciousness, which manifests through the instruments of action. The jnanatmic consciousness of the intellect and the kriyatmic consciousness of action have come into an awakened balance. The yellowish-white flame in the center represents pure awareness. The lightning energy in the center is the mysterious *rahasyatmic* energy that empowers all consciousness to unfold.

The heart-shaped, five-color outer band that surrounds the images represents the psychic heart, which is found in the Subtle Level. (Remember, the psychic heart manifests as energy.) The five colors represent the five subtle elements of the tanmantra that give rise to the five elements in the Physical Body. The blue background is akasha or etheric space. Balyogi says that this is the space where mind and heart can be active in an awakened balance. The result is divine love, peace, and well-being. In this space, harmony and balance are possible, whereas in physical space there is always tension, emotions, and confusion.

Balyogi says that the Om symbol combined with the brain represents tranquility. This tranquility is a result of the stillness and emptiness of the mind. This is the path that Buddhists follow to bring about the cessation of dukkha through awareness and wisdom, i.e., realization.

The Shri Yantra mandala is formed by nine interlocking triangles. In the illustration, we do not see all nine. The triangles radiate out from a central point, the bindu point, which I described previously as being the intersection between the manifest and the un-manifest. In the classic Shri Yantra, four of the triangles point upward and represent Shiva or masculine energy and five of the triangles point downward representing Shakti, the feminine, or the manifest. Thus, the Shri Yantra represents what Balyogi calls "the sun and the moon," the unification of the masculine and feminine. According to Balyogi, each person is capable of uniting these energies within the Subtle Level.[14] The image of the brain in the top part of the drawing on which the Om symbol appears represents the area that Buddhists access to go beyond dukkha though awareness and wisdom.

---

14 Because it is composed of nine triangles, the Shri Yantra is sometimes called the *navayoni chakra* ("nava" means "nine" in Sanskrit), which reinforces Balyogi's teachings of the nine chakras and the Nine Bodies. The nine triangles of the Shri Yantra are interlaced in such a way as to form forty-three smaller triangles. This web of triangles is said to symbolize the cosmos and is an expression of Advaita or nonduality.

▶ Meditating on the Shri Yantra and Om Mandala

Focus on this drawing for an extended period of time, and then close your eyes and continue your meditation. Allow knowing to arise. Revisit this drawing a number of times, always becoming aware of your felt experience of it.

Next, spend a few minutes chanting the sound of *Om* out loud. This sound has a specific frequency. Traditionally it is taught that *Om* is the sound of the manifest universe. After growing accustomed to saying *Om* aloud, start to notice how your body and mind feel as you say it.

Next, stop saying *Om* and then sit in silence. Notice whether you hear the inner sound of silence. This sound is high-pitched and you can use as it as the object of your meditation. (If you hear more than one inner sound, focus on the sound that is both full and high.)

Now, focus on the stillness of the silence out of which this inner sound arises. Such a suggestion can be confusing, but the silent stillness that is pure awareness does have an actual felt sense and it can yield great calmness and well-being when accessed. You may have to experiment for a while to be able to contact this awareness. Once you have a sense of the silent stillness, direct all your intention onto it, and invite the felt sense of the stillness to be the object of your meditation. Notice whether there are brief moments when the mind becomes empty of all thought and there is only luminous consciousness.

For Your Reflection

To get the full impact of this illustration, turn the page upside down. Notice how the leaves form a heart. When looked at from this perspective, Balyogi seems to be saying that the heart, not the mind, is most connected to pure consciousness and that the wanting, aversive, worrying, and deluded mind gets healed by freeing the heart. How does such a view affect the way you practice?

What do you feel now about the energetic presence of the lotus flower? Does this reversal of the drawing capture an important truth about the relationship of mind and heart that you may have missed before?

Now turn the page back to its normal position and imagine the drawing in three dimensions such that the flame of consciousness is arising from a mysterious depth beneath the lotus. This depth has dimensions that can never be known by the human brain, but its effect can be felt when the mind is still. Does reflecting on the image in this manner help you see how the extraordinary and mysterious nature of luminous consciousness is thus hidden in everyday thought?

The Nine Bodies and Liberation

YOU HAVE NOW completed your initial exploration of the Nine Bodies, the teachings that reflect the Nine Levels of Consciousness. As I stated in the beginning of the book, these are not teachings of liberating insights. Rather, these teachings are an orientation, a description, and a map for locating yourself in your meditation practice in terms of levels of consciousness. The Nine Bodies may be applied to your practice no matter the lineage or particular form of meditation you utilize. I want to close by offering a few suggestions about how you might incorporate these teachings into your practice in a manner that supports liberating the mind from greed, aversion, and delusion.

First of all, I suggest that you use the teachings to access the felt sense of the larger dimensionality of body-mind such that you are able to disengage from deep-seated habits of viewing yourself and the world strictly in concepts. You may not even realize how much of your inner experience, even in meditation, is based in conceptualizing, such that your thinking mind is acting as a filter between what you perceive and your actual experience.

Once you start regularly accessing a number of the Nine Bodies as direct experience, even for short periods of time, your habitual and narrow conceptual thinking starts to fall away. From this larger perspective, the suffering of the constantly wanting mind becomes abundantly clear, and the pointlessness of the aversive mind with its dislikes, anxieties, and disagreeableness is revealed to be just another form of attachment.

Second, you may well discover that repeatedly accessing a certain Body or level of consciousness eventually brings more concentration, bliss, or stability to your practice, or more access to insight. These stronger capabilities come about because you are intentionally using the mindfulness of a particular level of consciousness to align yourself with what you were already doing unconsciously. Or you may discover that just inviting the arising of a certain Body makes for more depth of practice, even if you are not able to stay with it throughout the length of your practice period.

Keep in mind that you can experiment with accessing various Bodies and then practice whatever form of meditation you currently practice while connecting to that particular Body. During the practice period, you may stay within that Body or forget all about it, but it will have gotten you started and helped you to become present, mindful, and in touch with your practice intention.

A third way to benefit from these teachings is to open your mind in a new manner that gives you more access to understanding how the mind becomes liberated. The Nine Bodies may well stir your imagination and open you to what you have already intuitively felt about the nature of reality. Imagination is often treated as an unskillful activity in spiritual practice. However, imagination opens us to possibilities that were present all along but had no access to previously. Imagination also invites creativity in applying wholesome skills we have learned and key insights we have experienced for still deeper learning and greater integration. We are capable of being mindful of and exploring many dimensions of awareness. And we are capable of *direct knowing* in ways that we have hardly touched upon previously. The teachings of the Nine Bodies can provide the imaginative, creative framework for us to discover and develop these capabilities.

A fourth way to apply these teachings is to use them to *ground* yourself while you practice meditation and during your daily activities. To ground yourself in meditation, select any one of the Bodies or any one of the illustrations that is of sufficient interest to the mind that you can place and maintain your attention on it for an extended period of time. The continuity of attention allows the mind to become collected and unified; as this happens, bliss and concentration arise, steadiness of mind is easily maintained, and a temporary letting go of attachment can occur such that liberating insights arise. Being grounded also protects the mind from the various hindrances of mind that arise—restlessness, worry, sensual desire, and doubt.

Being grounded in daily life means that you have a background object of experience that is your resting place for the mind while it is involved in the various activities of thinking and having emotions. For example, the easiest way to develop *ground* in daily activity is in the physical body itself. You can do this by staying mindful of the body when moving, sitting, doing activities, and interacting with others—not that you are mindful of the body each second, rather you return repeatedly to your awareness of your body as a direct experience.

As you repeatedly connect to the direct feeling of the body many times each day over a period of months, you will develop the skillful habit of being aware of body sensations or directly feeling the elements of earth, wind, fire, water, and space that compose the body without having to remember to do so or to make any effort. Body sensations become the interstitial experiences your mind registers when it is not actively thinking in a doing manner. As a result, you develop a continuous feeling of being present. Thus, you are grounded, you have presence moment to moment, you feel authentic to yourself, and others experience you as being present when they are with you. From the view of spiritual practice, being grounded means you have mindfulness, you are able to stay present in such a way that you avoid causing harm to yourself and others, and you are able to be an active observer of your speech and actions.

A fifth approach to using the Nine Bodies or levels of consciousness is to use the various bodies to explore the factors of mind that help create the conditions for spiritual awakening and release. For instance, energy and investigation are vital qualities for finding liberation from the clinging and attachment of the ego. You cultivate *energy* through the Vital Body, experiencing and nourishing the prana as described in earlier chapters. You cultivate *investigation* by being aware of the Emotional Body and how it affects the mind's clarity. You also utilize consciousness of the Etheric Body to cultivate vitality and to investigate the more subtle levels of physical and emotional experience.

A final way the teachings are useful for liberation is that they help you find the most mysterious dimensions of consciousness by connecting you to the direct experience of both the Etheric and Intuitional levels of consciousness and helping you stay with them until you can directly feel what lies beyond the ego mind, beyond mindfulness and any ego sense of a "me" or "mine." And if you are fortunate to be able to do so, you access the Intuitional Body, which enables a deep understanding to arise that connects the separate moments of experience to underlying spiritual truths. This means moving from simple mindfulness of arising and passing experiences in the mind to knowing directly the field of awareness and having insight into its empty, luminous, and radiating nature. Dwelling, being grounded in, and exploring the very nature of this empty awareness can lead to the insight that brings a *change in lineage*, as is said in Theravada Buddhism, meaning you experience a complete shift in how you view yourself and all of life.

The Nine Bodies: Real or an Analogy?

The Nine Bodies do exist—with practice they are locatable in any moment of time and space. But the nature or materiality of each is somewhat different. Each Body, from the most material to the most subtle or immaterial, is an *energetic body*. The form of the energy varies in its coarseness or subtleness and whether it is in manifest form or present as potentiality.

The Physical Body has a different elemental quality than the Emotional or the Vital Bodies, but each can definitely be experienced and each is always in existence, whether or not we are able to access that level of consciousness at any given moment. The Physical Body is easy to perceive and relatively easy to explore because the elements of which it is composed are quite detectable. Likewise, most people can feel the Emotional Body as it is manifesting, even if they cannot clearly identify the particular emotions that are being generated. Thus, you can know that the Emotional Body is strongly present or not and how it is affecting the Physical and Vital Bodies. But you have to remember to stay mindful in order to do so, which can be challenging because we are so identified with the Emotional Body as a "me" or "mine." On the other hand, it seems that most people can access the state of the Vital Body in terms of it being strong or weak, but seldom, if ever, do they stop to consider that it, too, is a Body, a level of consciousness that can be explored in the same way as the Physical and Emotional Bodies.

In a similar manner, the Etheric Body is a collection of energy in the body and mind that is always manifest and has its own defining characteristics, with or without your being conscious of it. As with the Vital Body, you often feel the Etheric Body, but are not identifying it as such. Traditionally, in spiritual teaching, this level of consciousness has been described or identified as the *tao* or *chi* or in modern terms as "the zone" or "flow." Such labels clearly indicate it has a Body, or level of consciousness, and one that is important to access. You now have the means to do so.

The Intuitional Body is the consciousness that is experiencing insight, realizing wisdom, or having an intuition, but is unlikely to be considered as a level or Body of consciousness that can be known in its own right by most people who practice. It is so easy with the Intuitional Body, as with the others, to simply categorize your experience as an activity of mind and fail to realize that you are accessing a particular level of consciousness with its own unique capacities and characteristics. Therefore, it takes a deliberate effort on your part to start to visualize and be open to having a direct experience of the energetic experience of the Intuitional Body.

Ending on a Personal Note

Once, many years ago, at the end of a long day of study and practice, Balyogi invited a group of students to join him for a traditional Indian fire pit ceremony celebrating Shiva. In the dark of the early winter evening, we sat around the fire chanting and meditating while Balyogi conducted several rituals. The night air was cold, and we were all wrapped in shawls or blankets. At the end of the ceremony, Balyogi stood up and walked around to my side of the fire pit. The rest of us remained sitting in silence since he had not indicated that the ceremony was over.

Balyogi then took his blanket off his shoulders and put it around mine. I was stunned and unsure of what Balyogi's gesture meant. He then disappeared inside his house and returned moments later with his *japa* (meditation) beads, the ones he had practiced with for twelve years while living in a small cave in the Himalayas. He bowed slightly as he handed them to me, saying they were now mine. My experience that evening of these two symbolic events was that a responsibility was being put on my shoulders that I could either accept or decline.

It has been both an honor and a burden to be entrusted with Balyogi's teaching lineage in this manner. In offering my meditative understandings that arose from his teachings, I feel as though I have fulfilled at least some part of that responsibility. I have done my best to live up to his trust and to wisely apply the knowledge I received while still pursuing my own path of awakening in the Buddhist Theravada tradition. At times, this has been difficult for Balyogi and for me, but we have stayed steadfast in our commitment to each other.

I have Balyogi's meditation blanket carefully stored. At times I still practice with his japa beads, and they, too, remain carefully cared for. Someday I will pass on the blanket and the japa beads to someone else. I am always alert to meeting this person, who is as yet unknown even though they may already be present in my life. I hold steadfast to the conviction that someday this someone will carry on the Nine Bodies teachings far better than I.

This completes the teachings of the Nine Bodies, at least for the present time and in this format. You now have access to the illustrations and possess at least the minimum knowledge of each Body that is needed for you to continue this exploration on your own. Please remember that knowledge brings with it responsibility. One honors knowledge; one does not use it for glorification or exploitation.

Much metta (loving-kindness) to you … Om Shanti, Shanti, Shanti

The Traditional Teachings on Levels of Being

IN ORDER TO fully appreciate Balyogi's teachings concerning the Nine Bodies, it is helpful to understand in more detail the historical teachings about the Levels of Being that have long existed in the Indian forest or mountain traditions of yoga.

In the classic yoga tradition, rishis living in the Himalayas taught that we each have three main Bodies—a Gross Body, a Subtle Body, and a Causal Body. The Gross Body is compared to ice, the solid phase of water. The Subtle Body is likened to water in its flowing, liquid form, such as a river. And the Causal Body is similar to steam, the form of water that is the most subtle and hardest to discern. Yet all three—ice, a flowing river, and steam—have the same essence, H_2O.

As discussed in Chapter 3, Balyogi's Nine-Body system is a refinement and elaboration of this classic system. Throughout this book, I have used the word Level to refer to the different layers in the traditional Three Body system, in order to avoid confusion with Balyogi's Nine Bodies. The chart below compares the two systems.

Traditional System	Nine-Body System
Gross Level	Physical Body Vital Body Emotional Body
Subtle Level	Etheric Body Astral Body Intuitional Body
Causal Level	Spiritual Body Divine Body Cosmic Body

In the traditional teachings, the Gross Level is made up of the "elements" of earth, air, fire, water, and ether (or *akasha* which translates into space), which combine to create bone, organs, and tissue. The Gross Level is experienced only during the time you are awake.

The Subtle Level is composed of the life energy (*prana*) and the subtle energies that create both physical and mental existence. The Subtle Level can be experienced when you are both awake and in dream states, but for the untrained mind the main way it is contacted is through dreams.

The Causal Level is the mysterious spiritual source from which conscious life arises. Being in touch with the Causal Level brings peace and bliss. In the untrained mind, the Causal Level is only experienced in deep, dreamless sleep, but with meditation practice it can also be experienced in the dream state and, most importantly, in the awake state. (In stable states of continual mindfulness meditation, it is also possible to be mindful during dream states. There are even "dream yoga" practices.)

All manifestations in these Three Levels can also be classified by the nature of the energy that is present. The energy can be characterized by one of three qualities or attributes, called *gunas*: It can be inert and lethargic (*tamasic*), active and highly stimulated (*rajasic*), or balanced and harmonious (*sattvic*). The more sattvic your mind state, the more access you have to directly experiencing the Subtle and Causal Bodies. In the forest tradition, this rebalancing happens through a complex regimen of restraints and correct actions, coupled with meditation for acquiring insights that bring consciousness into sattvic balance.

The Koshas or Sheaths of Existence

The Three Levels can be correlated with the five koshas or sheaths that comprise life. These sheaths can best be understood as energetic levels of existence that emanate from the most refined level to the most material or "gross" level. Each is a unique combination of the three gunas or types of energy. The hierarchy of koshas is similar to the manner in which Western science describes the human body, beginning with subatomic particles and then progressing to increasingly complex components—atoms, molecules, cells, tissues—and finally the whole body.

According to yogic science, life manifests from the bliss sheath (*anandamaya kosha*), which is the most ethereal energetic level and contains the Causal Body. In the water analogy, this would comprise steam or mist. The next most refined kosha is the *buddhi* or intelligence sheath (*vijnanamaya kosha*), which is composed of intuition, the "higher mind" (meaning self-awareness), and the capacity to reflect. The third is the mind sheath (*manomaya kosha*), which contains ordinary thinking, the intellect or "lower mind," the various sense gates, and what Balyogi calls the "psychic" or "psychological" mind. The fourth is the vital sheath (*pranamaya kosha*), which contains the vital life force and the Subtle Level from which it originates. The gross material sheath (*annamaya kosha*), which is also referred to as the food sheath, is taught as being the same as or containing the Physical Body.

Balyogi subdivides the anandamaya sheath, which contains the Causal Level, into three separate sheaths: the anandamaya kosha, or the body of joy; the *chitimaya* or *chinmaya kosha*, the sheath that contains individual consciousness; and the *atmamaya kosha*, the sheath that contains the Awakened Self. Other yoga traditions also state that there are two or more sheaths within the anandamaya kosha. Please note that the use of the word Self does not necessarily connote a personality self, but refers to a state of transcendence that is beyond ordinary mind states where one is free from the attachment and grasping that characterizes the ego-centered self.

In the discussion of the Nine Bodies in Chapter 3, I list the kosha or koshas in which each Body is located. That information is also displayed in the table below.

Body	Kosha
Physical	annamaya
Vital	pranamaya
Emotional	Between pranamaya and manomaya
Etheric	manomaya
Astral	manomaya
Intuitional	vijnanamaya
Spiritual	anandamaya
Divine	anandamaya
Cosmic	Transcends the koshas

Separate, Interrelated, and Unified

All Three Levels and all five koshas influence one another; therefore, they are regarded as interrelated rather than separate. Thus, an action at the physical level affects the capacity of mind and even spirit. Likewise, developing the higher levels benefits the grosser levels, both in refinement and healing capacity. The work of the yogi is to realize the interconnectedness of the Three Levels and the five koshas, clear the pathways between levels, and purify the entire system, moving from being tamasic (lethargic) and rajasic (active) to sattvic (balanced).

The koshas represent the various aspects of being human—having a body; having energy; having the ability to perceive and interpret the senses; having a mind that is reflective and self-aware; and having access to your true nature, which is inclined toward love, generosity, and selflessness and is the opposite of self-aggrandizement that characterizes identification with the ego.

There are many different and sometimes contradictory descriptions or maps of the Three Levels and Five Koshas and of the various structures within them. Still, throughout the centuries, there have been yogis who seemingly mastered an understanding of them to the degree that they gained extraordinary physical and mental capabilities. But even more importantly, these yogis manifested joy and peace of mind such that the tradition continues to attract many seekers of the knowledge and wisdom they possess.

ACKNOWLEDGMENTS

MANY INDIVIDUALS have contributed to the birth of this book, sometimes in such improbable ways that it often feels as though I am merely the servant of a body of knowledge determined to stay preserved. Here are just a few. The adventure started with my good friend Nikki Lastreto arranging an introduction to Sri Swami Balyogi Premvarni when we were traveling in India together in the 1990s. Over the next three years, we twice returned to his ashram together. Nikki was instrumental as my guide to Indian culture. An editor who wishes to remain unnamed worked with me throughout the early years of writing this book. She pushed me to write from my own experience with the teachings and would repeatedly call me on anything that was not clear.

I twice went to Rishikesh and read what was then the "finished" manuscript to Balyogi, only to come back and start all over again. The editing and guidance tasks for the manuscript that you have read came about with the great help of my teaching colleague Anne Cushman, an author herself. Anne fully immersed herself in the third and final manuscript, which reflects her clear mind and intellectual discipline. It also reflects the input of Dana DePalma, who in month-long silent retreats intensively studied these teachings with me while I was still clarifying them in my own mind.

I owe a great debt to many others, including Anam Thubten Rinpoche for writing the foreword to this book. Jack Kornfield and Guy Armstrong, friends and teaching colleagues, read the final manuscript and made important suggestions. Chip Hartranft, who translated and wrote a book on Patanjali's Yoga Sutra that re-examines the text from both the Hindu and Buddhist spiritual traditions, also suggested corrections. Hisae Matsuda did an edit of the manuscript when I was planning on self-publishing the book. Not only did she do a great job of editing, her husband, Ramana Erickson, who grew up in a yoga ashram, was able to help with the translations on a particular illustration! It was Hisae who suggested to North Atlantic that they might want to publish the book, thus giving the book a much larger exposure than was my original intention.

The Nine Bodies is in some ways two books in one and this presented a great design challenge, which designer Gail Segerstrom masterfully handled.

The book benefited from her patience and discipline as well as her creativity. Claire Auclavair took the photographs of Balyogi's illustrations, and I deeply appreciate her skill and her generosity. Balyogi's longtime student Gyana Bays was very helpful in providing historical perspective about Balyogi and his ashram.

Throughout these last years, it has been a struggle to balance my dharma meditation teaching and my work at the Life Balance Institute with the seemingly endless hours of writing and revising of this book. Jennifer Ward, program director here at the Life Balance Institute, managed the book project when it was to be self-published and then carried out all the negotiations when it moved to the publishing house.

My Buddhist teacher the Venerable Ajahn Sumedho's acceptance of the worthiness of this project provided much comfort during the years of doubt and frustration. While visiting him in Thailand at the monastery where he lives, I showed him the illustration called *Luminous Consciousness in the Spiritual Heart*. He looked at it steadily for some minutes in silence, and then looked up and said: "I understand this, I do not need an explanation." Although brief, it was such validation for the immense time it was taking to create this book.

Of course, there would be no beginning or ending without Balyogi Premvarni. Not only did he fully share his teachings, he and his daughter Divya were also generous hosts at the ashram. Among many other kind actions at lunchtime, they repeatedly fed me the best dal I have ever tasted, and at the end of each long day of study, wonderful chai as the shadows replaced sunlight.

GLOSSARY

Avyakta (Sanskrit). Invisible. The source of all that is manifest is said to be avyakta and to originate from the Causal Realm.

Ahamkara (Sanskrit). Ego consciousness. False identification with the body and personality.

Akasha (Sanskrit). Space or ether.

Akashic Field. An etheric field or storehouse consciousness in which a record of past events, experiences, and knowledge is imprinted. Contained in the Etheric Body.

Anatta (Pali). Not-self; the observation that our concept of a separate, solid self is an illusion.

Anicca (Pali). The reality that all things, including what we think of as the self, are impermanent and constantly changing.

Antah-karana (Sanskrit). The four instruments of inner knowing: the chitta (contents of consciousness), buddhi (intuitive intelligence), manas (mind), and ahamkara (ego).

Attention. The mind's ability to focus on an experience stimulated by one of the six senses (thought being the sixth sense).

Avidya (Sanskrit). Ignorance or delusion, particularly in regard to the nature of the self.

Bindu (Sanskrit). In the Tantric tradition, a point or dot where power or energy converges and can be accessed.

Bodhicitta (Pali). Compassion for all sentient beings, accompanied by a falling away of the attachment to the illusion of self.

Buddha (Pali). Literally, one who is awakened. The term can refer to the historical enlightened teacher who lived in India in the fifth century BCE or to an individual's own capacity for realization and freedom from greed, hatred, and delusion.

Buddhi (Sanskrit). Intuitive intelligence and higher wisdom; the capacity of the mind for discrimination and perception. When it is active, the ordinary mind and senses become still.

Causal Level. Traditionally known as the Causal Body. The highest, most subtle, or innermost of the traditional Three Bodies in yoga or Vedanta philosophy. It contains the Divine, Spiritual, and Cosmic Bodies of the Nine Bodies system. For a full description, see Chapter 3 and Appendix A.

Chakras (Sanskrit). Literally, "wheel." The chakra system is a map of the energy systems in the body and mind. On the energetic level, a chakra is the rotation of feminine Shakti energy in the body at a particular location.

Chit-akasha (Sanskrit). The inner subtle space of consciousness.

Chit (Sanskrit). The Sanskrit term for what is referred to in this book as pure awareness. See Chapter 2.

Chiti (Sanskrit). The Sanskrit term for what is referred to in this book as luminous consciousness. See Chapter 2.

Chitta (Sanskrit). Mind-stuff, mental substance. The contents of the mind and memory.

Chiti-shakti (Sanskrit)**.** The energy that radiates from the emptiness of pure awareness.

Dharma-megha (Sanskrit). Clouds of dharma. The deep state of meditative absorption in which the meditating mind becomes temporarily aligned with the pureness of awareness.

Dukkha (Pali). The stress, dissatisfaction, tension, or suffering that is inevitable in human life.

Electronics of the mind. In Balyogi's teaching, the instruments that produce thoughts: cognition, perceptions, hearing, and so forth. See Chapter 2.

Flame of consciousness. The unifying image in the teachings of the Nine Bodies. See Chapter 8.

Gross Level. The Physical, Vital, and Emotional Bodies. See Chapter 3 and Appendix A.

Gunas (Sanskrit). In Vedanta philosophy, the three interdependent qualities, attributes, or characteristics of existence: sattva, raja, and tamas.

Guru. A spiritual teacher in the Indian tradition. Literally, "a remover of darkness" or "one who shines light on the darkness."

Jhana (Pali). A meditative state of profound stillness and concentration in which the mind becomes immersed in the chosen object of attention.

Jnanatmic energy. The energy of knowledge, associated with the Etheric, Astral, and Intuitive Bodies.

Jnanendriyas (Sanskrit). The word is a contraction of *jnana* (knowing) and *indriya* (sense), referring to the five subtle sensory organs of knowledge in the Astral Body. They manifest in the material world as the senses of touch, taste, smell, vision, and hearing.

Karma (Sanskrit). Literally, action. The impact of action through the endless ripple of cause and effect.

Karmendriyas (Sanskrit). The word is a contraction of *karma* (action) and *indriya* (sense), referring to the subtle sensory organs of action in the Astral Body that manifest as the organs of action in the physical world: the mouth, hands, genitals, anus, and feet.

Kleshas (Pali). Hindrances or obstacles of mind that obscure clarity and lead to suffering.

Koshas (Sanskrit). Sheaths of existence—energetic dimensions of being that emanate from the most refined level to the most material level. For a detailed map, see Appendix A.

Kriyatmic Energy. Action oriented energy associated with the Physical, Vital, and Emotional Bodies.

Kundalini (Sanskrit). The latent energy coiled at the base of the spine.

Kurma nadyam (Sanskrit). In the Etheric Body, a tortoise-shaped tube or energy channel located in the area below the throat.

Kurma (Sanskrit). The tortoise, a symbol for deep samadhi.

Luminous consciousness. The capacity of consciousness itself that allows cognizing to happen. It is often described as radiant or timeless and can be directly experienced through meditation. See Chapter 2.

Mahakarana sharira. In Balyogi's illustrations, a figure sitting in the lotus at the navel area to symbolize the awakened self. It represents both the Divine Body and the Spiritual Body.

Manas (Sanskrit). Ordinary mental thinking or mind.

Metta (Pali). Loving-kindness, friendliness; unconditional positive regard.

Mindfulness. A quality of nonjudgmental and kind attention that can be systematically cultivated through meditation. Central to meditation practice in the Theravada Buddhist tradition.

Nada bindu (Sanskrit). The Eye of Enlightenment, the subtlest point of the Intuitional Body, the juncture between the un-manifest and manifest world. Located in the center of the forehead just above the third eye.

Nadi (Sanskrit). The energy pathways or subtle nerve channels through which the life force flows through the body.

Nibbana (Pali). Full spiritual awakening in the Buddhist tradition. Literally, the "extinction" or "blowing out" or "quenching" of greed, hatred, and delusion—and the freedom that brings.

Om (Sanskrit). A meditation mantra or sacred sound that appears at the beginning and end of most Sanskrit recitations, prayers, and texts.

Pali. An ancient language originating in North India, closely related to Sanskrit, in which the sacred texts of Theravada Buddhism are written.

Patanjali. The ancient Indian teacher or sage to whom is attributed the authorship of the classical Yoga Sutras, which codified the path of eight-limbed (*ashtanga*) yoga.

Pure Awareness. The ineffable source that generates the electricity of luminous consciousness. Mysterious and not comprehensible to ordinary mind states, pure awareness is beyond the personal, beyond time and space.

Prana (Sanskrit). The energy that animates all life and flows through the human body through a network of subtle channels. In the Nine Bodies system, it manifests tangibly in the Vital Body and originates more subtly in the Etheric Body.

Purusha (Sanskrit). In classic yoga philosophy, one of the words for spirit, luminous consciousness, or transcendent self.

Rahasyatmic energy. Mysterious energy, un-manifest, that empowers all consciousness to unfold. It emanates from the Cosmic Level.

Rajas, rajasic. Impassioned or active. One of the three gunas or characteristics of material existence.

Samadhi (Sanskrit). A state of intense concentration and inner stillness achieved through meditation.

Sanskrit. An ancient Indic language that is the classical literary language of India and the language in which the traditional yogic texts and Hindu scriptures were first recorded.

Sat-chit-ananda (Sanskrit). An elevated state of being, knowing, and bliss.

Sattva, sattvic (Sanskrit). Pure or harmonious. One of the three gunas or characteristics of materiality.

Sense-consciousness. The process of being conscious of something, i.e., the mental activity of cognizing. It is known through the experience of the senses and the mind, and it arises and passes away along with them. See Chapter 2.

Subtle Level. Traditionally known as the Subtle Body. The second of the traditional Three Bodies in yoga or Vedanta philosophy, containing the Etheric, Intuitional, and Astral Bodies of the Nine Body system. For a full description, see Chapter 3 and Appendix A.

Sushumna (Sanskrit). In kundalini yoga, the energetic channel of the center of the spine.

Tamas, tamasic (Sanskrit). Impure, inert. One of the three gunas or characteristics of materiality.

Tanmatras (Sanskrit). The five subtle elements of earth, water, fire, air, and space that originate in the Etheric Body (and then manifest in the physical world as the five material elements).

Tantra (Sanskrit). An ancient Indian tradition of philosophical texts, practices, and rituals designed to awaken and channel cosmic and personal energies for the purpose of spiritual awakening.

Ten Pranas. The energies that sustain the life force and that originate in the Etheric Body. There is a prana that is vital for breathing, one for digestion, one for circulation, and so on.

The Eightfold Path. Traditional Buddhist teachings on the wise practices that lead to liberation from suffering.

The electricity of consciousness. The capacity of luminous consciousness to provide illumination. See Chapter 2.

The Four Noble Truths. Traditional Buddhist teaching that describes the cause of suffering and the path to liberation from it.

Theravada Buddhism. The predominant Buddhism of Southeast Asia and Sri Lanka.

Three Bodies. Traditional yogic teachings about different manifestations or levels of being, referred to in this book as Three Levels: the physical, subtle, and causal levels of being. See Chapter 3.

Three Hearts. In the Nine Bodies teaching, the physical heart (which manifests as matter), the psychic heart (which manifests as energy in the Subtle Realm), and the spiritual heart (which manifests in the Subtle Realm as luminous consciousness).

Vijnana Chaksu (Sanskrit). The "eye of awakening." A location in the Subtle Level associated with a refined state of mind in which an extraordinary type of liberating knowing is accessed.

Vinnana (Pali). Sense-consciousness. See Chapter 2.

Vipassana (Insight) Meditation. Built upon the practice of mindfulness, it is a key aspect of Theravada Buddhism.

Vyakta (Sanskrit). Visible, expressed. All that is manifest in the world is said to be vyakta.

RESOURCES

ninebodies.com

On this website, you will find audio recordings of guided meditations, occasional blog posts by Phillip Moffitt, and information about teaching events based on *Awakening through the Nine Bodies*.

dharmawisdom.org

Phillip Moffitt has studied Theravada Buddhism since 1987. He is a vipassana meditation teacher and has been leading retreats and classes for twenty years. Phillip's teaching emphasizes living the dharma in daily life, and his articles and recordings of dharma talks and guided meditations are collected on his Dharma Wisdom website.

lifebalanceinstitute.com

Phillip Moffitt is the founder and president of Life Balance Institute, which offers group programs as well as individual consultation on how to skillfully manage major life changes and transitions. This approach is based on doing a strategic analysis of one's values, goals, and priorities with the aim of creating a sustainable life plan. You can find articles on change, decision making, managing pressure and stress, and more on the Life Balance Institute website.

Dancing with Life: Buddhist Insights for Finding Meaning and Joy in the Face of Suffering

Why do we suffer? Is there a purpose to our pain? Reflecting on his own journey from *Esquire* magazine CEO and editor-in-chief to Buddhist meditation teacher, Phillip Moffitt provides a fresh perspective on the Buddha's ancient wisdom, showing how it is possible to relate to your suffering in such a way that it does not define you. In *Dancing with Life,* Moffitt explores each of the Twelve Insights of the Four Noble Truths in accessible language that anyone can apply to their daily lives.

Emotional Chaos to Clarity: How to Live More Skillfully, Make Better Decisions, and Find Purpose in Life

This book evolved out of Phillip Moffitt's experience of working with both Life Balance clients and meditation students over the past twenty years. In *Emotional Chaos to Clarity*, Moffitt lays out a set of essential life skills that anyone can develop, which will lead to a profound improvement in their ability to respond wisely to any difficult life situation, as well as renew their enthusiasm for life.

Contact

For more information, please email info@lifebalance.org.

INDEX

avyakta, 55

absorption, 78–79

ahamkara, 28, 180, 192, 196

ajna chakra, 152–53

Akasha Sharir. See Etheric Body

akashic fields, 50, 144

amrita, 154

anahata chakra, 146, 152, 154

anandamaya kosha, 57, 60, 213–14

Anapanasati Sutta, 45

anatta, xvi

anicca, xvi, 105

annamaya kosha, 44, 214

antah-karana, 28, 180, 184, 192, 196, 197

Antehvahak Sharir. See Astral Body

asana, 4

ashram

    Balyogi's life in, 2–5, 9

    daily routine of, 4, 5

    location of, 2–3

Astral Body, 47–48, 51–53, 74, 77–79, 214

atmamaya kosha, 214

Atmik Sharir. See Spiritual Body

attention, 31

Auras of the Three Levels (illustration), 114–17

avidya, 7

awakening

    explosive, 144–48

    heart, 84, 146, 171

    kundalini, 135, 162

    in the Subtle Level, 143

awareness

    Eye of Awareness, The (illustration), 186–89

    pure, 32–33, 80, 100, 116, 135–36, 174–76

Back View of the Nine Chakras (illustration), 156–59

Balyogi. *See also individual illustrations*

    appearance of, 4

    ashram life of, 2–5, 9

    author's relationship with, xx–xxii, 6, 8–16, 210

cosmic view of, xiv

daughter of, 4

eco-therapy practices of, 9

forest tradition and, xviii–xix

illustrations of, xiv–xv, xix, xx, 86, 88–91

personality of, 5, 7

photographs of, xv, 3, 5, 6, 9, 11, 12, 13, 15

as teacher, 2, 7–9

Beatles, The, 5

Bhagavad Gita, 62

bhakti, 7, 189

Bhavanatmak Sharir. *See* Emotional Body

bindus, 118, 147, 154. *See also* nada bindu

bodhicitta, 84

bodywork, 77

brahma-viharas, 188

Buddha

    compassion and, 46

    enlightenment of, 98, 99, 200

    Intuitional Body and, 80

    as role model, 26–27

    spiritual heart opening and, 146

    teachings of, xx, xxi, 23, 33, 54, 60, 84, 116, 144

buddhi, 28, 53, 180, 181, 192, 196, 214

Causal Level

    Bodies of, 42, 128, 212

    description of, 213

Chah, Ajahn, xxii

chakras. *See also individual chakras*

    Back View of the Nine Chakras (illustration), 156–59

    balancing, 150

    definition of, 150

    nadis and, 42, 150

    number of, 150

    Side View of the Nine Chakras (illustration), 150–54

chid-akasha, 138

chinmaya kosha, 214

chiti, 25, 98, 180, 198

chitimaya kosha, 214

chiti-shakti, 32, 104

chitta, 28, 138, 139, 180, 192, 196

collective unconscious, 50

compassion, 46, 188

consciousness. *See also* Flame of Consciousness
>   definition of, 20–21
>   exploring, 34
>   freedom through, 26–27
>   illuminating power of, 132, 134–35
>   light bulb analogy for, 27–28
>   luminous, 21, 24–26, 28–32, 34, 94, 96, 100, 128, 156, 172–77, 180–81
>   pure, 35
>   sense-, 21–24, 27, 34, 96, 132
>   storehouse, 50
>   *Thousand Petals of Consciousness* (illustration), 166–70

Cosmic Body, 55–56, 61–62, 81–82, 84, 214

Cosmos in Movement, The (illustration), 102–5

Cosmos in Repose, The (illustration), 106–8

Dalai Lama, 40

death, 52, 99–100, 199

Details of the Flame of Individual Consciousness (illustration), 138–42

dharma-megha, 94, 96

diet, 44–45

Divine Body, 55–56, 58–60, 81–84, 214

Divya Sharir. *See* Divine Body

drugs, 52

dukkha, 60

eco-therapy, 9

ego, 14–16, 28, 138, 139, 140, 158, 166, 169

Eightfold Path, 23, 60, 116

élan, 45

Eliot, T. S., 175–76

Emotional Body, 43–44, 46–47, 68–69, 73–74, 209, 214

Energy Body. *See* Etheric Body

equanimity, 188

Eternal Journey of the Transmigration of Spirit and Consciousness, The (illustration), 94–101

Etheric Body, 47–51, 54, 74–77, 209, 214

experiential learning, 43

Explosive Awakening (illustration), 144–48

Eye of Awareness, The (illustration), 186–89

felt sense of knowing, 34–36

Flame of Consciousness
>   *Details of the Flame of Individual Consciousness* (illustration), 138–42
>   *Flame of Consciousness* (illustration), vii
>   *Flame of Consciousness with Nine Bodies* (illustration), 126–30
>   *Flame of Individual Consciousness* (illustration), 132–37
>   as unifying image, 200

Four Boundless, 59

Four Foundations of Mindfulness, 18

Four Noble Truths, xx, 60, 116

Ganges River, xix, 2, 3, 13, 14, 15, 38

Gross Level
>   Bodies of, 42, 43, 129, 212
>   description of, 213
>   Subtle Level and, 166, 168

grounding, 147, 207–8

gunas, 56–57, 97, 213

guru, role of, 5, 7

Hafiz, 189

Haridwar, 2

Harrison, George, 5

heart
>   awakened, 84, 146, 171
>   chakra, 152, 154
>   physical, 178, 180, 184, 200
>   psychic, 49, 178, 180, 181
>   *Radiating Heart* (illustration), 184–85
>   spiritual, 146, 172–77, 178, 180, 181, 184
>   *Three Hearts* (illustration), 178–82

Heart Sutra, 174

Henderson, Joseph, xx

hrita chakra, 153

Insight Meditation, xix–xx, 152

intention, 48

interdependent co-arising, 32, 126

Intuitive/Intuitional Body, 47–48, 53–55, 74, 79–81, 209–10, 214

intuitive understanding, 88–89

Iyengar, B. K. S., xix, 13

jhana. *See* absorption

jivatman, 196, 197

jnanatmic energy, 48, 133, 134, 202

jnanendriyas, 52–53, 134–35, 140, 162, 196

Jung, C. G., xx, 98, 153

Karan Sharir. *See* Cosmic Body

karma, 59, 60

karmendriyas, 52–53, 140, 162, 196

karuna. *See* compassion

kleshas, 7, 181

koshas, 42, 44, 213–15. *See also individual koshas*

kriyatmic energy, 48, 133, 134, 202

Kumbh Mela, 2

kundalini, 49, 77, 104, 120, 135, 156, 162–63

kurma, 160

kurma nadyam, 120, 160

Lakshman Jhula bridge, 2

liberation

    karma and, 60

    for mind and heart, 98–99

    Three Levels teaching of, 110–13

love

    as confusing emotion, 46

    Cosmic Body as, 61

    expression of, 45, 46, 47, 51, 53, 55, 58, 60, 62

    unconditional, 178

loving-kindness, xvii, 188

Luminous Consciousness in the Spiritual Heart (illustration), 172–77

mahakarana sharir, 110, 114, 118, 120

manas, 28, 162, 166, 169, 180, 181, 192, 196

mandalas

    definition of, 191

    Mandala of Antah-Karana (illustration), 192–93

    Mandalas of the Subtle Body, The (illustration), 194–99

    Shri Yantra and Om Mandala (illustration), 200–204

manipura chakra, 152

manomaya kosha, 46, 51, 53, 214

mantras, 8, 110, 160, 174, 188

meditation. *See also* Insight Meditation; meditation exercises; mindfulness

    altered mind states and, xviii

    breath as an object in, 67–68

    connecting to Nine Bodies in, xiv, 20, 41, 64–84

meditation exercises. *See also individual illustrations*

    Accessing the Astral Body, 77–78

    Accessing the Cosmic Body, 84

    Accessing the Divine Body, 83–84

    Accessing the Emotional Body, 73–74

    Accessing the Intuitional Body, 79

    Accessing the Spiritual Body, 82–83

    Accessing the Vital or Prana Body, 71–73

    Etheric Body, 75–77

    Locating Luminous Consciousness, 25–26

    Mindfulness, 23–24

    Physical Body, 69–71

    Sense-Consciousness, 22

metta, xvii, 188

mindfulness, xvi–xvii, 22–24, 175, 176, 181

moon, 144, 153, 158, 162, 188, 202

mudita, 188

muladhara chakra, 139, 141, 146, 152, 160

nada bindu, 144, 146, 147, 154, 162

nadis, 42, 50, 150

Nalanda International University, xxii

nature, role of, 9

neti, 175

nibbana, xiv, 81

Nine Bodies. *See also individual bodies*
    accessing, 66–84
    compared to Three Levels, 41–42, 212–15
    connecting to, in meditation, xiv, 20, 41,
      64–84
    definition of, 18
    Flame of Consciousness with Nine Bodies
      (illustration), 126–30
    Nine Bodies (illustration), 122–24
    reality of, 209–10
    as tool for teachers, xvii–xviii
    value of, xvi–xvii, 20, 40–41, 64, 66, 206–8
Nine Chakras. *See* chakras
nonattachment, 106
nonduality, 96, 97, 106, 202
nonordinary reality, 52
nonresistance, 22

Om, 49, 101, 105, 200–204
om mani padme hum, 110

Pali, xxi, 21
parasamgate, 81, 174
Patanjali, xvii, xxi, 7, 13, 26, 32, 33, 54, 60, 78, 84,
    97, 160, 174
Physical Body, 43–45, 68–71, 209, 214
prana, 44, 45, 50, 118, 192
Prana Body. *See* Vital Body
pranamaya kosha, 45, 46, 141, 196, 214
Pranamaya Sharir. *See* Vital Body
pranayama, 4
Psychic Body. *See* Astral Body
psychology, 50, 98, 178, 181
purusha, 33, 84

Radiating Heart (illustration), 184–85
rahasyatmic energy, 29, 84, 104, 106, 132, 133,
    136, 202
rajasic guna, 97, 213
Ram Jhula bridge, 2
reality
    ecology of, 94
    of the Nine Bodies, 209–10
    non-ordinary, 52

rebirth, 198–99
reflections, 105, 108, 112–13, 117, 121, 124, 130,
    137, 142, 147–48, 154, 159, 163–64, 168, 170,
    177, 181–82, 184, 189, 192, 198–99, 203–4
remote seeing, 52
Rishikesh, xix, 2
rishis, 41
Rumi, 189

sadhus, 3
sahasrara chakra, 153, 158–59, 162
samadhi, xiv, 4, 38, 94
Samkhya thought, xvii
Sanskrit, xxi
Satchidananda, Swami, 12
sat chit ananda, 96, 150
sattvic guna, 97, 213
sense-consciousness, 21–24, 27, 34, 96, 132
Shaivism, xvii, xxii
Shakti, 133, 135, 150, 188, 202
shatkarma, 45
Shiva, 3, 133, 135, 188, 202, 210
Shri Yantra, 200–204
shunya, 174
shunya chakra, 144, 150
Side View of the Nine Chakras (illustration), 150–54
skillful means, 40, 44
smriti, 22
Spiritual Body, 55–58, 81–83, 214
Sri Swami Balyogi Premvarni. *See* Balyogi
Sthool Sharir. *See* Physical Body
stillness, 174–77
storehouse consciousness, 50
Subtle Level
    awakening in, 143
    Bodies of, 42, 47, 129, 212
    description of, 213
    Gross Level and, 166, 168
    mandalas of, 194–99
sukshma prakriti, 196
Sumedho, Ajahn, xx, xxi, 80, 102
sun, 153, 158, 162, 188, 202
    -like figures, 94, 96, 97–98, 101
Supra-Mental Body. *See* Intuitive/Intuitional Body

surya chakra, 153

sushumna, 168, 169

svadhishthana chakra, 152

tai chi, 51

tamasic guna, 97, 213

tanmatras, 49, 140–41

Tanmatra Sharir. *See* Etheric Body

Tantra, xvi, 77, 146, 147, 156, 162–63

ten pranas, 45, 50

Theravada Buddhism, xvi, xvii, xx, 23, 59, 78, 140,
    174, 208, 210

third eye, 38, 146, 153, 163

Thousand Petals of Consciousness (illustration),
    166–70

Three Bodies. *See* Three Levels

Three Centers Awakened, The (illustration), 118–21

Three Hearts (illustration), 178–82

Three Levels. *See also* Causal Level; Gross Level;
    Subtle Level
        Auras of the Three Levels (illustration), 114–17
        koshas and, 213–15
        Nine Bodies compared to, 41–42, 212–15
        Three Levels Teachings of Liberation
            (illustration), 110–13

Tortoise Channel, The (illustration), 160–64

transcendence, 99

transmission, importance of, 10

Udana Sutta, 33

upekkha. *See* equanimity

vesica pisces, 137

vijnana chaksu, 38, 40, 102, 144, 153–54, 186

vijnanamaya kosha, 54, 214

Vijnanamaya Sharir. *See* Intuitive/Intuitional Body

vinnana, 21. *See also* sense-consciousness

Vipassana, xix–xx, xxii, 122

Vishnudevananda, Swami, xix

vishuddha chakra, 152

Vital Body, 43–44, 45–46, 68–69, 71–73, 209, 214

vyakta, 55

yoga
    Nine Bodies and, xvii
    purification techniques of, 45
    supreme, 144
    traditions of, xix

Yogant Foundation, 3, 5, 6, 8

Yoga Sutras, xvii, 13, 26, 60, 78, 84, 160

Yogeswarananda Maharaj, Swami, 11, 38

ABOUT THE AUTHOR

PHILLIP MOFFITT is a Buddhist meditation teacher and writer based in the San Francisco Bay Area. He has served as co-guiding teacher at Spirit Rock Meditation Center since 2010 and leads meditation retreats throughout the United States. His teacher, the Venerable Ajahn Sumedho, inspired his book on the Four Noble Truths, *Dancing with Life: Buddhist Insights for Finding Meaning and Joy in the Face of Suffering* (Rodale, 2008).

Prior to immersing himself in the study of Theravadan Buddhism, Moffitt spent over ten years studying and practicing yoga with teachers in the Sivananda and Iyengar traditions. He has written numerous articles for both Buddhist and yoga magazines and journals.

In addition to teaching meditation, Moffitt is the president of Life Balance Institute, which he founded in 1995. In his work at the institute, he trains individuals and groups in the principles of values-based leadership and living with an emphasis on how to skillfully make major transitions. His book, *Emotional Chaos to Clarity* (Penguin, 2012), presents many of the principles that he uses in Life Balance work.

Before becoming a meditation teacher and founding Life Balance Institute, Moffitt was editor-in-chief and CEO of *Esquire* and led the successful turnaround of the magazine in the 1980s.